Land
and
Freedom

Recent Titles in
Contributions to the Study of World History

The Myth of the Revolution: Hero Cults and the Institutionalization
of the Mexican State, 1920-1940
Ilene V. O'Malley

Accommodation and Resistance: The French Left, Indochina and the
Cold War, 1944-1954
Edward Rice-Maximin

Genocide and the Modern Age: Etiology and Case Studies of Mass Death
Isidor Wallimann and Michael N. Dobkowski, editors

Because They Were Jews: A History of Antisemitism
Meyer Weinberg

Societies in Upheaval: Insurrections in France, Hungary, and Spain in the
Early Eighteenth Century
Linda Frey and Marsha Frey

The Practical Revolutionaries: A New Interpretation of the French
Anarchosyndicalists
Barbara Mitchell

The Dragon and the Wild Goose: China and India
Jay Taylor

LAND
AND
FREEDOM

THE ORIGINS OF RUSSIAN TERRORISM, 1876-1879

DEBORAH HARDY

CONTRIBUTIONS TO THE
STUDY OF WORLD HISTORY,
NUMBER 7

Greenwood Press
NEW YORK
WESTPORT, CONNECTICUT
LONDON

Library of Congress Cataloging-in-Publication Data

Hardy, Deborah, 1927-
   Land and Freedom.

   (Contributions to the study of world history, ISSN
0885-9159 ; no. 7)
   Includes index.
   1. Terrorism—Soviet Union—History—19th century.
2. Revolutionists—Soviet Union—History—19th century.
3. Narodnai�a volia (Political party : Russia)   4. Soviet
Union—Politics and government—1855-1881.   I. Title.
II. Series.
HV6433.S65H37   1987   947.08'1   87-7509
ISBN 0-313-25596-2 (lib. bdg. : alk. paper)

British Library Cataloguing in Publication Data is available.

Copyright © 1987 by Deborah Hardy

Library of Congress Catalog Card Number: 87-7509
ISBN: 0-313-25596-2
ISSN: 0885-9159

First published in 1987

Greenwood Press, Inc.
88 Post Road West, Westport, Connecticut 06881

Printed in the United States of America

The paper used in this book complies with the
Permanent Paper Standard issued by the National
Information Standards Organization (Z39.48-1984).

10 9 8 7 6 5 4 3 2 1

CONTENTS

PREFACE

This manuscript grew out of my fascination with puzzles and contradictions. In connection with some other research, I found it necessary to go through some early twentieth-century Russian radical journals almost page by page. In spite of myself, I was soon absorbed in the many romantic and ingenuous reminiscences published there by Russian revolutionaries of earlier decades.

One is struck at once by the strangest dichotomies. Women who told of teaching peasant children turned instead to the dynamiting of trains. Men who sought social utopias of wealth and honey stabbed other human beings until their hands as well as their daggers were red with blood. Young people whose original dreams had been to cure the ailing poor traveled in disguise from city to city distributing bombs that they carried in suitcases and paper bags. And fifty years later, they published tales of their heroism and martyrdom as if their methods had been vindicated, although actually the tsar's assassination had only resulted in the destruction of their comrades and their cause.

Who were these people? What did they seek, and why? Above all, why did they decide on violence, and what did they think to achieve by it? I had read much about them, but it seemed to me that the richness of the sources as measures of character, personality, and intent had not been thoroughly exploited. These puzzles and questions led me to write this manuscript. Whether they are really answered herein is something else altogether.

The research that led to this manuscript is so entangled with other projects and dates so far back in time that it is difficult accurately to acknowledge kindnesses and assistance. I am grateful to the American

Council of Learned Societies and to the American Philosophical Society for grants-in-aid many years ago. I have greatly benefited from my use of the University of Illinois library during the Summer Research Lab on Russia and Eastern Europe. The University of Wyoming has provided generous support on more than one occasion. I am grateful to excellent archivists and librarians in more places than I can mention: from the Lenin Library in Moscow to the University of Helsinki, the Hoover Institution at Stanford, the International Institute for Social History in Amsterdam, the British Library, the Library of Congress, and elsewhere. Family and colleagues have been consistently supportive, even to the point of reading and criticizing the manuscript. Without the patience of Diane Alexander, who cheerfully typed her way through several versions, I might still be editing rough drafts.

It should be noted that dates herein accord with those of the old Russian calendar, which ran thirteen days behind our own. In notes and citations, dates of course are either Russian or Western, depending on the source.

INTRODUCTION

Historians of the Russian revolutionary movement between the years 1860 and 1881 have painted a dreary landscape of failure and futility, and indeed a similarly gloomy picture haunted young radicals of the time as they struggled to remold Russian society. Determined to foment a massive social (or sometimes more strictly political) revolution, these youthful rebels were driven by successive failures from one method to another, from attempts at one type of revolution to another—at least according to traditional evaluations.

In the 1860s, after the first flood of hope that followed the Crimean war and the emancipation proclamation, the intelligentsia (and particularly the students) operated as conspirators, forming small underground groups, reading forbidden radical literature, and devising plots and plans for the future. Beyond the publication of occasional leaflets and the unsuccessful attempt of Dmitrii Karakazov to assassinate the tsar (1866), they could point to few accomplishments. Therefore in the early 1870s they charted a new course; discouraged by their lack of success, repelled by the "immoral" actions of Sergei Nechaev,[1] and inspired by a new light, they abandoned conspiracy for learning.

The following few years saw the major radical circles (particularly the group known as the Chaikovtsy, located in Russia's major cities) concentrating on the pursuit of knowledge. Educating themselves first (they said), they soon moved to the education of others and developed an extraordinary system for distributing illegal literature to the intelligentsia in the provinces. No revolution resulted (if indeed revolution was intended), and the frustrated radicals turned in 1874 to a new device: a mass movement of the intelligentsia out to what they saw as the mute, oppressed, suffering Russian peasantry, which now became the focus of hopes, the core of revolutionary plans. If some of these educated young people sought out the peasant in order to draw close to him, to share his miseries, and thus to expunge the burden of guilt they had chosen to assume for Russia's centuries-long exploitation of the serfs, other youths went clearly to foment revolution, to persuade the peasant to rebellion against master and tsar. In this too they did not succeed.

The ebbs and flows of conspiracy, radical learning, and *buntizm**
in great measure reflected the advices and admonitions of Russia's three contemporary revolutionary theorists: the conspirator Petr Tkachev, the scholar Petr Lavrov, and the anarchist Mikhail Bakunin. Caught up in one enthusiasm after another, the Russian students—for most of them were attached at least temporarily to one or another institution of higher learning—avidly read, adopted, and then just as avidly rejected the dicta of these radical emigrés, as pronounced in books and journals smuggled in from the free atmosphere of Switzerland. True, on occasion ideas merged and muddied each other, for *buntari* could become conspirators, and scholars could seek out the peasants. One Russian returning from abroad in 1878 was startled to find that the St. Petersburg Lavrists had little in common with the Lavrov he had come to know in Paris.[2] Still it would be a mistake not to grant these revolutionary mentors their due in terms of the influence they exerted on young and enthusiastic minds.

From the patterns of revolutionary activity, scholars have frequently concluded that the wave of terrorism and violence that caught up the young radicals between 1878 and 1881—a wave culminating in the successful assassination of Alexander II, but involving violence beforehand on many levels—was the result of the failure of the revolutionaries in the countryside. Having adopted a plan based on the ideas of Bakunin and Lavrov, the propagandists (it is said) found it to be inadequate and switched to a scheme more closely resembling the plans of Tkachev. Because they were unable to rouse the peasant to rebellion, the radicals took revolution into their own hands and, as Adam Ulam has put it, "in the name of the people"[3] went ahead with a program of individual violence and assassination.

*A *bunt* was a local, spontaneous, violent uprising, such as advocated by Bakunin's followers, who called themselves *buntari*.

Scholars have frequently pointed to failure in the countryside as a major reason for the switch to terrorism as a revolutionary method— or in other words, as the participants themselves tended to put it, the switch from social to political revolution as a first goal. In this regard, Soviet historians have consistently taken a strong and positive line. Thus B. P. Koz'min, great scholar of the Russian revolutionary movement, has written:

The transfer [of the populists from agitation and propaganda among the peasants to terrorism] was the direct consequence of the failure of "going to the people" and the "fixed settlements" in the village. The propagandistic experience of the populists . . . led them to the conclusion that efforts to rouse the peasants to revolution were doomed to failure.[4]

His views were later echoed by P. S. Tkachenko, a historian of the group called Land and Freedom, the leading St. Petersburg revolutionary organization of the mid-1870s: "Disenchanted with the previous forms of work in the village, the Land and Freedom group transferred its hopes to the intelligentsia, to its potential for independent revolutionary action,"[5] and by another Soviet scholar, L. Berman:

Bitter experience in the seventies of the last century, [experience] acquired at a dear price, demonstrated that under the existing political regime, propaganda of revolutionary ideas was impossible. This called forth the appearance of a new direction in the revolutionary movement.[6]

Franco Venturi, great scholar of Russian populism and socialism, writes in somewhat similar vein.

As they began to defend the peasants, [the propagandists] at once felt ahead of them a huge wall, made up of all the dominating social forces from the kulak to the Tsar. And so the need to fight against the State itself became inevitable. . . . Returning from the colonies, individually and in groups, the Populists came to the towns, convinced that a change was necessary. It was they who developed the campaign of terrorism and who wrote the programme of *Narodnaya Volya* [the People's Will].[7]

American scholars, while less dogmatic in their analyses than their Soviet colleagues, have on the whole agreed that the failure of propaganda among the peasantry was at least a major factor in the coming of terrorism. "The attempt to rouse the masses had obviously failed," writes Avrahm Yarmolinsky, and he adds that therefore "the idea of an offensive against the monarchy . . . was coming to the fore."[8] In his biography of G. V. Plekhanov, revolutionary leader and early Marxist, Samuel Baron writes that "terrorism was attractive to many revolutionists who were discouraged by the lack of success among the peasants."[9] Philip Pomper, in his study of *The Russian Revolutionary Intelligentsia*, on the whole agrees that "continuing frustration in the countryside during 1877 and 1878 forced more and more *narodniki* [populists] to search for new modes of revolutionary expression,"[10] and Ronald Seth believes the radicals of the seventies saw in terrorism "the only means of arousing the masses, of dispelling the inertia which was a much greater enemy even than the Third Division [the secret police]."[11] These thoughts appear also in other scholarly works.

Careful examination of the sequence of events in the years 1878 and 1879—the period of the origins of the People's Will, the leading Russian terrorist organization—indicates that the reactions and actions of propagandists and terrorists alike were emotional, intellectual, rational, irrational, complex, and unpredictable. This book should be seen as an effort to enlarge the picture painted by many historians because it adds shadows, mutes colors, and perhaps contributes complicated perspectives.

Without presuming to reduce broad spectra into simplistic schemes, this book will attempt to demonstrate that many "villagers" or propagandists, (those young revolutionaries who favored work directly among the peasantry) did not regard themselves as unsuccessful in the countryside. From the beginning, their plans had involved several stages of development before any revolutionary attempt was forthcoming, and according to their schedule they were moving forward toward their goal. Their personal experiences among the peasantry were often, although not always, less disheartening than heartwarming. Thus terrorism does not seem to have been inaugurated by discouraged "villagers." With few exceptions, it was an urban phenomenon, designed by urban revolutionaries for protection against the urban police. Until the spring of 1879, no single terrorist action was perpetrated by a propagandist partial to the program of 1876. Indeed, violence was disliked by many "villagers" because police retaliation in the provinces made their work dangerous.

There is reason to believe that the leading revolutionary organization called Land and Freedom was deliberately destroyed by urban

proponents of violence who had only scorn for provincial propagandizing. Thereafter many one-time propagandists were persuaded into
the terrorist camp primarily through a deliberate campaign on the
part of their urban colleagues. A number of leading members of the
terrorist core that assassinated the tsar were at first reluctant to turn
to violence. Although thoughtful and intellectual arguments played
their role in converting these skeptics, a major element in the terrorist effort lay in its appeal for action and heroism and in the promise
of membership in a close-knit, dedicated group. Even so, the would-
be terrorists found it difficult to convince the "villagers" that they
had failed in the countryside and needed to change course.

But a reassessment of the roots of Russian terrorism must begin
in the year 1876, when those of the revolutionaries not already behind bars for propagandizing among the peasantry began their efforts
to reassess the situation for themselves.

Land
and
Freedom

1

THE NEW POPULIST PROGRAM

The renewed optimism and enthusiasm of the Russian *narodniki** in the years 1876 to 1879 emerged from their conviction that they had found a different, more mature, and sounder approach to winning support among the peasantry—an approach demanding more sacrifice and patience, but promising in the long run greater success. The new program for revolution was not easy to devise, for the radicals' experience in the Russian countryside in the summer of 1874 had proved so traumatic that it took the young propagandists years to recuperate and regroup. Once they had analyzed their difficulties, argued out their differences, and set their new plans, the reinspired *narodniki* went back to the villages filled with determination and hope. Their failures and successes, the weaknesses and the strengths of their convictions form the backdrop against which the turn toward terrorism must be viewed.

The program that these young revolutionaries formulated in 1876 was based upon a careful analysis of the lessons of the past. Indeed, the "crazy summer" of 1874 had devastated and demoralized revolutionary ranks. The almost spontaneous movement of *narodniki* "to the people" had notoriously failed to convince the Russian peasant of the benefits of revolutionary socialism.[1] Instead, the most telling response to the propagandists' efforts had come not from the peasants

---

*Much has been written about the definition of *"narodnik,"* the exact translation of which is "populist." Without entering the debate, the author has chosen to use the term as it was generally used in 1876: as a designation for those who supported village work and propaganda, as distinct from those who preached terrorism or "disorganization."

1

but from the police. Hundreds of young radicals had been arrested, and throughout several years many of them languished in prison while tsarist officials prepared the lengthy, detailed accusation to be set against them at their trial, eventually held finally in the winter of 1877–78.[2] Some of the erstwhile propagandists escaped abroad. Those who remained at liberty were only somewhat better off than their imprisoned comrades, for their spirits were shattered. Russian circles were disorganized and contacts disrupted. Many young radicals—even those who had escaped arrest—were discouraged to the point of giving up the revolutionary cause.

Vera Figner found them so on her return to Russia in December 1875. At first optimistic and cheerful—so much so that she shocked some of her Moscow comrades[3] —she was soon so deeply drawn into their misery and depression that she too sank into a spiritual morass and even contemplated suicide.[4]

In her perceptive autobiography, Figner has described the situation. Government persecutions, she wrote, had effectively destroyed all major revolutionary circles. Citing statistics proffered by Count C. I. Palen, Minister of Justice, Figner averred that in Moscow

about a hundred persons were investigated, and the number of people treated to short-term arrest and to searches was, of course, many times greater. The plague had struck in a certain stratum of society; everyone had lost a friend or a relative; a mass of families had experienced grief.[5]

But worse even than devastation by arrest, Figner found the pervasive discouragement and general inertia that traumatized the movement. Even the loss of comrades, she wrote, might be endured more easily than

the moral shock that was incurred by the failure of the propagandist movement. All hopes were dashed; the program that had seemed so realistic did not lead to the anticipated results. [The propagandists'] faith in the correctness of their methods and in their own abilities was shaken. The stronger the enthusiasm of persons going to the people for propaganda, the more bitter their disenchantment. All previous convictions disintegrated into dust. Criticism, skepticism, and lack of faith were characteristic of these times. The old was destroyed, but new outlooks had not yet evolved. In the course of the seven years that I lived through with the [revolutionary] party, I never saw anything like it. This was a crisis in the full sense of the word.[6]

Unable to help as she had intended, Figner observed with increasing misery the hopelessness and lassitude of her companions.

Figner's situation is revealing, for not only does she give us the most detailed available report of the revolutionary centers in these times, but she observes and judges what was happening from the perspective of a new arrival, an outsider. She had not participated in the "crazy summer," for she was then in Switzerland, studying to become a doctor. Her decision to return to Russia just a few months before her course was completed was reached only with great difficulty and soul-searching.[7]

For Figner, leaving Bern and abandoning her studies meant giving up a dream in exchange for less happy reality. She had gone to Switzerland because medical education was not open to women in the Russia of her day, but she had always meant to return, for she had seen herself as a doctor among the peasants. To give up was not easy. She was influenced in her decision by the crisis in the revolutionary movement, as it was described to her by propagandists who had fled abroad, and by the pleadings of Mark Natanson, a revolutionary returned from exile, who sought her help in reviving the movement. Above all, she was upset by the plight of her dearest friends from the women students' circle in Zurich, called *Fritsche* after their Swiss landlady. These friends had gone home before her to propagandize among the Moscow textile workers and with their companions (a group of young male radicals mostly from the Caucasus) had suffered arrest and imprisonment.[8] Among them was Vera's sister Lidiia. Thus with no clear sense of what she might do to help but with a fervent desire to assist them, Vera Figner finally threw over her studies and came home.

Her lot was more difficult than she might have anticipated. First there was the meeting with her mother—dearly beloved by her and her sisters—who was greatly distressed by Vera's abandonment of her studies. Then there was the necessity of finalizing her separation from her husband, named Filippov, who had earlier moved from Switzerland and was living in Kazan.[9] Moreover, once arrived in Moscow, Figner despaired of aiding her imprisoned friends, for she feared that her very appearance as their visitor might have engendered police surveillance and endangered the comrades at liberty with whom she was in touch. She did not dare to communicate with her sister at all.

Denied contact with friends, acquainted with few individuals and caring for fewer, she settled unhappily in Moscow in the early spring of 1875, in a so-called "conspiratorial apartment," where she was assigned a task she hated: that of decoding messages, day after day. Little wonder she felt depressed.

For a time, I lost myself. Not having had the slightest experience in the revolutionary cause and not knowing where within it was an appropriate place for me, I passively submitted to whatever they asked of me and did whatever they assigned. These were people hastily summoned from various areas, called partly from far away, and united in the task of continuing that which they had not begun and in which they had not previously taken part. And now, without previous common agreement between them, without having decided on a plan of action, these replacements for the arrested members of the circle each carried on his segment on his own without coordination between them—contacting one another more physically than spiritually. True, a strict cohesion of organizations was not generally characteristic of the revolutionary milieu at that time, but here it was completely nonexistent, in the sense that people did not identify with each other, did not merge together for the common cause, as was the case earlier with the Chaikovtsy [the famous radical circle of the 1870s], the Fritsche, the Caucasians, but [instead] met in one place, called by some outside force for a goal chosen, but not freely chosen.[10]

Indeed, efforts to reunite and revitalize the revolutionary movement had consistently failed, one after another. The great gathering to analyze the achievements of the "crazy summer," as enthusiastically scheduled for the autumn of 1874, had never materialized, owing to the arrests of many propagandists, the flight of others, and the demoralization of all.[11] In 1875 in St. Petersburg, some of the old members of the Chaikovskii circle attempted to build a united front with some followers of P. L. Lavrov, whom they too had once supported, but lack of enthusiasm and philosophical disagreement caused the entente to disintegrate within weeks.[12] Later that year conferees in Moscow found themselves unable to establish a united revolutionary front, and the effort was termed "unsuccessful" even by its sponsors.[13] In the same city in 1876, Figner was instrumental in organizing a meeting of radicals to hear out an unidentified St. Petersburg revolutionary leader, but she reports that he was only greeted with cynicism when he attempted to infuse the Moscow groups with a sense of unity and purpose; "pushers," such agitators were called, less with irritation than with sad humor and hopeless shrugs.[14] That same spring, sixteen narodniki from Moscow went to spread propaganda in Nizhegorod province, but scarcely had they arrived when they turned back, blaming their defection on police restrictions, although Figner was wise enough to recognize what was really lack of cohesion, energy, and purpose.[15]

Figner was a woman of energy and spirit, lucky in that she had not shared in the previous defeats, but she might never have pulled herself free had it not been for a friend. He was Anton Taksis (real name: Aleksandr Sergeevich Buturlin), a follower of the philosophy of Lavrov and deeply committed to educative revolutionary propaganda among intelligentsia as well as peasantry. To Taksis, Figner turned for succor and advice. Where was her work with the people? she asked him. Where was her propaganda? Was this what she had studied medicine for?[16] Taksis understood her purposes and her mood. He urged her to set clear goals for herself. When she explained her ambitions, he insisted that she not set them aside in favor of mundane tasks she had been assigned. He advised her to find out for herself what propagandizing was like, to settle in a village, to "observe what kind of sphinx this 'people' is."[17] Without promising her a life of excitement or of heroism—and indeed she wrote later that his words were not designed to be comforting—he set her back on track.

Under Taksis's influence, Vera left Moscow in late spring 1876 for Iaroslavl, where she had an introduction to a medical doctor. After working for several months in a hospital under his supervision, she took and passed her exams for paramedic (fel'dsher), although she felt and feared the suspicions of the local examiner, for she knew medicine better than might be expected and Latin better than he.[18] In August she came to St. Petersburg, where a few months later she took additional exams in midwifery at the Medical-Surgical Academy. She was thus in the capital city in the autumn of 1876, when the revolutionaries there slowly began to pull themselves together and come back to life.

In the long run, credit for reorganizing the revolutionaries under a more or less common banner must go not to Figner but to Mark Andreevich Natanson, a Jew born in Lithuania, who was primarily responsible for the regathering of forces in the capital city in autumn 1876.[19] A one-time student at the Medical-Surgical Academy, Natanson had already won his credentials in the radical movement, for in 1871 he had assembled the original "commune" on which the important Chaikovskii circle was based and had then become a leading member of the latter group. Through his work with the Chaikovtsy in the so-called "book affair"—the distribution of illegal volumes to student and intelligentsia groups throughout Russia—he had established contacts with many provincial radical circles. In 1873, he was exiled by administrative (that is, not judicial) order. He and his activist wife Ol'ga Shleisner, who followed him, spent three years away from the capital city, first in Siberia, then in Voronezh, and finally in Finland, the home of Ol'ga's relatives. Figner reports that Natanson devoted his exile to completing his education, even borrow-books long-distance from his St. Petersburg friends.[20]

Released in 1875, Natanson returned at once to the capital to observe first-hand the demoralization among revolutionary ranks. Like Figner, he had not participated in the movement "to the people" and like her, he was able to reactivate his hopes and renew his energies more rapidly than could those who had been more directly devastated by a sense of personal failure.

And reactivate he did. Immediately upon his return from Finland, Natanson set to work to reestablish friendships and to call the revolutionaries back together. Making arrangements through unidentified sources, he slipped abroad: to Berlin, to Paris, and to Switzerland, contacting his old Chaikovskii circle comrades, many of whom had been able to flee from Russian arrest into West European safety after 1874. Figner gives him credit for convincing many individuals of energy and dedication that it was time to return home, and indeed he so persuaded such later important revolutionaries as Aleksandr Ivanovich Ivanchin-Pisarev, nobleman propagandist; Dmitrii Klements, writer and radical; and Mariia Pavlovna Leshern-fon-Gertsfel't, one of Figner's own circle of friends.[21] He was also instrumental in persuading Figner, whom he sought out in Bern; she could hardly refuse him when he told her that her Fritsche friends, imprisoned in Moscow, begged her to come, although she discovered later that Natanson had told a little white lie and her friends had not actually asked her aid at all.

It was Natanson who proposed to unite his friends and the Lavrists into one Union of Russian Revolutionary Groups, and he who negotiated such a united front with Figner's friend Taksis in the autumn of 1875.[22] When in the winter of that year Natanson journeyed to London, it was to meet Lavrov, in the hopes of subsuming the latter's emigré journal *Vpered!* (Forward) under the new revolutionary umbrella. But Lavrov was not impressed; Natanson's "conditions" would have deprived the old radical of all editorial decisions and left such judgments in the hands of the St. Petersburg revolutionaries.

"What is he," wrote Lavrov to a friend, "a proconsul or a dictator?"[23] While Natanson returned home to confer with colleagues, Lavrov hesitated, but a few months later the proposed Union fell apart. Natanson, Taksis wrote to Lavrov, had alienated the St. Petersburg Lavrists with leadership too domineering and programs too militant.[24] Because Natanson was no theorist, Lev Deich wrote later, he failed to understand the importance of theoretical differences among revolutionary groups.[25]

His failure to merge with the Lavrists scarcely slowed Natanson down. Back in Russia, he traveled to cities where his contacts still stood him in good stead—to Moscow, Kiev, Odessa, Voronezh, and Kharkov.[26] Here he sought out old comrades, uncovered what revolutionary circles were still in existence, and attempted to persuade young radicals out of apathy, back to the firmness of conviction and feeling for unity that might build a new and stronger movement. In Kiev, he made contact with the circle of Lev Deich, Iakob Stefanovich, and Valer'ian Osinskii; although these Southern *buntari* offered communication and camaraderie, they insisted on continuing independence of action. From Dmitrii Lizogub, a young and wealthy revolutionary sympathizer, Natanson obtained a pledge of money, some of which he willingly turned over to Deich and Stefanovich, who were planning their revolutionary efforts in Chigirin province.[27] Sometimes Natanson was accompanied by his wife, but often she remained in St. Petersburg. Ol'ga Natanson was, says Figner, "a woman rare in intellect, discretion, capacity for work, and energy," "unusually persistent in the pursuit of her goals."[28] In her husband's absence, Natanson's wife gathered around herself a small group of devotees, including Aleksei Oboleshev (pseudonym Saburov), who suffered from pleurisy and was to die in Petropavlovsk fortress, and Aleksandr Dmitrievich Mikhailov, who became a vital leader in the terrorist movement.[29]

Since Natanson was often on the road, it was probably Ol'ga's friends who coordinated the revolutionaries' first new dramatic move. In June 1876, they helped to engineer the escape of Petr Kropotkin, member of the Chaikovskii circle and later leading anarchist, from the medical hospital where he was a patient. Kropotkin designed the scheme himself: released to walk in the prison yard for the sake of his health, he slipped off his dressing gown, ducked past a startled guard, and raced through the open gate into the waiting carriage supplied by the Natanson group. The effort involved cooperation among at least a dozen young radicals, including Dr. Orest Veimar and his brother, patrons of the revolutionary cause; Aaron (called Moishe) Zundelevich, strong partisan of activism who came to be the revolutionaries' liaison with European exiles; Iurii Bogdanovich, propagandist who was soon to join Figner's circle; and not least of all, the infamous revolutionary stallion Varvar'. All served in various disguises in the escape plot: as signalmen, coachmen, watchmen, and escorts.[30] The daring and successful feat—Kropotkin was spirited away through Finland to Western Europe, where he lived as an anarchist leader until his return to Russia as an old man in 1917— sent a shiver of hope through the gloom-filled revolutionary underworld.

Thanks in part to the notorious Kropotkin escape, the mood was turning by the autumn of 1876, and those young radicals not still in prison were beginning to seek each other out again. Natanson's efforts to gather his friends in the capital city were so successful that Lev Deich referred to him as the movement's "gatherer of lands," and Ivanchin-Pisarev later laughingly dubbed him their Ivan Kalita, after the Muscovite prince who was notorious for "gathering" lands by buying his way to power and influence.[31] Urged by Natanson, a handful of the 1874 propagandists returned to St. Petersburg from their hiding places abroad, and more friends arrived from circles in the south. Ol'ga Natanson's companions were already on hand to form the nucleus for a close-knit circle. A scattering of young sympathizers who had spent the summer working in the provinces came back to the capital city, and students were arriving again to take up their classes at the university and other academic institutions. G. V. Plekhanov and his friends were spreading propaganda among the St. Petersburg workers. On these reconstituted groups, the Natansons drew for support and advice.

After August, Figner's presence lent much support to the radical movement, for she had the determination, the vitality, and the personal attractiveness that drew together a second circle to work in the revolutionary cause. At first she was discouraged to find so little support. She looked up her old friend N. I. Drago from the Chaikovskii circle, but although he shared her viewpoints, he was about to head south to his family and was shortly to leave the revolutionary movement altogether. She met some women from the same circle—she mentions particularly the Kornilova sisters—but they were too absorbed in their efforts to keep in touch with their imprisoned friends (who awaited mass trial with the 193 propagandists) to devote themselves to restructuring any radical organization.[32] Figner might have given up, but she was unable to find a paramedical job in the provinces and was rejected too as a volunteer in the Turkish wars. Finally she made contact with the propagandists recently summoned by Mark Natanson back from Switzerland. Many of them she had met there before her own return: Iurii Bogdanovich, Ivanchin-Pisarev (of whom her first impressions had been highly negative), and perhaps others. First in Moscow, where they engaged in futile plotting for the rescue of several of the Fritsche women (inspired perhaps by Kropotkin's escape), and soon in St. Petersburg, they came to form a tight and devoted circle, separate from the group clustered around the Natansons. In the capital city that autumn, Figner reports, she and her friends met constantly, almost daily, at the home of the writer I. A. Gol'dsmit, editor of the journal *Znanie* (Knowledge), and his radical wife Sof'ia. Here for hours on end they attempted to analyze what had gone wrong in the "crazy summer" and tried to put together a stronger revolutionary program.[33]

Both groups—that of the Natansons and that of Figner and her friends—began by an analysis of the summer of 1874, and this critique of the past served as a basis for their program for the future. What had gone wrong in the "crazy summer?" There was no lack of information, for Ivanchin-Pisarev had been there, and so had Bogdanovich, and others like Vladimir Debagorii-Mokrievich were already beginning to publish their bittersweet tales. Looking back (and we find these conclusions in testimony, depositions, and memoirs of later years), the new radicals found much to criticize in the old. Since the program they eventually devised was based on these criticisms, it is important to review here the nature of the propagandist drive of 1874 and the major grounds on which the new groups objected to it.

Their primary objection to the efforts of 1874 was that the young, eager students who poured out "to the people" had never stopped to coordinate their ideas or their goals. Zealous as they were about their country crusade, they had never taken time to determine the principles on which their activity was based nor to attempt any statement of what they hoped to achieve. They could hardly share a common direction, for they did not really know where they were going.

Evidence of philosophical disharmony and disorder in the propagandist ranks has been confirmed by many contemporary observers. It must have been emphasized in the tales told to the Natansons and Figner by such 1874 leaders as Ivanchin-Pisarev and Bogdanovich. Debagorii-Mokrievich had been there, and in his half-humorous, half-sad analysis in the Geneva journal *Obshchina* (The Commune), he pointed out that the men of 1874 did not really have goals at all.

Many went to the people with purely reconnaissance aims, to identify a village for settlement, to try their strengths, and finally, simply to view these people about whom they had talked so much and who were as remote from the socialists as the Chinese wall. If before they went to the people one had asked the majority of most serious propagandists how they saw their future activity, what form of propaganda they preferred, the answer would have been: I do not go to the people, I live among the people![34]

In her later description of the great trial of 1878-1879, for which the government detailed movements and activities of the propagandists, A. Iakimova, who became an ardent terrorist, emphasized the diversity of the young people's aims.

Some went in the hopes of provoking immediate social revolution, and some hoped to activate local *bunty* and later to unite them; others to clarify the consciousness of the people and gradually to organize a "true popular party;" a third [group] with the aim of coming to learn from the people for the sake of future action; and finally [there were] those who wished to merge with the people, to share their poverty with them . . . and to teach them by their own example.[35]

Part of the problem was that each was inspired by his own particular creed, his own particular background, reading, and studies.

There were *narodnik* anarchists, *narodnik* Jacobins; there were also those in whose minds the most extreme economic radicalism peacefully accommodated itself to the most intolerant political conservatism. Such important social factors as political organization were consciously and systematically ignored.[36]

Young people of all radical persuasions had in common only their desire to "go to the people" as rapidly as they could get there.

To the revolutionaries of 1876, this lack of common purpose and philosophy led by definition to an inability to coordinate propagandist efforts. Although later observers have pointed out that the propagandists of 1874 traveled in pairs and groups, kept in touch through correspondence and rendezvous,[37] their critics rejected this informal coordination as insufficient. Both Figner's circle and the Natanson group sought first of all to devise a clearly stated program, detailing goals and purposes, in order to achieve the cooperation they deemed essential. As one of them put it,

It was necessary above all to establish the fundamentals of *narodnichestvo*, [fundamentals] which would serve as criteria for deciding individual problems of a theoretical nature as well as all practical questions. . . . It was necessary that the *narodniki* themselves firmly clarify and consolidate these principles.[38]

Not just a program but some sort of coordinating organization came to be regarded as essential by the two new propagandist circles.

But their criticisms of the earlier *narodniki* did not stop with philosophical and organizational laxity. To these new colleagues, the summer propagandists seemed childish and green. If the *narodniki* of 1874 shared no common aims, what they had in common was lack of experience, romantic expectations, and naiveté. As one of them later admitted, they had been "poetical" rather than realistic in their expectations when they set off for the village. They had approached the peasant with a romantic and "utopian" vision of his life.[39] What the Soviet scholar V. N. Ginev has called their "mystical conception" of the peasantry[40] is given substance by the contemporary description of the "spirit of '74" written by O. V. Aptekman, one of the radicals summoned by Natanson to judge the new program and compare it with the old.

To the people! What did this mean? This meant not only to give the people one's strengths, one's knowledge in the name of and for the people's revolution, but it meant also to live [the people's] joys and sufferings, to share with it its bright hopes and bitter disappointments. And this once again meant: It was necessary to abandon institutions of higher learning, formal scholarship, to part with relatives and friends, shaking all this dust from oneself as unjust, unserving, and harmful, in order to plunge into the very depths, the very sediment of the people's all-suffering existence! . . . It is necessary, perhaps once and for all, to shed one's cultural skin and to appear before the people in [the people's] hardworking skin. . . .[41]

Filled with romantic notions of self-sacrifice and suffering, the propagandists had their heads in the clouds. The object of their crusade was foreign to them, whether they sought to merge into his soul or to raise the level of his sights by educating him to their own convictions. A common criticism of the *narodniki* of 1874 was that they had been too doctrinaire, that they had attempted to educate the peasant far beyond his actual abilities, that they propounded intricate socialist theory to illiterate toilers who could not understand.[42] Thus in the view of their critics, the early propagandists came to the village totally unprepared for what they found and unable to give the peasantry what it really needed.

One can imagine the tales told to Figner and the Natansons about the "crazy summer" by their comrades who had been there. They had gone to the people to make friends, but for all that they were usually awkward and did not know how to act.[43] Thus they had meticulously donned peasant disguises, at various centers (especially in Moscow) set up to provide such clothing, in a generally futile effort to blend into village life. For many of them, accustomed to better clothes and more elegant standards, even the disguises represented a hurdle that had to be uneasily negotiated.[44] They then armed themselves with literature especially written in the form of simple folk tales, such stories as might be expected to appeal to the unsophisticated peasant; particularly popular were the "Tale of Four Brothers," a folk-like, peasant-oriented allegory written by Lev Tikhomirov, budding journalist from the St. Petersburg Chaikovskii circle and now imprisoned awaiting trial; and "The Story of a Kopek," a tale of peasant life with a strongly moralistic tone, written by Sergei Kravchinskii, now fled abroad, later renowned for his works about Russia published under the name of Stepniak, or "man from the steppes."[45] Dressed in peasant clothes, carrying peasant literature, armed with such knowledge of the peasantry as might be compiled in the halls of academe or the homes of the landed gentry, the propagandists poured into the villages of the Volga and the Ukraine, expecting to attract followers with their stories and evoke faith with their appearances. Their meetings with peasants on side roads or in the back rooms of local taverns (reserved for the lower classes), their juxtaposition of educated speech—and often they did not know the dialects of the areas where they found themselves—with made-up rough exteriors, their "little books" read out loud because the peasants could not read—all these subjected them to suspicion, mistrust, occasional betrayal to the police, and the tragedy of mass arrests. The peasantry rejected its propagandists because the propagandists did not understand how to proceed.

Figner's writings indicate that she and her friends—and probably the Natansons too—debated at length the methods of propagandizing, rejecting some and approving others. It must have been clear to them that the propaganda of 1874 had been conducted in two different ways. A historian of the revolutionary movement was later to write:

The most widespread was *letuchaia propaganda* [literally: flying propaganda], with the aid of which [the *narodniki*] strove to carry revolutionary discontent to the broadest possible strata of the population. The propagandist traveled from village to village, from one district to another, using every appropriate encounter, beginning with any petty case that demonstrated exploitation or oppression, in order to develop before the listener his whole anarchistic program. The settled propagandists [on the other hand] conducted their business very carefully, making friends selectively and thus preparing circles of the more conscious peasants and workers. People of specific professions—teachers, paramedics, and others—usually propagandized by this method. The majority of the settlers did not have definite trades. Nevertheless, they established durable settlements which often served as a convenient waystation for the itinerants and also supplied them with news about different people and points of interest.[46]

"Flying propagandists," at least according to Soviet analyses, gained a reputation among their colleagues for the most daring deeds, the most exciting adventures, and the wildest, nearest escapes. "In the eyes of youth," reports a Soviet scholar, flying propaganda was "considered the highest manifestation of revolutionary activeness."[47] Those who swept through villages distributing pamphlets by day and by evening, surreptitiously moving on in the dark of night, seldom pausing in their peregrinations for fear of police retaliation, gained a reputation for courage and ingenuity.

Nevertheless, they came in for the greatest criticism in 1876, and their dramatic schemes were rejected by their analytical colleagues. Few of the "flying" *narodniki* could report conversions, for few of them paused long enough to follow through. There was little evidence that they had made an imprint on the peasantry. In many instances, as Nikolai Morozov (later leading terrorist) insisted on his return to Moscow following his own propaganda odyssey of 1874, their efforts at distributing literature were haphazard at best. "The majority of them," Morozov reported,

did not honor our books as I did. The itinerant propagandists gave them out to anyone they met, or even scattered them right along the road, in the hopes that someone who needed them would find them for himself and read them through.[48]

As a result, he added, much literature simply disappeared and did no good at all, as might be concluded from the fact that "not a single one of those [booklets] tossed away at random even evoked a police investigation!"[49] Both the Figner and Natanson groups agreed with Morozov's evaluation and in 1876 they rejected flying propaganda as unsuccessful in spite of its dramatic and exciting approach.

Instead, the new revolutionaries chose to draw on the example of the "settled" villagers. Although not one of their colleagues had managed to foment a *bunt* in 1874, those who had tried to integrate themselves into peasant life were at least able to report that they had made friends and perhaps laid some groundwork. Strong young men like Sergei Kravchinskii and his friend Dmitrii Rogachev—among the first wave of propagandists to move to the people from the Chaikovskii circle—had worked side by side with peasants in a woodcutters' artel in 1872, and all Moscow youth had been electrified and inspired by the closeness they felt they had achieved with their co-workers and by their efforts thus to spread the revolutionary gospel.[50] In 1875 Lev Deich, later a convert to Marxism, spent the summer working on a farm for a family of religious dissenters, who heard his stories and came to love and respect him.[51] Powerful and energetic as always, A. I. Zheliabov (later executed in connection with the tsar's assassination) abandoned his checkered university career and went back to labor in the fields.[52]

Others sought more skilled employment, and some of them had avoided imprisonment and were still at it. Sof'ia Perovskaia, later hanged for her role in the tsar's assassination, had helped to found a village school in Stavropol province as early as 1872; thereafter she took lessons in vaccinating from a licensed doctor, who supplied her with instruments so she could travel from village to village offering vaccinations against smallpox.[53] Then, like Figner, she trained as a paramedic, pointing the way to a generation of young women revolutionaries—and even to several men like N. A. Sablin, later a suicide in St. Petersburg, who attempted to become a paramedic too.[54] In 1876, Perovskaia was still working in a hospital in Kharkov. Porfirii Voinaral'skii, who became to his friends one of the heroes of the mammoth trial of 193 propagandists (1877–78), had worked in a carpenters' artel in Samara before he went to ply his trade and spread the revolutionary word in various Volga-area villages. Even among the itinerant propagandists, it often seemed valuable to profess a trade so as to explain one's presence in the countryside; thus Vladimir Debagorii-Mokrievich and Iakob Stefanovich, along with several others from their Kiev circle, posed as traveling shoemakers, although they soon found themselves not up to the intricacies of the art and changed their identities to cloth-dyers.[55]

Soon several communes of radical young men began efforts at providing some training for these less nomadic "villagers," as the settled *narodniki* came to be called. In Toropetsk district, on an estate called Voronin, N. N. Bogdanovich (later to die in prison; he was the brother of Figner's friend Iurii) and his wife Mariia set up a smithy; although Bogdanovich insisted that his aims were strictly "commercial," his enterprise soon became a training school for young men interested in learning the blacksmith's trade in order to seek village employment and draw close to the peasantry. Among the commune's residents at different times were such illustrious radical figures as Dmitrii Klements, writer, editor, and later Siberian archeologist, and Aleksandr Konstantinovich Solov'ev, who attempted regicide in 1879.[56] Bogdanovich trained his brother Iurii there, and Iurii must have described the smithy to Figner in the course of their daily meetings in autumn 1876. Iurii later started a smithy of his own with similar revolutionary motives.[57]

Another blacksmiths' artel had been organized by the wealthy Ivanchin-Pisarev, a member of Figner's group, on his estates at Potopovo in 1873. Here young peasants worked side by side with Ivanchin-Pisarev's revolutionary friends, who gradually fanned out into the surrounding villages.[58] Morozov (who was in prison in 1876) went to Potopovo in the first exciting months of the movement to the people, and on the advice of Ivanchin-Pisarev, he shortly moved to work for a blacksmith in the village of Koptevo, twelve kilometers away. Here he lived with a peasant family, worked at his newly-acquired trade, made friends with his coworkers, and managed to convince (he thought) several of his acquaintances that the order of the day was unjust. At the end of the summer, Morozov returned from his propaganda efforts with heavy heart, considering himself a failure in that he had not single-handedly fomented a *bunt*. To his astonishment, he was greeted by his Moscow colleagues as a hero, or at least so he reports. He had accomplished something the itinerant propagandists had been unable to achieve: he had gained trust and made friends. Kravchinskii, hearing Morozov's stories, became so enthused that he wanted to strike out for the same village at once.[59] Ivanchin-Pisarev must have told Figner about the Morozov example, for he was there to observe it firsthand. To the new radicals, the possibility of persuading the peasant to revolution by becoming part of his life, by offering him special aid and support, seemed more likely to succeed than the more dramatic "flying" approach.

In Figner's circle of 1876, the decision in favor of settled instead of itinerant propaganda was surely commended by Bogdanovich and Ivanchin-Pisarev, both of whom had supported the plan (with their blacksmith artels) during the 1874 campaign. For Figner herself, settling in the countryside embodied her dreams; from her early student years, she had hoped to combine peasant doctoring with propagandizing for the cause. The settlement plan evoked the spirit of Anton Taksis and the advice he had given her earlier in the year in Moscow, when she had been so deeply depressed. Figner wrote:

Knowing the conditions of Russian life and considering revolutionary activity from a sober point of view, he tried with all his might to dispel the romanticism which had been established through my readings and personal encounters. He said that I should not expect great feats and sparkling deeds in the village, that life there is much more primitive and unattractive than imagination might concede, that work among the people is slow work, and that one must advance towards the goal by means of constant efforts, while experiencing a number of failures and disappointments.[60]

The conclusion that revolution could best be made by beginning with "small deeds"—the exact words used by Taksis—rather than through heroic pretensions formed the basis of the program worked out by Figner and her friends.

Although we have no records of their debates, it seems clear that the Natansons and their circle came to a similar conclusion. This group too was working intensely, and through the autumn of 1876 its plans continued to gather momentum. Better known than Figner's circle and probably larger, the group carried with it the prestige of the old Chaikovtsy and drew on the many contacts all over the country developed during the "book affair." By autumn, the Natansons had attracted to their meetings what Aptekman—who arrived on the scene in early 1877—described as "all kinds of propagandists."[61] Among them were members of the Chaikovskii circle, students of many political shades, probably several members of the small group propagandizing among St. Petersburg workers, and at least one Ukrainian Bakuninist, namely, the highly militant Kievite Valer'ian Osinskii, later hanged for political murder, who was apparently a member of the circle from the start. Ol'ga's devoted friends Saburov/ Oboleshov and Aleksandr Mikhailov were there as was a young revolutionary named A. S. Emel'ianov (pseudonym: Bogoliubov) whose later punishment by flogging would hurl the revolutionary movement further toward violence by a giant step.[62]

The participation of young G. V. Plekhanov in drafting the Natanson program is more problematic, although Plekhanov was present in St. Petersburg that autumn and was in touch with the Natanson group. Aptekman lists him as an original member of the nascent but yet unnamed revolutionary organization, but Lev Deich, who knew him well in later years, reports that Plekhanov said he did not consider himself a member of the Natansons' immediate circle. Still the Natansons, by Figner's report, lent Plekhanov moral support in his effort to foment a demonstration at Kazan cathedral in December 1876—an effort that proved unsuccessful not only in the fact that few workers appeared at the appointed time but also in that Plekhanov was later blamed by many radicals for arrests of innocent bystanders that took place.[63] In any event, Plekhanov temporarily gave up propagandizing among St. Petersburg factory workers, escaped abroad, and was not in Russia during the final debates about new plans; he returned to join the propagandists only in August 1877, months after the program had been approved and put into effect.

We cannot be certain of the exact chain of events nor even know all the names of the participants in the Natanson circle, for there existed no Figner to leave descriptions of the meetings and their results. What we do know is that the Natansons worked just as intensely as Figner and her friends in attempting to clarify new aims and specify new procedures. Mark Natanson, a man of great energy, carried on "day and night," in Aptekman's words.[64]

In the end, the two circles agreed. Sometime in the late autumn of 1876, the two groups got together. At the invitation of Figner and her friends, some 25–30 individuals from both circles attended a meeting in order to compare programs and notes. Reviewing the results of the labors of each group, those present found them amazingly similar.[65] From the particular questions addressed, it seems clear that both circles had similarly analyzed the failures of 1874. Both had worked out similar statements of purpose and philosophy. Both proposed to found an organization structured to coordinate work of the *narodniki* in the villages; both suggested a system of "settlement," whereby propagandists would live in the countryside and would organize their efforts around the specific, practical, realistically perceived needs of the peasant himself. Although the program drawn up by Ivanchin-Pisarev for the Figner group has not been preserved, that devised by the Natanson circle has come down to us in a version dated by Soviet scholars as "no earlier than 1876."[66] It is impossible to tell whether this particular edition of the program was written before the joint meeting or afterwards; as adopted, it may well have incorporated suggestions or phraseology drawn from Ivanchin-Pisarev's efforts. In any event, it became the official program of the *narodniki* and (after some revisions) of the organization later known as Land and Freedom.

Most noteworthy among the principles stated in the Natanson program is the view, widely attributed to Bakunin, that the revolutionaries had to begin with the peasantry—with its traditions, its problems, its hopes, and its fears—and base their propaganda upon the immediate cycle of peasant life, abandoning efforts, broadly associated with Lavrov's outlooks, to spread the gospel of socialism and revolution from the elevated position of the educated man. Although one may debate the exact interpretation of the views of these two Russian revolutionary leaders and the measure to which they differed or coincided, it seems quite clear that the decision of the new radicals reflected the failure of the flying propaganda of 1874 to alter the lives and outlooks of the Russian peasantry.

To the radicals of 1876, the Bakuninist nature of their plans seemed clear, and they acknowledged it in their written program. Indeed, the program begins with a startlingly out-of-place statement in support of Bakunin's cause—"We wholeheartedly sympathize with the federalist international, that is, with the anarchists"[67] —although no further reference is made to European socialist movements anywhere in the document.

Thereafter in the program and by its contemporary interpreters, Bakunin is awarded primary credit for the organization's concept of its necessary relationship to the peasantry, for its decision to base its work on practical peasant needs. To the observer, there is much of Lavrov here, in that the act of revolution is clearly postponed until local peasants can be sufficiently educated, organized, and inspired. But the absence of Lavrov's name in contemporary and memoir literature is telling: it reflects a rejection of the old revolutionary that may be based on Lavrov's parting of ways with the Chaikovskii circle or on Natanson's inability to persuade the St. Petersburg Lavrists into cooperation. In essence the new program may be considered a blending of the ideas of Bakunin with those of Lavrov, but its composers referred only to the former.

Thus the program clearly recognizes:

... on the one hand, that the party can be influential and powerful only when it bases itself on popular demands and does not violate an economic and political ideal which has evolved through history, and on the other hand, that the basic traits of character of the Russian people are so socialistic that should the wishes and strivings of the people be activated at a given time, this [socialism] would stand as a strong foundation for the successful course of social action in Russia.[68]

The indebtedness of these particular phrases to Bakunin seems clear, and it was recognized by both Aptekman and Stepan Shiriaev (who was not present, but who soon returned from abroad and contacted the new organization).[69] Such recognition is tacitly granted by Figner, who devotes a long paragraph in her memoir to analyzing that oft-debated Bakuninist *bête noire*—the faith of the peasantry in the tsar.[70] Osinskii, as most of the Southern *buntari*, claimed strong orientation toward Bakunin's approaches, and this section of the Natanson program may reflect the power of his arguments.

Comments of individuals who were present or who shortly joined the new propagandist organization also make it clear that the core of the new approach lay in its accounting for the peasant's own traditions and needs. We must take advantage of the "conscious striving and instinctive habits of the masses," wrote Shiriaev, later terrorist and manufacturer of dynamite, when he explained the movement to the court procuror in a deposition after his arrest.[71] One must begin with what the peasant really was and what he really wanted. "No party in the world, no matter how numerous, under such conditions as exist in Russia ... is in a position to change the people's world view as it has been assembled through centuries of existence,"[72] wrote another of the new *narodniki*. Aleksandr Kviatkovskii, later dedicated terrorist, added: "In practical activity, in the tasks that we set for ourselves, we are anarchists insofar as the people themselves are anarchistic; we are socialists insofar as the people are socialistic in their ideals and strivings."[73] In the words of Iurii Bogdanovich, a member of Figner's circle, "Any system not corresponding to the concepts put together in the people, to its intellectual and moral nature, will not serve to better popular life."[74]

Two years later, in the journal *Zemlia i volia* (Land and Freedom), an anonymous author insisted that even the future was best left to the tradition of the peasants, who "understood incomparably more deeply and broadly than the so-called educated strata."[75] And the program was defended later by the terrorist Zheliabov, in one of his powerful speeches to the court that was about to condemn him to death.

In the popular consciousness, there is much that one must preserve, on which one must base oneself until a certain time. Considering that because of the impediments set up by the government it was impossible to carry socialist ideals *in toto* into the popular consciousness, the socialists transformed themselves into *narodniki.* We decided to act in terms of the interests that the people recognized, not in terms of pure doctrine, but on the basis of interests inherent in popular life. From dreamy metaphysics [we] transferred to positivism and stood on solid ground—this is the basic trait of *narodnichestvo.*[76]

But in spite of their resolution to let the peasants determine their own goals, the Natanson group—and by all accounts Figner's as well—could not help but include in their new program a statement of what they were convinced the peasant believed. The peasantry wants land, they insisted.

The orthodox popular view recognizes the injustice of that order under which land is alienated into private property; by the popular concept "God's land," each farmer has the right to land in that quantity which he can work by his own labor. Therefore we must demand the transfer of all land to the hands of the agricultural working class and its uniform distribution.[77]

The peasant sought a government based on a Bakunin-style federation of communes (*obshchiny*) and therefore the propagandists must strive for "the transfer of all public functions to the hands of the communes." Unfortunately, that might not be easy.

It is impossible to call this demand universally popular; there is a group of communes striving for this, but the majority of them have not yet attained such a moral and intellectual level, and, in our opinion, each union of communes will determine for itself what share of public functions it will give to the government and what share it will keep for itself. *Our obligation is only to strive to increase this share as much as possible.*[78]

The people, their propagandists were sure, would want the Russian empire divided "into parts, corresponding to local wishes," a clause probably insisted upon by Osinskii and his Ukrainian friends.

To seal their promise that the people would get what they wanted, the new *narodniki* adopted an old slogan.

... "Land and Freedom"–that has served as the slogan of so many popular movements ... even now serves as the best expression of popular viewpoints about the ownership of the land and the structure of communal life. Recognizing the impossibility of innoculating the people under present conditions with other ideals that are perhaps even better from an abstract point of view, we have decided to write on our banner the historically-evolved formula, "Land and Freedom."[79]

The formula will be recognized as derived from a proclamation written by Nikolai Ogarev in Alexander Herzen's famous emigré journal *Kolokol* (The Bell). It became the name of an underground organization with which the radical critic N. G. Chernyshevskii was associated in 1861, and more recently, Plekhanov had used it on a placard at his Kazan Square demonstration. It was to become the formal title of the Natanson organization later–perhaps not until 1878.[80]

Of course, the program asserted, this "formula" could only be attained in Russia by means of forceful revolution. Anticipating the later Marxist viewpoint and drawing perhaps on the thinking of Tkachev, the *narodniki* realized that such revolution must be made as rapidly as possible because

the development of capitalism and the ever increasing penetration into popular life ... of various evils of bourgeois civilization threaten the destruction of the commune and the perversion, to a greater or lesser degree, of the popular world view...[81]

As to the exact methods by which revolution might be fomented, the program remains vague. It states that propaganda and agitation should be conducted among broad strata of the population, and it specifically mentions the intelligentsia (for which purpose a journal should be founded); university students; factory workers (the propagandizing and educating of whom had been carried on by Plekhanov in the Chaikovskii circle tradition); and non-Orthodox religious sects (known for their anti-government stances). It states that "settlements" (*poseleniia*) must be constructed among the peasant populations of those regions where dissatisfaction traditionally was most keen.[82] Beyond this, no exact techniques for propagandizing or for making revolution are specified, and we must turn to Figner's account—as verified, to be sure, by the procedures the *narodniki* clearly adopted.

Although it was not specifically included in the written program that has come down to us, a plan was laid, according to Figner, and this time flying propaganda was rejected in principle. Instead, the *narodniki* of 1876 vowed to go back to the village to stay, in accordance with the example of those of their earlier colleagues whom they deemed most successful. Among the peasantry, they would first engender trust, confidence, and support. They would thus seek out a core of village activists, and only then would they work to foment revolutionary action.

Figner pours her own enthusiasm into her description of the new course. "In order to intensify the courage of the people and its ability to stand up for its own interests," she writes,

the revolutionaries needed a systematic procedure; they must live among the people in such a manner that the habits and weaknesses of civilized man were not too obvious, but that still permitted the revolutionaries to be close to the people in a so-to-speak semi-intellectual profession (be it local scribe, treasury bookkeeper, paramedic, shopkeeper, etc.) and must then use all opportunities in peasant life to elevate the idea of justice, to share the general interests of the peasants, and to promote the dignity of the individual.[83]

Figner's report suggests a model approach.

In his position as, say, village or local scribe, the revolutionary should use his influence on the local court to dispel grossness and corruption, in order to make it a real court of popular conscience; he should enhance the significance of the village commune and the district court to make them into real expressions of public opinion and not let them remain a playing ball of some sort of village scoundrels as in the past; he should force village usurers and bloodsuckers out of village business and elevate the standards of the village poor; should suggest and support lawsuits against property owners, village usurers, government officials, and should, whenever possible, insist that the peasants stand up for their rights and achievements; in short, he should develop in the peasantry a spirit of self-protection and protest and at the same time seek out those energetic natures, natural leaders, who will particularly take on village interests; he should bring them together into groups so that he can support them in that battle which, beginning with legal protests, will eventually lead to the path of open revolution.[84]

That others understood the program in the same way is indicated by Kviatkovskii's less detailed version of the same procedure.

... the party had to set for itself the goal of realizing those wishes, those strivings which already exist among the people. The method for realizing these particular goals was the colonization of an area more or less important (in party eyes), with the aim of becoming, so to speak, a citizen of this locality, acquiring for oneself the trust and respect of the people, calling them forth to active declaration of their needs and demands—both on a legal and an illegal basis.[85]

First settling among the peasants, then building their self-esteem and self-confidence by minor (even legal) protest, then isolating those who might form nuclei for violent revolutionary action, the *narodniki* would do best, they thought, to take up employment in positions particularly useful to the peasantry and traditionally respected in the villages. As a historian of the movement later wrote:

The previous dogmatic assertion demanding that a revolutionary go to the people in the form of a black [or unskilled] laborer lost its absolute force. The position of a person engaged in physical labor was recognized as before as very desirable and useful, but the situation of a wandering itinerant was unconditionally contraindicated, for it could in no way evoke the respect and trust of the peasantry, which was accustomed to respecting personal, financial independence, settlement, and property ownership—and thus it seemed immediately necessary to achieve a situation in which the revolutionary, with full material independence, would have a strong possibility of working in closest cooperation with the inhabitants of a given locality, of sharing their interests, and benefiting from influence in public affairs.[86]

The positions deemed most desirable for propagandists under the new system were those involving skills: the management of retail shops, of mills, or of farms, jobs as district scribes or local teachers, work as paramedics or physicians.[87] The *narodniki* who formulated the new program agreed that it was desirable for at least one person native to a given area and familiar with its particularisms to work among the propagandists there.

Some question remains as to whether the St. Petersburg *narodniki* actually drew up a separate constitution for their new organization as early as 1876 or 1877. Although Soviet scholars have presumed such a document existed,[88] it has not come down to us. Figner's broad description of the organizational system probably represents the oral debate that ranged around the sections of the written program labeled "organizational" and "disorganizational." The notes of O. V. Aptekman, who was called from the South to review the new program in January 1877, probably also represent minutes of a meeting rather than an actually written document; they are clearly a version of notes that Aptekman put into definite form much later, for internal evidence indicates that in their published form they date not from 1877 but rather from later years.[89] The first official constitution published (only in draft form) by S. N. Valk *et al.* is dated 1878, and it contains no reference to any similar document from earlier days;[90] it probably represents not a constitution but an addendum to the 1876–77 program described above. Although they discussed organizational matters, the propagandists of 1877 do not seem to have felt it necessary formally to found a society, to set up a written constitution, or to limit their actions by any schematic, specific strictures, defining the relationship of one to another.

One further plan, according to Figner, was adopted by her circle and the Natansons' in the early spring of 1877. The two groups, apparently working together, spelled out an idea for a system of provincial support centers from which propagandists would fan out into the surrounding countryside. The scheme obviously drew on the experiences of the earlier *narodniki*, who had established occasional centers dedicated to the distribution of booklets (such as those published by the Chaikovskii circle or those distributed by Ippolit Myshkin's Moscow underground press) or to the acquisition of skills (such as the smithies set up by Ivanchin-Pisarev and the Bogdanovich brothers) to serve as focal points from which propagandists went to work.

More specifically, the new *narodniki* determined not to center all organizational work in St. Petersburg, but rather to establish "settlements" in appropriate provincial towns. These communes, permanently inhabited by a handful of radicals, could serve as administrative and organizational capitals for local revolutionary efforts. They would act as distribution points for propaganda materials to *narodniki* in the remote country villages. Their members would cultivate close ties with local intelligentsia, in an effort to provide village jobs for propagandists who sought such positions. They would keep in touch with leaders in St. Petersburg and Moscow with the aim of transmitting messages to the "villagers" regarding policies, activities, and threats. Their conspiratorial quarters in provincial cities would serve as communication posts, bringing together on any desirable occasion the scattered propagandists in the area; spreading the word about danger and arrest, and—although the *narodniki* may not have anticipated the necessity when they debated their plans—providing that which many propagandists of 1874 had found wanting: social centers, meeting places, homes-away-from-homes, where the articulate and gregarious revolutionaries, otherwise isolated in desolate peasant communities, could gather to recoup themselves, to exchange notes on their experiences, to gossip about friends, to relax in empathetic company, and to seek advice and succor from each other.[91]

So far, Figner reports, the Natansonists and her own circle were in perfect agreement. On one point, however, there was trouble, and after their joint meeting late in 1876, Figner and her circle opted not to join the Natanson association on this account. The problem lay not in organizational structure but in organizational principle. The Natansonists, Figner reports, chose to adopt "business-like" criteria for membership in the group and association with its projects. Having lived in close ties of camaraderie with the other members of the Chaikovskii circle and perhaps having suffered from police suspicion of such a commune, they may also have worn out their tolerance for intense interrelationships. Instead all they asked is that any prospective member be judged by his honesty, reliability, and sympathy with the principles of the organization. To Figner and her circle—and it is interesting that none of them had been Chaikovtsy, although they had undoubtedly enjoyed similar relationships with others of like mind—this was not enough. Having come to know each other through their daily meetings and appreciate each other through their intense soul-searching debates, they sought an organization based on sympathy and understanding such (Figner writes) as the Chaikovtsy, the Fritsche commune in Zurich, and others. To them, devotion and warmth were an essential bond; sincerity, honesty, and agreement would not suffice. For Figner personally, the lonely experience in Moscow undoubtedly still hurt.

On this matter and not on the principles of the program, she and her group declined to join any new organization that might be set up by the Natanson circle.[92] Apparently without rancor, the Natansonists agreed. Both groups proceeded to activate the identical program in different geographic arenas. The Figner circle came to be known as "separatists." That the Natansonists succeeded to a greater degree than the separatists caused Figner embarrassment, second thoughts, and even apologies when she reported later. Nevertheless, the two groups worked in harmony and when a constitution was finally drawn up by the Natanson segment, the separatists and their operations were accorded special treatment.

Having debated their program with the Figner circle and perhaps even having revised it in accordance with the results, the Natansons called to St. Petersburg representatives of the Southern *buntari* or Bakuninists in an effort to achieve nationwide coordination. Osinskii, from Kiev, was already with them; to the capital city in January 1877 came Aptekman, later historian of the movement, with his friends I. M. Tishchenko (nicknamed Titych), N. N. Moshchenko, and S. A. Kharizomenov from Rostov-on-Don and Kharkov.[93] Natanson sought them out at once in their conspiratorial quarters, and here Aptekman met him for the first time. Natanson was a little over medium height, Aptekman reported, with a small beard, lively (although shifty) eyes, and a "tall, white, philosophical forehead." He did not stay with them long, but told them, "There is much, much work to be done," and acted as though the program were already in operation. That evening they went to the Natansons' apartment, where they approved the program and its tactics and agreed to a division of functions among themselves. They left at midnight, Aptekman reports, and shook hands with vigor all around. They were full of hopes for revolution.[94]

But was their program really revolutionary? One Soviet scholar has referred to it as "the transition from the propaganda of socialist ideas to the political education of the people on the basis of everyday needs and current interests" and has noted that the goal of revolution was postponed in favor of legal action.[95] Lev Tikhomirov (then in prison; later ardent terrorist) called it "petty agitation on the basis of peasant needs; the struggle with landlords, with the administration."[96] These judgments are surely correct in that the new program never anticipated revolution in the immediate future.

But most of the young propagandists thought that upon it revolution might one day be built. As Taksis had told Figner, "For the revolutionary cause, one needs not so much stormy enthusiasm as patient, tenacious, and durable small deeds."[97] Later Zheliabov contended that the new *narodniki* had abandoned not revolution but romanticism by setting their struggle on a more practical foundation.

Thus the character of our activity was changed and so were the methods of struggle—from the word, one switched to the deed. Instead of propaganda of socialist ideas, agitational stimulation of the people in terms of their conscious interests moved into first place. Instead of the peaceful word, we deemed it necessary to transfer to actual struggle. This struggle always corresponds to the magnitude of accumulated forces.[98]

And using Taksis's exact phrase, he added, "It was decided first of all to try small deeds."

Others answered that the propagandists' work must be regarded at first as preparatory because, as Kviatkovskii put it in his deposition to the court, "in the long run the realization of popular ideals can occur only by means of a popular revolution. That is the essential trait of the program of the *narodnik* party."[99] Under similar circumstances, Iurii Bogdanovich wrote a similar analysis. Revolution, Bogdanovich believed, was something the people had to decide for themselves. The intelligentsia could not succeed without the people, could not make revolution without the peasantry's aid. They could only do their best to encourage the popular forces. "The party should not strive to evoke revolution," he testified,

for this latter is the result of general conditions of living, and synthetic evocation makes its success more than doubtful. Each member of the party, taking advantage of existing rights and institutions among the people—as for instance village and district meetings and courts, the right of representation in the zemstvos [local assemblies], schools, communes, and artels, etc.—must raise these institutions to their full significance, arouse in the people and in society a consciousness of communality of interest, defend the people from oppression by the nation's parasites, and then try to arouse in the people a sense of its own worth, consciousness of its rights, etc.[100]

Awaiting trial, Bogdanovich no doubt deliberately played down the final, drastic objective that the new program proclaimed. Still that objective was surely as vital to him as to his colleagues.

These statements underline the *narodniki*'s conviction that revolution could not—and should not—be made overnight. Dedicated to the idea of broad based social revolution, they were certain that the peasantry could be persuaded into activity only slowly. Having drawn from Bakunin the conviction that the peasantry would make revolution only when it was convinced rebellion was necessary on the basis of its own needs and desires, the *narodniki* found it propitious to adhere to Lavrov's plan for educating the populace to recognize its needs, for postponing any outbreak until the time was ripe. The patient work in the countryside with revolution as its eventual endpoint was more Lavrist than its proponents admitted.

Whether the new program was "revolutionary" or not, whether it might have slowly convinced the peasant to take up arms remains one of those "what if" questions left to us by history. More important to this study is the way the new propagandists viewed their plan and their successes and failures thereunder. As it turned out, they had set themselves no timetable, and within a few years they were to alter their methods for attaining the objective they professed. Instead of strengthening their resolve in view of local successes, the "villagers" threw in the towel in the face of local threats, which indeed they might well have anticipated. The program of 1876–77 might never have brought on revolution at all, but it was not thoroughly tested because its proponents changed their minds and abandoned it.

Nevertheless, the spirits of the new *narodniki* at first were wreathed with hope. Having devised their new tactics in response to and repair of the failure of 1874, they began their move back "to the people" three years later, in the spring of 1877.

2

THE VILLAGERS
AT WORK

Young people from the Natanson circle and from Figner's separatists moved to put their new program into action in 1877. Inspired by their hopes to agitate for peasant reform and thus gain support for peasant revolution, they proposed to settle in the countryside and gradually build that consciousness from which revolution might be made. An evaluation of their successes and failures among the peasantry is vitally important in this study, but for the researcher the task is a difficult one.

In the first place, few statistics are available. We do not even know exactly how many young radicals left St. Petersburg for the provinces in 1877. It is likely that we are dealing with a small number, perhaps three dozen or less. Figner mentions a program-devising meeting of twenty or thirty people, but this statistic does not include last-minute recruits made by Natanson—who (to Figner's irritation) usurped the entire list of suggestions—nor those summoned to approve the program, adhere to the cause, and return to the provinces whence they came.[1] When the St. Petersburg *narodniki* arrived at designated provincial towns, they frequently found like-thinking propagandists who joined them in their village destinations; surely this was true at such a center as Saratov, although even in this case we have no clear statistics.[2] On the other hand, testimony indicates that an unknown number of *narodniki* from the capital city moved to the provinces and settled not in villages but in provincial towns, where their propaganda was directed towards students, workers, and intelligentsia rather than towards peasants.[3] Among these, the best known was G. V. Plekhanov, who devoted his efforts to worker circles in Saratov as he had previously to those in St. Petersburg.[4] Two years later, when members of the organization Land and Freedom met at Voronezh (together with certain of the Figner separatist group), fewer than two dozen people were present, although some carried proxies for friends. The truth is that we are dealing with such small numbers that statistics about individuals who took up work in the village and thereafter abandoned it in distress or continued it in determination are meaningless in terms of evaluating success and failure. The "large number of men of high quality" postulated by Franco Venturi (a figure he estimates at sixty to seventy individuals) undoubtedly includes radicals living in the provincial centers as well as those who, acting under the new program, joined them from St. Petersburg.[5]

More importantly, the very nature of success or failure is difficult to define. Clearly, no one of the new revolutionaries succeeded in fomenting a *bunt* in the image of Bakunin, their professed mentor. Still their new program made it clear that the actual act of revolution was not to be expected soon—not until the propagandists earned the respect of the peasantry and isolated a prospective village revolutionary core. These tasks would demand patience and time. Since it is their own evaluation of their success (rather than ours) that is important to us, we are bound to accept the standards of accomplishment that they set for themselves. Were they discouraged by their experiences or encouraged to continue? Memoir literature—which must always be interpreted with caution—remains the best source available.

We have, at least, some idea of the course of events. In the spring of 1877, the St. Petersburg radicals headed for those areas where they thought their activity most likely to find success—to the Volga, particularly the centers of Saratov, Samara, Astrakhan, and Tambov; to the Don; to many parts of the Ukraine—everywhere where traditions of jacquerie, acute agrarian problems, or schismatic religious views might aid them in their agitational work. Thus although Natanson remained in St. Petersburg as a national coordinator, his wife Ol'ga (who was a paramedic) and her friend Aleksandr Mikhailov slipped into Saratov, where they established a communal "settlement," apparently at the home of a sympathizer who was serving in the zemstvo administration.[6] Here they made contacts with Saratov radical groups, including some individuals who intended like themselves to work among the peasantry. In August, having returned from abroad, Plekhanov joined them, and he remained in the provincial city—as did, apparently, both Ol'ga Natanson and Mikhailov, the latter settling in the merchant quarter in order to propagandize schismatic traders who lived and worked there.

For reasons unknown, Figner remained in St. Petersburg while others in her separatist group proceeded to Samara that spring. She joined them only in August. Her contacts in Samara commended her to a young physician named N. S. Popov, and she went to see him at the village where he was practicing. They liked each other at once. He had actually been in Zurich, where he remembered meeting her and her sister Lidiia, still imprisoned for propagandizing among Moscow workers. At her request, he assigned her to the village of Studentsy, and there she went, determined and fearful, to work for the peasant cause.[7]

Later Figner was to write:

Here for the first time in my life I met the village face to face, alone with the people, far from friends, acquaintances, far from educated men. I must admit I felt lonely, weak, wanting of energy in this sea of peasants. Besides I had no idea of how to act with the common man. Until now I had never seen poverty-stricken peasant life close at hand; I knew the desperate need of the people only from theories, from books, newspapers, statistical charts. In order to get out of the narrow rut of family concerns, the kitchen, the visiting cards, the search for profit, I had seized on knowledge as a means to reach the people. . . . [Here she describes her education and the years in Switzerland.] But where all this time were the real people? Now at twenty-five, I stood before them like a child in whose hands someone has pressed something frightening, [something] never seen before.[8]

As things worked out, Figner did not have an easy time. Her account of life as a traveling paramedic based in Studentsy is heartwarming and sad. She describes disease, dirt, and depression that she had never suspected existed. For eighteen days each month, she traveled among the twelve villages in her assigned district, setting up her mobile clinic in some public building, examining and prescribing from early morning until late at night, sometimes with tears of sympathy streaming down her face. She found influenza and tuberculosis, headaches and abscesses, skin disease and syphilis. She slept at night on a pile of straw provided for her by whatever village she was visiting. She was overwhelmed with doubts: How could casual medical treatment be any more than hypocrisy in such conditions of sanitation and general health? How could one expect a peasant suffering from lung disease to rise in revolution? "I never opened my mouth to propagandize," she wrote later.[9]

Through the autumn she worked and into the winter of 1877–78, and she would have stayed longer but for an emergency that presented itself. In January 1878, she was urgently summoned by her friend Ivanchin-Pisarev and hurried to the Samara headquarters that very day. They were revealed, Ivanchin-Pisarev told her, endangered by a letter from her sister in St. Petersburg, a letter picked up by the police. Ivanchin and his colleague Iurii Bogdanovich, who had been working as scribes in a nearby district, urged her to throw over her job and flee while she could.

At first, Figner refused. She could not leave Studentsy, she told them, nor abandon the ailing for whom she was caring. Her friends were alarmed. Would she so risk her freedom when arrest could be imminent? It was only when Bogdanovich threatened to return at personal risk to his own scribe's position that Figner relented. The three, probably with A. K. Solov'ev, slipped out of Samara and returned to the capital city.[10]

Within a few months Figner was back. This time it was more difficult to find a position, and not until summer 1878—through the auspices of a friend of Ivanchin-Pisarev in Saratov[11] —did she manage to locate a job. But this time things went better. She and her sister Evgeniia settled together in a village in the Petrovskii district, Vera again as a paramedic and Evgeniia as a schoolteacher.

Now their success was immediate, great, and unforgettable. Under living conditions that were at least somewhat better than in Studentsy (although they made a point of eating black bread, avoiding meat, and maintaining themselves on an approximation of village standards), the sisters became a center of village life.[12] Peasants lined up at Vera's door for treatment, and Evgeniia's school attracted 25 boys and girls who came regularly from as far away as twenty kilometers. Evenings, having finished their work, the sisters would walk into the village to visit (on invitation) the homes of peasant families. Here the atmosphere would be that of a feast-day; relatives and friends gathered, food and drink were served. Evgeniia and Vera read aloud to the assembly until their voices cracked. They met with excitement and urgings to continue. Vera reported later that they almost always chose readings that unveiled problems in peasant life, in government, or more broadly regarding social justice. The discussion often took, she said, a reform if not revolutionary turn. More than once the

Figners were asked by peasants to visit the local court or the local gentry landowner to help redress some wrong.

During their stay, they established themselves in the heart of the village. The sisters were asked to stand as godmothers to newborn babies. Women begged them to help raise village children in their own image. As time went on, they met with opposition: from the priest, the local scribe, and certain local government officials. But they never forgot the warmth and affection with which the peasants came to regard them. Years later Figner wrote, "The affection of these simple souls carried such delightful charm that even today I am filled with joy when I think back on this time. Every minute we felt we were needed."[13] When finally they knew they must leave—in the spring of 1879 they were threatened by the arrest of Solov'ev, who had visited them and subsequently called national attention to himself in an assassination attempt—the president of the local assembly begged them not to go. They were actually ashamed to do so.[14]

Figner's comrade Ivanchin-Pisarev later reported similar experiences. If he met with greater tests, it was in part because of the specific goal he set for himself. In his memoirs of his life as a scribe from 1877 to 1879, Ivanchin clearly states his personal intention: "To unite the peasantry on questions of the day."[15] The phrase was probably drawn from the program (now vanished) that he had devised for the Figner circle. That the aim seemed to him highly specific and not just a broad Bakuninist declaration seems certain from his repetition of the phrase in his writings. In 1879, he reaffirmed it to his friend N. K. Mikhailovskii, who proceeded to convince him that on this basis he had failed in his mission.[16] In choosing the job of village scribe (instead of teacher or blacksmith, which he was well able to handle), Ivanchin was attempting to put himself in a position to achieve his goal by legal agitation. He hoped, he tells us, to influence the way village peasants responded to economic and administrative pressures, to persuade them that they possessed legal means to combat their enemies, and (in the long run) to change the way they thought of themselves, in preparation to mobilizing for revolution.

Ivanchin set the commune at the center of his plans. This age-old communal cooperative of village householders had for decades inspired Russian radicals to idyllic hopes for peasant socialism and democracy. To the defense of the commune and to its reestablishment in the positive worldview of the peasantry, this young nobleman (himself an owner of considerable estates) prepared to devote his effort. He was not, he wrote later, deceiving himself; he was aware that the commune had lost prestige in the eyes of the peasantry, gentry, and administrators alike. In many villages, peasants carelessly turned its functions over to a handful of village officials, and too often these administrators had only their own profit, not that of the community, in mind.[17] But Ivanchin was convinced that the commune could be rebirthed; strengthened and inspired, focused on its own legal rights, it could become powerful among the peasants again—a present force for reform and a future rallying point for revolutionary coordination. So he saw the commune, and so he used it during his months in various villages of the Volga region. The story of Ivanchin's life as a scribe—a recorder, administrator, and legal advisor to the village—is as extraordinary as Figner's and more meticulously told.

At first, like Figner, Ivanchin-Pisarev found village conditions unfavorable for agitation, inhospitable for propaganda, and depressing for morale.

Arriving in Samara in spring of 1877 with his friends Iurii Bogdanovich and Mariia Pavlovna Leshern-fon-Gertsfel't (one of Figner's Zurich comrades), Ivanchin found Bogdanovich's old acquaintance A. K. Solov'ev already installed there, for Solov'ev had left early for the countryside and had already abandoned his first job as a blacksmith.[18] Ivanchin was lucky: through a casual acquaintance in Samara, he received a recommendation to a permanent member of the local Office of Peasant Affairs. Shortly he had accepted a scribe's job in a nearby district. But in the village where he settled, Ivanchin found himself at a loss; the population here was mixed, composed of Ukrainians, Russians, and Tatars, and the Tatar language was unfamiliar to him. "Uniting" these diverse ethnic groups with their sundry cultural backgrounds seemed impossible. Even the village population saw it so, for the communal government never met, owing to its previous consistent record for dissent and disagreement. Ivanchin found his time devoted to recording and supervising court sessions—many of them quite lively[19]—focused primarily on family relationships (wife and child beating). Soon he asked for a transfer.

In Strakhov district lay his second assignment and here—in the spirit of camaraderie that the Figner group had found so essential—he managed to bring Bogdanovich with him as his assistant.[20] By now Solov'ev was working nearby as well. Bogdanovich and Ivanchin found another unusual situation, for the local landowner was an Aksakov (a brother to Ivan Sergeevich Aksakov, leading Slavophil), who devoted time, money, and conscience to protecting the peasants, serving as their chief justice, and maintaining for them one of the most prosperous economic standards in the province. The other local gentry too were sympathetic.[21] Revolutionary instincts seemed superfluous and nonexistent.

Here Ivanchin's efforts went into a fight against local officials. He saved a man from a charge of horsethievery and caused the local policeman, responsible for the false arrest, to be chastised by Mme Aksakova herself.[22] He so carefully investigated each case of redemption dues arrears as to gain the cancellation of many debts and the congratulations of other scribes, village elders, and provincial officials.[23] He moved freely and easily among the peasants, as he had in his own village where he had operated a blacksmiths' artel in 1874. Meanwhile Bogdanovich earned the admiration of priest, peasant, and landowner alike for his powerful singing in the local church, and when he left—trained by Ivanchin for a scribe's job of his own— Aksakov himself volunteered extra salary if he would change his mind and stay.[24]

Ivanchin might have stayed too, had he not been betrayed to the police through a letter misdirected by Evgeniia Figner, who wrote from St. Petersburg. The letter remained so long at the wrong railroad station that the stationmaster opened it and revealed its coded contents about revolutionary activity and arrests in the capital city. Warned by a village comrade that the police intended to arrest him, Ivanchin fled in the middle of the night.[25] To Samara, their settlement headquarters, he summoned Figner and Solov'ev, and together with Bogdanovich they slipped away to St. Petersburg. It was just as well, for within hours their friend Vera Chepurnova was arrested near the capital city, and she was carrying ill-advised conspiratorial letters addressed to all of them.

Beginning again was not easy, especially since the conspirators felt that Samara must now be abandoned as dangerous. In 1878, Ivanchin, Bogdanovich, and Figner, accompanied by Solov'ev and Figner's ardent pursuer Nikolai Morozov, sought out their comrades in the settlement at Tambov. Although they spent nearly two months waiting, they were unable to find positions nearby. Thereafter they transferred to Saratov, where the old Natansonist settlement had been dispersed by police, and here they had better luck. Through a notary known to Ivanchin, they were introduced to a liberal-minded marshal of the nobility from a nearby district called Vol'sk. Taking the bull by the horns, Ivanchin and Bogdanovich admitted to Marshal Florov that they were not the ordinary job applicants: that they sought to enhance peasant self-administration, end the stifling of the peasantry by economic exploiters and corrupt village administrators, and raise the self-consciousness and self-confidence of the rural population as expressed through a revived commune.[26] They were delighted to find Florov sympathetic, although he was amused at their assumption of false passports and false names. Now Figner and her sister found work as paramedic and schoolmistress in Petrovskii district; Bogdanovich went as a scribe to a village in Vol'sk; and Solov'ev—always the loner—opted to wait in Saratov until some opportunity arose. After a few miserable weeks in a village widely known for drunkenness and another short period working with a sympathetic inspector of local administration,[27] Ivanchin took a position as scribe in a community called Baltai. Here he set his plans to work. One after another, he picked up peasant causes and made each into a crusade through which the villagers themselves might discover the legal power of their communal organization to vanquish corrupt local officials and even defeat wealthy landlords or kulaks who attempted to take advantage of them.

First there was the matter of insurance, for many village homes had recently burned down. Ivanchin infuriated the local moneylender and the priest by insisting that the law did not permit the peasants to pay debts from their insurance money but commanded them to use such funds only for rebuilding. A hundred and fifty people showed up at the meeting when he explained:

A feeling of joy seized me when even from a distance I noted the crowd, consisting of three or four times the number I had expected. It was clear that a great many peasants, enmeshed in debt, wanted to find out about their rights in "insurance" and hoped that their voices would not be stifled either by the local elder Senotov, who was clearly an enemy of all the Khakhalins [the local kulak family], or by the new scribe, who had already proclaimed himself a partisan of the "poor."[28]

"*Buntovshchik*," one of his antagonists shouted, when Ivanchin explained the system, but Ivanchin was not dismayed.

His next attack was against a district policeman, who had been pocketing fees from the village treasury with the consent of peasants too frightened to question his manipulations. This time the villagers were nervous and had to be persuaded to stand firm, but Ivanchin got the man fired by taking the case first to the communal and then to district authorities.[29] Next he delighted the peasantry by abolish-

ing a special loan fund from which a series of local officials had traditionally helped themselves, leaving the peasants to wonder why their
debts increased from year to year in spite of their regular payments.
He challenged the local landowner by insisting that the peasants exercise their legal right to check through wage and working agreements
before they committed themselves. He insisted that the rich pay their
taxes and talked the local elder, his strongest supporter, into bailing
out those villagers who were hopelessly in debt. He called on the
commune to evict a "kulak" who had set up a liquor market on the
village square without communal permission.[30]

That the peasantry understood Ivanchin's efforts and rallied behind him emerges from a dozen episodes that he describes in his
memoirs. Villagers besieged his office with requests for help with
their accounts as debtors. In spite of their fears, they stood up to
testify against the district policeman who had manipulated the account books. They came quietly to Ivanchin to report any chicanery
against him on the part of the leading local kulak family. The discovery that he would not only refuse a ruble offered in gratitude but
would severely rebuke whoever offered one caused astonishment, de-
light, and rising confidence among the village population.

At the meeting to consider local salaries—having insisted that his
own not be increased—Ivanchin heard panegyrics in his favor. "In my
opinion," said the local elder, "you can see at once how the scribe
was sent to us by God."[31] And another spoke out:

As for the scribe, you must at once say: For another year, for another two, the
peasants must have help from him. . . . This [scribe], he defends us from exploiters, he got the policeman off our necks, he got rid of the treasury fund, he won't
take your passport without reason. Before, you went to the local administration—before the [village] fire—with something in your pocket [meaning a
bribe] . . . And they paid a better salary [to the scribe], but everything was no
good. . . .[32]

And yet another:

Take the post office now. . . . You went to get a letter—you paid. For keeping
things . . . the same. . . . And if on the side you wrote a letter, the scribe asked
something for everything: for his labor, and for the paper, for the envelope, a
good price! And now? If you need to send a letter, you go the sister of Aleksandr
Ivanovich [actually Mariia Pavlovna Leshern-fon-Gertsfel't]. With a kind word
everything is done and nothing is demanded. . .[33]

In what was probably for Ivanchin his greatest accomplishment, the peasants lost their indifference to their communal organization. They turned up at village meetings in increasing numbers, if only to get in on the action and (as the elder pointed out) to watch their rich enemies get their tails twitched.[34] Ivanchin himself had only a few complaints: that the peasants were abysmally uneducated; that in such matters as hygiene they took no interest and indeed resentfully ignored administrative orders; that their superstitions were deep and unshakable; that their mistrust of local officials was so extreme that it sometimes impeded their rational decision making.

In his sojourn in the countryside, Ivanchin-Pisarev discovered something else: Advocates of reform and enlightenment, of peasant self-government and prosperity, existed there and were willing to offer him succor and support. Unlike Figner, who found hostility mounting against her, Ivanchin found increasing approbation. The local elder, Vasilii Mikheevich Senotov, supported him with glee in all he attempted. N. M. Kostritsyn, the inspector with whom he had worked, appreciated and approved of his activities. Even his fellow scribes, impressed by his energy, his insistence on the letter of the law, and his defense of the peasantry, came to look up to him as a model. Later, owing to circumstances affecting himself and his friends, he in some distress revealed his identity to Inspector Kostritsyn, who was impressed, moved, and delighted.[35] Instead of betraying Ivanchin to the police, Kostritsyn saved Bogdanovich from losing his job and in a sense became part of the *narodnik* underground.

What betrayed Ivanchin-Pisarev and caused him to leave the village was—as in so many cases—his association with his friends. It was not (as in Figner's situation) Solov'ev who was to blame. Ivanchin had found a position for Solov'ev in a village near his own, but the latter left the area first, determined to assassinate the tsar; Solov'ev spent a few last days as a guest of Ivanchin, but never had the courtesy or courage to reveal to his friend his dramatic future plans. Bogdanovich too lived and worked nearby. His constant contact with Ivanchin was probably dangerous to them both, and this is what caused them to reveal their status and identity to Kostritsyn, who turned out to be sympathetic to their cause. But the most urgent suspicions came to rest on Leshern-fon-Gertsfel't, who was living with Ivanchin as his sister while working as village postmistress. To certain officials with whom her job put her in contact, she had always seemed suspicious, if only for her literacy. When, in connection with a query about signatures, Mariia Pavlovna's passport was politely confiscated for recertification, Ivanchin realized the game was up. Her passport was false as was his own, and neither could have withstood official scrutiny. In mid-March 1879, Ivanchin decided they had to leave.

At the last moment, moved by the closeness of their comradeship, he confessed to the Elder Senotov who he really was. "It's this way, Vasilii Mikheevich," said Ivanchin,

I love you so, I have such faith in you, that I am telling you the truth. . . . We are not those people whose names you know. I am not the son of a Deacon Strakhov, but a nobleman, Aleksandr Ivanovich Ivanchin-Pisarev, a one-time landowner in Iaroslav province. I could live as a lord lives, but I gave up that life and came to serve the peasants. They need so much protection! . . . Now you know everything. . . .[36]

At first Senotov protested, "I will go to the governor. . . . What will become of the district without you? Oi, lad, get those thoughts of leaving out of your head. My heart knows that you will never return."[37] But Ivanchin explained the danger, and eventually Senotov understood. "Thanks for your love," he said. "Stay healthy, stay well."

To the last, the elder addressed the nobleman as *ty*, and at their final parting, tears streamed down his cheeks. Ivanchin took his hand.

"So let us say goodbye, Vasilii Mikheevich. . . . I wish you everything good. . . . Permit me to kiss you. . ." He strongly embraced me and kissed me at length. . . Saying goodbye to me and Mariia Ivanovna at our quarters, Vasilii Mikheevich took from his shoulders a sheepskin coat from expensive lambskin . . . and said, "Take it, it will be warm. . . . Keep it in memory . . ." We once again kissed warmly. For a long, long time he stood by the wing of the local administration building.[38]

Late in March 1879, only a few days before Solov'ev's attempt on the life of the tsar, Ivanchin-Pisarev returned to the capital city.

Many other *narodniki* who settled among the peasantry had equally positive experiences. Although he was not among those who journeyed to St. Petersburg to devise the new program of 1876–77, Lev Deich—a Kievite who considered himself a *buntar'* and Bakuninist—decided to settle among the people in the summer of 1875, when the revolutionary movement was still at low ebb. Deich and his companion, one Iosif Shchepanskii, chose not to claim any special skills. They opted to work among the sectarians known as Molokany, but, having had difficulty locating the village they sought, they settled for jobs in a railroad repair shop where they determined to propagandize for revolution among the railroad workers.[39] Unfortunately, the work demanded great physical exertion. In a few days Shchepanskii gave up and went back to Kiev. Lonely and exhausted, Deich shared some of Figner's discouragement. "All of this," he wrote later, "could drive one to despair."[40]

Although after a time he became accustomed to the physical labor, Deich still longed to be among the peasantry and by midsummer found his way to a small Molokan village where he settled for several months. He located a hospitable family that gave him bed and board in exchange for his help with haying, at which he was so unskilled as to be mortally embarrassed at first. Gradually, however, he became part of the family life, rising early, working hard, participating in lively discussions and arguments, and even becoming a kind of reference consultant on life in the outside world. Deich records that his propaganda failed, for although the principles of socialism seemed interesting to his new family, the Molokany were too prosperous, too steeped in the virtues of hard work, too satisfied and proud of their accomplishments to seek a different way of life.[41]

When autumn came and the crops were in, Deich insisted on leaving, but the family begged him to stay—or at least to return. They told him they would help him convert to their own faith; they promised him a strong and beautiful bride. In the end, he left with sorrow. They had never said a sharp word to him, in spite of his initial awkwardness at work and his tendency to become absorbed in reading to the detriment of his cattle-watching chores.[42] He refused any payment for his services, and he never saw them again.

A similarly warm reception was accorded to Mikhail Rodionich Popov in several peasant villages of the Voronezh district. In 1878 the revolutionary organization had determined to establish a "settlement center" in Voronezh, with the aim of directing propagandists to work in the surrounding villages. While a pair of revolutionary women (Mariia Oshanina, friend to the Natansons, and her sister N. N. Olovennikova) remained in the town, Popov and Aleksandr Kviatkovskii (later off-and-on terrorist) donned peasant garb, stowed their possessions in rough packs, and with a horse, a cart, and a tent traveled from village to village as itinerant pedlars, checking the lay of the land for suitable employment and propaganda purposes.[43]

Their odyssey makes a remarkable story: the annual market in a small town, with Kviatkovskii the center of a circle of young people as he played the harmonica; the sturdy family, with whose daughter

Kviatkovskii promptly fell in love; the grateful peasant women, whose cloth they measured free instead of at a charge. In the evenings, the young revolutionaries were invited into peasant huts where they deliberately sought out local grievances. Here they heard long complaints about the wolf hunts by members of the gentry, who regularly evacuated peasants from their homes to provide shelter for themselves, and about administrators particularly renowned for the volume of bribes they collected.[44] Surprisingly, villagers took to the young men at once and seldom seemed doubtful or suspicious. One peasant offered to build them special quarters if they would open a permanent store in his village.[45] In light of their reception, they were eager and optimistic, but they too left and never returned, for plans for the Voronezh settlement were shortly inundated by the flood of violence issuing from urban areas. Popov records that they were sick at heart to leave. Several years later when one of his terrorist friends suggested that he take shelter abroad, Popov reacted with scorn. If the worst came to worst, he said, he would go back to the villages near Voronezh. The peasants would protect him; he would always be safe there.[46]

Not all revolutionaries "succeeded" in this first stage of their mission to bolster the morale of the peasantry and gain its support; it is not the intention of this essay to suggest that they did. There were many reasons for their failures. Some of them picked areas or groups almost impossible to revolutionize, as witness Deich's experience with the wealthy Molokany (who in spite of being schismatics were never of revolutionary nature) or Ivanchin's among the peasantry who already could count on Aksakov's support. Figner could no more propagandize among the mortally ill than Ivanchin could unite villagers of many ethnic backgrounds or persuade hopeless alcoholics away from their drink. The necessity of picking and choosing one's subjects for propaganda boded ill for the eventual conversion of all peasant Russia.

Other *narodniki* were clearly improperly trained for the jobs they undertook. Solov'ev, for example, got all the way to Samara before he realized that he really did not know how to shoe a horse, although he had spent months in Bogdanovich's revolutionary communal smithy attempting to learn; the fact is that Solov'ev was never physically powerful, was affected with lung trouble, and had little aptitude for the blacksmith's trade.[47] Others complained later that the physical labor they undertook so exhausted them that they found little energy for propagandizing. One pictures S. E. Lion, from Odessa, working on a tobacco plantation in the hot summer sun,[48] or Lev Gartman, later a *cause célèbre* when France refused to extradite him back to his homeland, with his legs trembling after a day chopping wood from sunrise to sunset.[49] This situation of G. F. Cherniavskaia-Bokhanovskaia was not without its humorous aspects. With her friend Praskovaia Ivanovskaia, she went to work for the summer on a village farm.

I will only say that for me it was sheer physical torture. It was very difficult for me to draw a bucket of water from a well. I had never held either spade or rake in my hands; I did not know what to do with them, and my palms were covered with the blisters they gave me. Once when they sent me to the steppe to fetch sheaves (which was considered one of the easiest and most pleasant tasks) I did not know what to do with the oxen harnessed to the huge cart; I had heard that one shouts "tsob" or "tsoba," but when to use one and when the other, I did not know, and I ineptly called first one, then the other. In the end the oxen turned around and took me back with an empty cart. They had to laugh at me, of course. Bringing in the sheaves, I could never keep in step with the harvesting machine. . . . My lack of know-how I explained by the fact that I had grown up in the city and always worked as a servant.[50]

The best prepared of the propagandists, of course, were those who took jobs within their own experience and particularly of a semi-intellectual nature, like the Figner sisters and Sof'ia Perovskaia, who worked long years as a paramedic in the South. Such traditional professional positions were encouraged by the early St. Petersburg group which made an effort to coordinate the new movement through town settlements and through the central organization that later came to be known as Land and Freedom.

Other problems pursued the young propagandists. Settlements—established by necessity in provincial capital cities—were frequently raided and closed by the city police, who were by training more sophisticated about tracing revolutionaries than were their village cousins. The commune in Samara, founded by Figner, Bogdanovich, and the other separatists, was one of the first to close in response to police activities, and the larger Saratov settlement was dispersed in a police raid in 1877, although the separatists reestablished a center of sorts in Saratov the following year. In 1877 too the settlement commune at Nizhnyi Novgorod (directed at first by Kviatkovskii) also fell. Those at Tambov and Voronezh were among the survivors.[51]

Thus although they played an important role in coordinating local revolutionary activity and perhaps in distributing revolutionary literature to village propagandists, urban settlements induced police suspicion by becoming meeting places for radicals of all strains. One might speculate that the movement would have been better off without them, but indeed they proved to be essential. Most of these gregarious young people could not maintain themselves long without contact with each other. For a few it was easy; Perovskaia—independent, stubborn, and taciturn—worked on different occasions as teacher and paramedic, living for months with only minimal, sporadic contact with fellow radicals. On the other hand, Morozov could not tolerate village life without company, and Zheliabov's wife sometimes huddled in the fields, weeping in loneliness and in nostalgia for the life she had abandoned.[52]

As dangerous to the village workers as the provincial settlements were other modes of contact between one revolutionary and another. Thus Ivanchin and Bogdanovich, as we have seen, endangered their positions by their frequent nocturnal meetings, while many a village propagandist was compromised by a visit from a comrade who had already incurred suspicion. Others were betrayed by letters sent or delivered by companionable urban comrades from areas where police security was tight.

Some of the young people were by nature restless and found it impossible to settle for long in villages dreary, tiny, and remote. Solov'ev was perhaps the prime example. From one village to another he threaded his way, stopping for company at the Saratov center or for friendly visits with other propagandists, whose position his presence immediately endangered.[53] Others—primarily men—also circulated from job to job, unable or unwilling to stay. Although women seemed to work better than men, reception was not always warm, and considerable patience was often necessary to overcome initial suspicion. Observing these peregrinations, the historian must conclude that the ubiquitous claim of danger from the police was often a cover for boredom, restlessness, loneliness, or impatience. Having committed themselves to a program calling for patience and time, activist souls remained pledged to immediate rebellion. The "flying" spirit was clearly still at large. Nevertheless, at one time propagandists were apparently holding seven jobs as district scribes, three as zemstvo paramedics, and an unspecified number as village teachers in the Saratov province alone, with others uncounted working in Samara, Tambov, and elsewhere.[54]

Memoir literature reflects what its author wishes to remember, and one might expect both the worst and the best of the *narodnik* experience to become engrained over future years. Still in the accounts that they wrote later, many of the propagandists reported that they were treated with affection, that they evoked little bitterness or suspicion, that they found support, good humor, and respect among their peasant hosts. Those who remained in the villages more than a few months felt they had made warm friends and left lasting impressions: witness Popov's reactions, when after years in exile he returned to his home,[55] and Figner's, when accidentally in St. Petersburg she ran into a woman from the village where she had worked.[56] Some propagandists even claimed that they escaped arrest thanks to the forewarning and assistance of good peasant friends. Thus local acquaintances apparently saved Ivanchin-Pisarev when he was working near Samara, and in the village of Peski (Voronezh province), peasants armed themselves with spikes to hold off the police when the latter came to arrest their scribe, a propagandist named Mozgov.[57] A government prosecutor, who met Popov casually on a train and did not know his identity, told the young *narodnik* that he never realized what deep roots the propagandists could lay among the peasantry. He described a group of peasants who spoke of the local paramedic as if she were a noble person, a holy soul, and refused to believe she was an "enemy of the tsar." We in the cities, he said, have no real concept of what the revolutionaries are doing in the countryside.[58]

Popov may have exaggerated the incident; he was always a strong *narodnik*, and the village program was dear to his heart. Still many of his colleagues also looked back with nostalgia. The very warmth of their reminiscences testifies to the sense of accomplishment they carried with them into later years.

O. V. Aptekman, like Popov a *narodnik* by all his inclinations, contended later that the propagandists had not failed.

Looking back on the path we had taken—a path strewn not with roses but with bumps and pitfalls—and laying hand on heart, we have the right to say: Our work was not without traces in the village! Our voice was not a voice crying in the wilderness! True, we had not yet succeeded in creating among the people a militant party, a fighting force in opposition to the existing enslaving government structure. This is true. But we succeeded with our various preparatory revolutionary work in *significantly narrowing that terrible gulf* that our ruthless, severe history had wrenched between us, the *intelligenty*, and the people. Let us not forget that then in the seventies we were almost the first *pioneer-educators with revolutionary aims.* Our various cultural activities directed to the benefit of the people were permeated through with *revolutionary* elements. We taught the people—and not as aliens, strange to them, but as their own—as people curing them, teaching them, glad about them—in mobile clinics, in village and government schools, on market squares, in shops and stores—we taught them how they must liberate themselves from an age-old yoke. We awakened the feeling of protest slumbering within them, we threw the light of day onto their yet dark consciousness. . . . Practice fully demonstrated that where the revolutionary settlements existed about a year, the revolutionaries succeeded in earning the respect, love, and trust of the peasantry. Not without reason did certain representatives of the administration and the zemstvos . . . say that if all socialists were like this, then they would rapidly win over the people.[59]

Like Popov's, Aptekman's viewpoint was overly positive. Not only had the revolutionaries constructed no uprising in their years among the peasantry, but they had created only the smallest ripple on the great sea of the Russian countryside. They had literally been forced to pick and choose their villages, and their converts to activism numbered in total not many more than themselves. The presence of these few dozen young people, quietly working with the Russian peasantry, could be counted no more than a drop in the ocean. Their failure to foment revolution might be considered inevitable.

Still there is little doubt that most of them had—in spite of privations and difficulties—emerged with a sense of pride and accomplishment. On a personal basis—and that was little enough—they had aided some peasants to educate their children, to regain a modicum of health, to seek support in their communal assembly or among certain local officials, and to oppose local corruption and tyranny. Later testimony indicates that they emerged from their personal experience less depressed than exhilarated, less discouraged than determined. They had followed their program, and by its lights they had not failed in their immediate tasks. Few of them—and surely not those whose writings we know the best—were ready to give up. Their optimism and their determination, in spite of the mammoth tasks that remained to be done, belie the historians' conviction that they deliberately abandoned their program in a sense of frustration and failure.

3

THE ORIGINS
OF VIOLENCE

From its origin, the organization that came to be called Land and Freedom was bifurcated, its members divided in purpose, method, and perhaps even personality. The principles of "organization" that have come down to us in written form as worked out by the Natanson circle in the autumn of 1876 were supplemented by principles of "disorganization"—or, in modern terms, violence and terrorism. In subsequent years, violence turned out to be frighteningly contagious; as it increased, one deed begot another, and the intent of the perpetrators thundered forward from strictly confined motives of self-defense to local schemes for political revenge to a compelling drive to assassinate the tsar himself. Within Land and Freedom, the flourishing of the terrorist mystique was accompanied by a growing emphasis on conspiracy, discipline, and urban rather than rural activity.

Eventually the propagandists, for whom Land and Freedom was founded, became the group's second-class citizens, and the "disorganizers" began to predominate over their leaders, much as the palace guard once made itself master of its Russian tsars. As L. Barrive has put it in his history of this era, the "disorganization" group

took advantage of its commissioned powers, ever more and more absorbing into its activity the better forces of the society. But even the very formation of the group attests in considerable degree to the growth of a political [that is, a non-social revolutionary] mood.[1]

The propagandists had never objected to "defensive" violence executed in their own behalf. But nobody among them apparently

47

anticipated where violence might lead. Eventually, the once-balanced program was tilted toward an extremism that few were able to resist.

The original program of the Natanson circle, as this plan was devised in the autumn of 1876 and approved by associates in the months thereafter, contained clear reference to the element of "disorganization." Here the new and yet unnamed society set as one of its tasks "to weaken, to shatter, that is to disorganize the power of the state, without which, in our opinion, the success of even the broadest and best devised plan for revolution will not be guaranteed."[2] Outlining the tasks of the "disorganizers," the written program specifically entrusts them with:

a) The institution of ties and organizations in the army, for the most part among officers.

b) The attraction to their support of persons serving in one or another government institution.

c) The systematic extermination of the most evil or prominent individuals in the government.

d) On the day of reckoning [revolution], the mass extermination of the government and in general of individuals by whom is preserved or might be preserved one or another structure that we deplore.[3]

It is impossible to determine who within the Natanson and Figner groups argued the merits of "disorganization," for even the exact membership of those circles remains uncertain. Surely Valer'ian Osinskii, one of the Southern Bakuninists who participated in the debates of 1876, must have been one of the strong proponents of terrorism; throughout his revolutionary career, he favored violent solutions. Along with him, Figner mentions Iosif Ivanovich Kablits, later writer and scholar, "who although he did not enter into the organization, was in constant touch with its members, and even earlier had busied himself with thoughts of dynamite, and had gone to England in order to become acquainted with its preparation."[4]

During the winter of 1876–77, when circles and individuals were called upon to debate the Natanson program, proposals for violent action were developed in writing and debate. Figner, who saw the Natanson program in the autumn of 1876 when she and her circle invited the other group to a joint meeting, writes particularly of the concept of a "blow to the center" at the moment of popular uprising, as suggested by the last of the disorganizers' programmatic tasks.

To Mark Natanson or to some one of the persons around him belonged not only the innovative idea of actively rebuffing the government in the person of its high ranking gendarmes, judges, and administrators who were most distinguished in the matter of seeking out and persecuting socialists, but also the idea of the need for a "blow to the center" simultaneous with the successful popular attack. By this blow they meant a direct attack on the tsar and his family. The idea of the need for resistance to arrest and for rendering harmless the most zealous servants of the autocracy was already hovering in the air.[5]

In another account, Figner seems to indicate that such a "blow" had not been a part of the Natansons' original plans but was suggested and added at the joint meeting, perhaps by Kablits.

... at these meetings it was first realized that no uprising could be secure in its success unless part of the revolutionary forces were directed to struggle with the government and without preparation of a "blow to the center" at the moment of uprising in the provinces—such as would throw the state mechanism into confusion, [bring about] its destruction, and grant the popular movement the possibility of strengthening and increasing. The possibility of blowing up the Winter Palace by dynamite and burying the entire tsarist family under its ruins was discussed. This [and another] amendment were unanimously approved by those present.[6]

It was Kablits who proposed to drive a carriage loaded with dynamite into the Winter Palace at the moment of revolution and explode it there—a scheme later partially realized by the detonation set by Stepan Khalturin (February 1880) at a time when popular revolution was not yet in sight.[7]

But not all "disorganizational" activities were to await the moment when the outbreak of social revolution gave the signal for a central blow. Plans for ongoing violence were also clearly formulated in the Natanson program. Of the meeting her group shared with the Natansonists in 1876, Figner writes that "it was decided to protect by force of arms the honor and dignity of comrades and control with blows of the dagger the arbitrariness of excessively zealous government agents."[8] When early in 1877 Aptekman and his comrades came to St. Petersburg to review the program at Natanson's and Osinskii's request, the notes he took (and later published), probably representing minutes of resolutions and debates that focused around the Natanson circle's written program proposal, demonstrate that "disorganization" was discussed in considerable detail.

In Aptekman's notes, a "disorganization group" appears as a branch of Land and Freedom to carry out terrorist activities. Aptekman indicates that this group was regarded as one of five specialized branches (the others, all mentioned in the written program, being an administrative core and segments for conducting propaganda among workers, peasants, and intelligentsia). From the first, however, the "disorganization group" was envisaged as occupying a very "special situation."

Disorganizational activity, in the broad sense of the word, had as its aim the weakening of the government structure by infiltrating into it hostile and disruptive elements, by means of a series of different actions and events. Members of this group were charged, among other things, with the obligation of establishing relationships with various persons in government circles, thus opening up the possibility, with their help, of filling posts important to the revolutionaries [with revolutionary partisans]. In its special sense, disorganizational activity included the following goals:

1. Liberation of comrades from arrest;
2. Defense from government arbitrary acts. It was already known that government men, especially in prisons, were permitted to torture the imprisoned in order to extract necessary testimony from them. In view of this, the society Land and Freedom, without deciding on the primary priority of struggle with the government, nevertheless saw it necessary to create a group for *special* cases in this struggle when, for example, the honor of the entire revolutionary party was at stake.
3. Self-defense. Already at this time there had been instances of betrayal, and in view of the continual expansion of the revolutionary movement, such instances would naturally be expected in the future as well. Thus the society charged the disorganizers with the obligation—in the event of undeniable evidence of a betrayal by one or another person—to "withdraw the latter from circulation," that is, to murder him. The necessity and possibility of this action has been demonstrated by experience.[9]

"By the constitution of the society," Aptekman wrote—and it seems likely that he refers here to the earliest Natanson program, since the "disorganization squad" is not mentioned in the statute of later years,

the disorganization group was assigned broad authority and significant material means. The disorganization group had the right to set up a section with its particular structure anywhere where circumstances made it necessary. All undertakings of a disorganizational nature were to be strictly conspiratorial. The administration or the council [of the core organization] should merely be informed, in the most general terms, about the ideas of disorganizational action; any details should remain in deep secrecy.[10]

Such secrecy, such self-sufficiency of the shadowy group—if indeed a formal group existed—was eventually to contribute to the split of Land and Freedom into two separate organizations. As one historian of the movement has written:

From the very beginning, at the heart of Land and Freedom there stood two large and influential groups—the villagers, on the one hand, and the disorganization group on the other. The history of Land and Freedom is the history of the relationship of these two groups that were contained in one and the same organization.[11]

From the start, the propagandist majority was unable to control the "disorganization squad" through any administrative rulings and strictures. Since it is likely that the new revolutionary group never adopted a detailed, written constitution until later in its history, the division of sympathizers into sections that were to perform those functions outlined in the program was probably based on volunteers who were never subjected to central control. This informal arrangement did not make for discipline. Actually, Aptekman's notes indicate that the need for secrecy seemed paramount, to the point that no central administration was expected to know about plans for violence, much less to coordinate or to approve them.

Although anxious to provide the coordination of effort lacking in 1874, the Natanson circle also sought to preserve freedom of action on all levels. An apparently voluntary group, later termed by Aptekman an "administrative core," remained in St. Petersburg working on the "business" of the society. Comprised of the "group most active in founding the [yet unnamed] society," this core was to serve as a coordinating bureau for provincial workers, set up a subdivision to manufacture false passports, and busy itself with the raising and allocating of monetary resources. Natanson was its leader. It was he who favored subjecting sympathizers to formal but cursory scrutiny before enrolling them in whatever activity they favored for themselves. The principle was coordination without compulsion, and to this end the early organization demanded little in the way of disciplined responsibilities from its members.

Thus the society Land and Freedom was distinguished at first by organizational looseness and flexibility. Those willing to settle in the villages retained considerable freedom of choice and action. As Aleksandr Kviatkovskii, who was involved in the organization of a settlement at Nizhni Novgorod, later stated:

The center of activity is the village; the party must strive to settle with its agents a more or less broad region. . . . The character of the settlement was not defined. Anyone was permitted to take such a position as appropriate (scribe, teacher, paramedic, director of agricultural enterprises or of factories, worker, trader) so long as he did not in essence contradict the aims of the *narodniki* and did not evoke mistrust (by undertaking any governmental duties).[12]

Aptekman writes that there were no strictures on individuals and that one could change one's mind and move freely back and forth from one group to another.[13] Stepan Shiriaev, who had begun his revolutionary propagandizing with the Saratov circle, wrote:

The society divided into two natural groups: city and village. Constancy in the organization of this or that group did not exist; one and the same persons, depending on their inclinations and desires, settled or roamed among the people— in the guise of simple workers or district scribes, paramedics, etc., and then they appeared in St. Petersburg and other cities, while at the same time a transfer went on in the opposite direction, to the village. At least so far as I know, many of the strongest activists of the organization thus changed their situation without leaving the society.[14]

Local town settlements—like the individuals working in villages— retained considerable freedom of action. Iurii Bogdanovich, describing the Land and Freedom organization in a deposition to prison authorities in 1882, insisted that from the start the society was federative, with local affiliated groups acting independently of the center, and both the situation of the Figner circle, to which he belonged, and the provisions of the 1878 written constitution indicate that Bogdanovich was right.[15] Each provincial group was expected to work out its own organizational structure and principles, and indeed the Soviet scholar B. P. Koz'min has unearthed and published such a statute for the Land and Freedom settlement in Tambov—a constitution that was obviously locally designed and adopted.[16] The town circles mandated to conduct revolutionary propaganda among students and factory workers seemed no more stable in composition than the "fully autonomous" village propaganda groups, as the experience of the Saratov settlement indicates.[17]

Even the St. Petersburg center was subject to vicissitudes. Aptek-man reports that the *sovet*, the council composed of members lo-cated in the capital city, was unstable in number and composition.[18] With the rush of people to the countryside, Figner and her group felt that the St. Petersburg core lost vitality and that only those of "little energy or organizational capacity" remained; she was probably speak-ing of the period following Natanson's arrest in 1877. At any rate, her separatists soon ceased to maintain regular contact with the cen-tral group.[19] Under the circumstances, the strictness and discipline that might have controlled the "disorganization squad" were just not present. An activity which, in the words of Kviatkovskii, was in-tended to be "a secondary, even a tertiary part of the program—[it] had to do with the defense and protection of members of the party, not with attaining its goals"[20] too soon took on independence and importance never anticipated by the majority of the propagandists.

In actuality, the early members of Land and Freedom might not have been able to control the escalating mood of violence even had they not formed a murder squad or had they been able more effec-tively and systematically to define and discipline its activities. His-tory has occasionally seen movements that, in the manner of wildfire or of a plague, have spread out of control from one area to another, leaping from community to community through an indefinable kind of contagion. The call to violence, the adoption of terrorism as a mystique, is not unknown in contemporary times. In Russia after 1877, one deed seemed to generate another of even more drastic nature than the first and of even more sweeping intent. Most of the individual events have been chronicled in English-language works.[21] It is not the intent of this essay to report details. Nevertheless, an overview of the nature of terroristic deeds is essential to an under-standing of how terror came eventually to take over center stage.

The "disorganizers" of 1877 had firm examples of the usage of violence as model and inspiration. Although most of the propagan-dists of 1874 had gone to the people armed only with their illegal leaflets, violence had broken out from time to time.

Occasionally, trapped revolutionaries had drawn guns against the police in an effort to defend themselves and their comrades from arrest. Thus in 1875 a young radical named A. K. Tsitsianov (appar-ently a prince by title) had fought back when police attempted to search his quarters. The following year Ippolit Myshkin (operator of a Moscow printing press during the "crazy summer" and later to become a hero to his colleagues because of his dramatic speech to the court in the trial of 193) fired on government agents when they moved in to arrest him. Myshkin had devised what turned out to be an abortive mission to free the writer N. G. Chernyshevskii from Siberian exile. He was fully armed, for he had disguised himself as a gendarme for the occasion, but he had apparently incorrectly placed some of the accessories on his uniform and was recognized as a fake.[22]

It was in the South, however, particularly in the southern Ukraine, where many authorities argue the real roots of terrorism took life. There was more "fuel" in the South, wrote Serebriakov in his history of the society Land and Freedom, and "the battle with the government with arms in hand appeared more powerful in the revolutionary world."[23] It seems likely that the Southern *buntari* profited from their ties with the Ukrainian independence movement. Venturi suggests that a political revival struck the Ukraine as a response to independence movements in neighboring Slavic countries during the Balkan wars and that Russian revolutionaries benefited from the ferment.[24] Indeed, the Southern revolutionary circles seem to have maintained considerable contact with the Ukrainian nationalist movement. Osinskii is known to have been in touch—through his friend Debagorii-Mokrievich—with the student constitutionalists at Kiev University. He and his comrades apparently later (1878) conducted "conversations" with leading Ukrainophiles (A. F. Lindfors, I. I. Petrunkevich), although these negotiations never resulted in agreement for common action.[25] Most Ukrainian nationalists were not committed to violence, but their orientation to constitutionalism provided a "political" direction that may also have inspired the revolutionaries to favor direct "disorganizational" attacks on the government, which ordained political repression.

Many—perhaps the majority—of the later leading terrorists emerged from Southern *buntari* groups. Among them were A. I. Zheliabov, Mikhail Trigoni, G. D. Gol'denberg, Nikolai Kolodkevich, M. F. Frolenko, and N. I. Kibal'chich. The government was aware of this fact, and one of its spokesmen wrote:

The vitality of the circles of the South, which functioned much more actively than those of the North during the entire duration of the terrorist movement, is a fact worth remarking. It is among them that the idea of creating a revolutionary organization with a central core and discipline in special forms triumphs. . . . Energetic and capable leaders were never lacking in the South; those who fell into the hands of the police were rapidly replaced by others, which explains the fact that while the anarchists of the North and even their "center" (the Executive Committee [of the People's Will]) went through a violent crisis, the circles of Kiev continued at peak activity.[26]

In the South, the *buntari* set a pattern for the torture or murder of "traitors" to the revolutionary cause. In their elimination of government spies who had infiltrated into the movement or of revolutionaries who were thought to have succumbed to attractive offers to report activities to the police, the Ukrainians might be judged to be returning to the example set by the notorious Sergei Nechaev in 1869, when he murdered a student member of his revolutionary organization whom he presumed (or said he presumed) to be working for the police.[27] Although his primary crime lay in his accusation against a colleague later proved innocent of "spying," Nechaev became a symbol of manipulativeness, mystification, and unjustifiable violence that young radicals at the time deplored. Many young people (including particularly Natanson's circle) had been shocked by the "Machiavellian" morality of Nechaev in killing his own under accusations later demonstrated to have been false, and this deed has been credited with temporarily directing the whole revolutionary movement onto a nonviolent course.[28]

But by 1876, the code of revolution had changed. In Odessa in that year, a man named Gorinovich, suspected of spying for the police, was not murdered but tortured; he was attacked with a club and badly mutilated by acid sprayed in his face. He survived as a cripple.[29] Testimony from the circle that sponsored the deed indicated that the revolutionaries had no proof of Gorinovich's guilt, but based their attack on "suspicions," "guesses," and "rumors."[30] As instigator of the crime, the police sought the Kievan Lev Deich, one-time propagandist, who only a few years before had deplored Nechaev's "immoral" deed.[31] In approving murder in self-defense, in the liberation of comrades, or in coping with traitors, the revolutionaries of 1876 were taking a page out of the code of their predecessors, and even dedicated "villagers" seem to have agreed that this violence was justified.

In the long run, however, it was not projects to liberate colleagues, to eliminate traitors, or to defend one's person that roused the terrorist spirit. Rather it was the concept, vaguely expressed (in Aptekman's words), that the "disorganizers" might utilize violence against "government arbitrary deeds" when "the honor of the whole revolutionary party" was at stake—a suggestion subject to wise and unwise interpretation and never carefully defined at all.[32] Under this loose charge, with "broad authority and significant material means," the supposedly disciplined "disorganizing" squad got out of hand almost from the start.

This group from its origins was so shrouded in secrecy and deceit as to shed doubt on its existence as a specific and definite unit. Membership was defined only by the disorganizers themselves, and it is probable that several different circles were engaged in violent deeds in several parts of the country at the same time with little coordination. Valer'ian Osinskii and his Kievan friend Mikhail Frolenko, later deeply involved in efforts to assassinate the tsar, considered themselves "disorganizers;" we need only follow their activities as described below. Osinskii had been close to the Natanson circle and thus intimately involved in discussions of violence and its purposes. In the South, these leaders found many temporary assistants, who may or may not have belonged to any clear subgroup—or even to Land and Freedom itself. Less has been written of "disorganizers" elsewhere, but a later historian has unearthed evidence that Aleksandr Kviatkovskii, A. K. Presniakov, and N. S. Tiutchev (the latter a longtime friend of the Natansons) formed a "separate section, a militant brigade (*druzhina*)" within the disorganization group itself, and that the three comprised a "militant *troika* . . . welded by links of revolutionary comradeship."[33] Although they were always mobile, this *troika* of murderers operated primarily in the cities of the North.

Not just in membership but in plots and activities, the "disorganizers" proved to be self-defining and self-motivated. Acts of violence came to be committed by regional terrorists whose allegiance to the central organization was negligible, even though they may have participated in negotiations with the Land and Freedom core. Murderous deeds in the South, planned and executed by the *buntari* there, were often not ordained or even approved by the St. Petersburg center, as evidenced by the fact that the proclamations claiming responsibility for the murders of several Kievan tsarist officials (Procuror M. M. Kotliarevskii, Police Chief G. E. Geiking) were published and distributed locally (not by the St. Petersburg revolutionary press) and signed by a Nechaev-like mystifying local "Executive Committee" (not by the central Land and Freedom core).[34] The links of the Southern *buntari* to the Northern *narodniki* were often tenuous because of the scorn of the former for the concept of limited, defined terrorist action. On one occasion Osinskii, angered at the restrictions imposed by the central group, left St. Petersburg in a huff to return to his own headquarters in Kiev, where terrorism found more sympathy and support.[35] In spite of his commitment to the Natansons, Osinskii always considered himself a free agent, able to act as he saw fit. He and Frolenko slipped back and forth between North and South, plotting acts of violence on their own initiative, at the instigation of comrades or circles, or occasionally (as in the case of Governor General F. F. Trepov) as St. Petersburg requested. They seem to have acted as hit men, working on assignment from others but operating often on their own. Very probably the Kviatkovskii brigade functioned in the same manner, although its location nearer the capital city may have encouraged closer coordination with the Land and Freedom core.

Under the circumstances, it is not surprising that once violence began in earnest, it fed upon its own dramatic nature, intoxicated its proponents, and soon gathered momentum beyond the ability of any individual or group to control it. Although scholars have devoted more attention to the highly-publicized campaigns of terrorism in 1878, the year 1877 had seen a dramatic increase in revolutionary crimes.

That spring, Mark Natanson was arrested. He was one of the few who had remained in St. Petersburg while his comrades hurried to the provinces. His loss was a heavy blow to the revolutionary cause, and as Figner pointed out, it was a great tribute to his organizational ability that Land and Freedom survived at all.[36] The revolutionaries blamed a worker named Finogenov for what they believed to be the betrayal of Natanson to the police, and shortly Finogenov was murdered, by a hand unknown.[37] On June 19 of the same year, Presniakov and his brigade murdered a "traitor" named Sharashkin in Nova Derevna, near the capital city; Sharashkin too was suspected of aiding the police in Natanson's arrest. The northern murders slowed to a halt when Presniakov was arrested in the autumn of 1877. But early the next year, two of the Southern *buntari* ambushed and stabbed one Adam Nikonov in Rostov-on-Don for his supposed betrayal to the police of over thirty Southern radicals. Nikonov died two weeks later. Historians of the revolution later credited the murder to the "disorganizers" (probably self-styled) Ivan Ivichevich, well known Southern Bakuninist, and his friend Ludovic Brantner, but according to one source, a worker named Sentianin was also involved.[38]

Meanwhile, in the North, Presniakov's comrades devised plans to "liberate" him from prison, and in early March such plans resulted in the arrest (and exile to Siberia) of Presniakov's friend Tiutchev, who was hanging around a fish market day after day, watching the prison gates and noting prison routines. Tiutchev was probably betrayed to police by a worker. In spite of his arrest, his comrades continued to plot, and on April 16 Presniakov was liberated and whisked away in a coach drawn by the revolutionary stallion Varvar'; he had befuddled the guard who was taking him to the baths by throwing cigarette ashes into his eyes.[39] By early 1879, Presniakov was back in action. In February he single-handedly killed the "spy" Aleksandr Zharkov, who had supposedly betrayed to the police the location of the new Land and Freedom press. Presniakov approached Zharkov—a small, thin man—on the banks of the Neva in broad daylight and read him a formal sentence. Zharkov never said a word, nor moved, nor objected. Presniakov shot him, weighted the body, tossed it into the river, and walked off. A man of "iron confidence and calm, relentless self-control," Presniakov told a friend that he thought of spies as vicious animals and felt no remorse when called upon to shoot them.[40] He was subsequently caught by the police and hanged on November 4, 1880, in connection with various assassination attempts.

By 1878, many more militant terrorists were making a point of carrying arms and using them when attacked. In January of that year, in a spectacular display, I. M. Koval'skii, later hanged for his efforts, shot it out with Kiev police who attempted to search his "conspiratorial quarters." When he was ordered to empty his pockets, Koval'skii pulled out a revolver and fired on the gendarmes, wounding several of them and the doorman as well. The police quickly retreated and regrouped. When they returned, the militant rebel went for them with a dagger, but they overpowered and captured him.[41] Koval'skii set a pattern for revolutionaries when threatened with arrest, but it was basically an urban pattern. In the villages, propagandists were seldom armed. They suffered fewer betrayals to the police, and when threatened with arrest, they tended to face the music or slip quietly away. Nevertheless, if Vera Figner may be considered a model, the narodniki had little quarrel with the early "executions" of spies or with violence undertaken in self-defense, in spite of the fact that under similar circumstances their own reactions were less dramatic.[42]

The instinctive tendency to reach for violence as a solution led the revolutionaries to their wildest efforts in the early months of 1878, and thereafter the escalation of assassination to regicide was probably inevitable. The episode that inaugurated a series of acts directed against important government officials was a simple one. In August

1877, the Governor-General of St. Petersburg, one F. F. Trepov, visited a prison then under his charge and was met with an act of petty insubordination by an imprisoned revolutionary named A. S. Emel'ianov (pseudonym: Bogoliubov), a member of the Natanson circle of 1876. Summoned to a review by the governor-general in the prison yard, Emel'ianov first tried to approach this official and later sassily refused to remove his cap in deference. The angry Trepov ordered him flogged, and indeed he was. That the punishment did not fit the jibe might be argued by anyone; by the revolutionaries, the episode was deliberately magnified into a *cause célèbre*. From the Ukraine, Frolenko, Osinskii, Dmitrii Lizogub, G. A. Popko, and others hurried to the capital city, intent on revenge.[43] Violence was their first thought. Still they never had the opportunity to avenge Emelianov because before their plans were complete, their task was surprisingly assumed by a young woman named Vera Zasulich.

The case of Zasulich is unique, and it set a new course for the Russian revolutionary terrorists. This radical-minded, 29-year-old woman had been teaching and working in St. Petersburg nine years before at the time of Nechaev's futile efforts to foment conspiracy and revolution among university students in the capital city. She knew Nechaev and his friends, although she never completely fell under the spell of the dark-eyed, magnetic young leader.[44] Nevertheless, for her association with the conspirators she was arrested, temporarily imprisoned, and exiled in spite of being officially proclaimed innocent. By 1875 she had found her way back to Southern Russia, where her awkward efforts to work among the Ukrainian peasantry (she did not even speak the language with any fluency) met with little success. Distressed by her failure to manage as a propagandist, she moved to Kiev with considerable relief.[45] Her friend (and soon her lover) Lev Deich was there, and he drew her into revolutionary circles. For a time, he attempted to teach her how to use a gun.[46] In 1877, he persuaded her to move to St. Petersburg in order to protect her from involvement in the fateful "Chigirin affair," the effort of Deich and his friends to foment revolution among the peasants of the Chigirin district by deceiving them into thinking the revolutionists were agents of the tsar himself.

Zasulich was a woman of courage and commitment; she was to dedicate her lifetime to the Russian revolutionary movement and never hesitated when she felt commanded by the cause. Still in St. Petersburg, she felt miserable and shy. She was ill at ease in the company of the sophisticated radicals of the capital city and did not easily mix with the articulate, argumentative, outgoing Land and Freedom group. She lived alone with a Kiev friend—Mariia Fedorova/Zagorskaia/Kolenkina, later arrested only after armed resistance—and worked as an assistant typesetter on the Free Russian Typography, a radical press.[47] From dreary routine she came alive when she heard that Deich and his companions had been arrested and were being held in Kiev central prison.[48] She agonized to see them set free.

Desperate for assistance from her Kiev acquaintances who were then in the capital city, Zasulich found herself in a dilemma. As agents of Land and Freedom, Frolenko and his friends were busy planning to avenge Emelianov's painful and humiliating fate at the hands of Governor-General Trepov. They had made a commitment, and they could not undertake any enterprise in the Ukraine until their St. Petersburg plot was laid, hatched, and executed.[49] Zasulich and Kolenkina were already aware of the conspirators' planning. They were perhaps even scornful of the amount of time that these Southern *buntari* were dedicating to its realization, for six months had passed since the Emel'ianov incident. At any rate, for Zasulich, her lover's plight was the last straw, and she and Kolenkina determined to take matters into their own hands. They waited only until sentences had been announced for the 193 propagandists then on trial, apparently aware that any deed might well cause the government to increase what turned out to be unexpectedly light punishments for those accused of antigovernment actions in the "crazy summer" of 1874.[50] Once sentences had been determined, Zasulich moved. She shot Governor-General Trepov herself.

The story of Zasulich's attempt on the life of Trepov has been told often before and need not be repeated here in detail. Briefly, after having drawn straws for the honor with her friend Kolenkina, who refused to let her walk alone into disaster,[51] Zasulich acquired a gun through her Southern acquaintances. On January 24, 1878, she went to Trepov's office as an ordinary petitioner. Politely waiting until her name was called, she then stepped forward and shot the governor-general in broad daylight and in the presence of several witnesses. With what might be considered typical revolutionary ineptitude, she failed to kill her victim but winged him seriously enough so that he required hospitalization. She made no attempt to escape and submitted calmly to arrest.

At the prompt trial by jury (a government error that scholars have long sought to explain), Zasulich's attorney cleverly turned the procedure into a trial of Trepov and an evaluation of his policies and behavior. The astonishing result was that Zasulich was exonerated. As she left the courtroom, she and her friends feared immediate retaliation by the police in the form of administrative (that is, not judicially-ordained) exile. Outside in Senate square, confusion, excitement, and near-rioting reigned. It was perhaps prophetic that violence broke out again and that a young man died, apparently a suicide, either seeking martyrdom of his own or distracting attention for the heroine.[52] Did Zasulich feel herself responsible for his death? In the confusion, she slipped away to safety at Dr. Orest Veimar's apartment, whence she shortly escaped abroad, aided and accompanied by the radical writer Dmitrii Klements and Land and Freedom's foreign ambassador, Aaron Zundelevich.

Zasulich's deed accomplished exactly what she wished. Immediately, to her pleasure, Frolenko and Osinskii (relieved of their burden of revenge) slipped south to engineer a *tour de force* rescue of Deich and his friends, Iakob Stefanovich and I. V. Bokhanovskii, from Kiev central prison. Frolenko got himself a job as prison guard and at an appointed time simply released the conspirators from their cells, let them out of the gate to which he had a key, and escorted them to an escape riverboat, manned by Osinskii.[53] Deich stopped briefly in St. Petersburg to command a hero's welcome and some revolutionary assistance, and within a few months he had joined Zasulich in the safety of Switzerland.[54]

Meanwhile, Zasulich received enormous publicity; her name became a household word among the radicals of her day. In Russia, the radical press and public saw her act as a deed of highest heroism.[55] The 193 propagandists emerging from prison and trial in early 1878 gasped in admiration, although (as Zasulich had feared) many of them found themselves victims of government retaliation when their sentences—prison, exile, or surveillance—were increased on the basis of police irritation and alarm. Propagandists in the provinces reported their excitement when they heard of Zasulich's exoneration.[56] Abroad, in the emigré journals of Switzerland, she was hailed as a heroine, and in the radical press of France her case was followed in detail.[57] Never comfortable with publicity and fame, Zasulich chose to withdraw as quietly as possible into her Geneva circle.[58]

Still she could never withdraw from the impact of her attack on Trepov, and she never seems to have anticipated its results on a broad scale. For this first terrorist attack on a government official accelerated violence and set the revolutionaries on a new and dangerous path of which Zasulich herself could never approve. The gunshot from her uneasy hand propelled terrorism on its way. The Zasulich affair, Sergei Kravchinskii wrote later (having recognized it as inspiring his own violent deed), was "one of the turning points in the history of the Russian revolution" and "at once changed the character of our struggle with the government."[59] Mikhail Popov, never a terrorist, wrote that "the shot of V. I. [Zasulich] was a call to the revolutionary world to a new path of struggle. . . . Many revolutionaries of our time so understood it."[60] On the basis of Zasulich's heroism, N. I. Kibal'chich, manufacturer of bombs, decided to join the terrorists, and without him they would have been lost indeed.[61] Deich himself later wrote that his lover's shot had activated revolutionaries of all kinds, and he called it the forefather of terrorism.[62]

Zasulich had never been a terrorist, and for years she suffered pangs of remorse when she came to understand the broader ramifications of what she had done. Never cheerful or outgoing, she was emotionally devastated as she watched deeds of violence escalate in number and intent. More than a year later, when word reached Geneva of the attempt on the life of Alexander II in the spring of 1879, Zasulich "hid herself from everyone in a state of deep depression."[63] She had acted the assassin when impelled by deep commitment, but she was seldom a propagandist and never a terrorist at heart. It was clearly agony for her to recognize that her attempt on the life of Trepov inspired the terrorists to an exaltation of violence that gripped them until the assassination of the tsar and beyond.

Again the lead came from the Ukraine. Again it seems in great measure uncontrolled by order from Land and Freedom or its administrative center, although one historian of that organization strangely credits this society for all assassination attempts.[64] On February 23, inspired by the Zasulich example, three men attacked the acting procuror for Kiev province as he approached his home late at night. They have been variously identified (Alexei Fedorov, Ivan Ivichevich, P. N. Fomin/A. F. Medvedev, Southern *buntari* all), but it seems likely that Osinskii, who had returned south after the Zasulich attempt, was the leading perpetrator of the deed and perhaps even a participant;[65] always rebellious and independent, Osinskii was caught and hanged the following year. This attack on M. M. Kotliarevskii, who survived, was lauded and explained in a proclamation issued locally in Kiev, a fact that indicates that Land and Freedom, centered in St. Petersburg, was not in charge.[66] A few days after the Kotliarevskii episode, a young revolutionary named Ladislas Izbitskii, whose brother had murdered the "spy" Nikonov the year before, pulled a

gun on a policeman who attempted to arrest him while he was post-
ing the proclamation mentioned above.[67] The government blamed
these terrorist activities for an increasing rebelliousness among university students. All through March there were riots at Kiev University, from which 120 students were eventually expelled, and one student lay dead after violence erupted at the Petrovskii agricultural
school in Moscow.[68]

The unsuccessful Kotliarevskii attempt was almost immediately
followed by threats against the life of Kiev Police Chief G. E. Geiking,
threats distributed throughout the city in a proclamation devised by
Osinskii and signed with the deliberately mysterious designation
"Executive Committee," the logo of which was the dagger and the
pistol crossed. On May 24 in Kiev, G. A. Popko attacked Geiking as
he returned home late at night; the weapon was a dagger, but as
Popko turned to flee he was pursued by a peasant, at whom he fired
a gun; by a masonry worker, whom he shot and killed; and by a
policeman, whom he wounded. Geiking died of his wounds five days
later.[69]

Escalating violence could hardly go unremarked by the propagandist members of Land and Freedom. Within that organization and in
its central core, disagreements attest a growing bifurcation and an
increasing uncertainty and nervousness among central administrators.
The first crisis concerning the nature and importance of violence
occurred in spring 1878. The presence in St. Petersburg of Valer'ian
Osinskii precipitated the debate; in the winter of 1877–78 he was
living in the capital city, along with the group of Southern terrorists
(Frolenko, Popko, and others) who had come there with the aim of
eliminating Governor-General Trepov. Mariia Nikolaevna Olovenni-
kova/Oshanina was there too; a Jacobin from Orel, she had not
joined Land and Freedom, but she was a friend to the "disorganizers"
and became a leading member of the terrorist faction after the
society split. At frequent meetings in the quarters of Aleksandr
Kviatkovskii (colleague of Tiutchev and Presniakov in the subgroup
of the "disorganization" squad), even Ol'ga Natanson, whose husband was still in prison, was apparently swayed by the arguments for
increasing violence.[70]

Osinskii pressed the cause of violence at a meeting of St. Petersburg radicals in May 1878. The growing crisis about revolutionary
methods and the accidental presence of so many young Land and
Freedom supporters in the capital city made this an ideal time for
debate. It is possible but not likely that an earlier agreement called

for annual reviews of Land and Freedom's policies and activities, but our only reference to such a document comes from Aptekman, whose notes were written later and remain fuzzy in regard to exact dates.[71] Whatever the basis, a meeting of all society members who were currently in the capital city—the group that Aptekman calls the council—occurred at this time, and here Osinskii set forth his demands and those of his comrades.

The Southern terrorists insisted that measures be taken to strengthen the "disorganizational activity" of the society. In particular, Osinskii proposed increasing financial support for violence and suggested that such could be achieved through the estate of the wealthy Dmitrii Lizogub, a revolutionary sympathizer from the South who had been approached earlier by Natanson, and if necessary through "expropriation" of government, public, and even private wealth. He apparently argued his case with all the passion he could so often muster.

But Osinskii went too far and lost his cause. For one thing, he did not have majority support. Several of his own friends had recently left for Kiev, and it is probable that many of them were not official voting members of Land and Freedom anyway. On the other hand, the St. Petersburg group had been temporarily expanded by several *narodniki* whose provincial settlements had recently been raided and abandoned. M. R. Popov was there; an old friend to the Natansons, he never abandoned his propagandist dreams. Aleksandr Barannikov (later to be converted to terrorism by Frolenko and Oshanina), Adrian Mikhailov, and perhaps even Kviatkovskii, whose appetite for violence came and went, may still have been oriented toward the *narodnik* faction. Plekhanov (a natural orator) and Aptekman spoke strongly against the escalating terror. What support might have been offered to Osinskii by Aaron Zundelevich, Aleksei Oboleshov, and Ol'ga Natanson was apparently hesitant and certainly insufficient to carry the vote.

The result was that Osinskii was sharply rebuffed. The majority of the council opposed the use of violence and "cautioned against excessive attraction to this ill-defined and dangerous method, which can become a source of very serious confusion."[72] The victors cited the organization's original purposes and called on the Southerners to recognize that "disorganization," like the central administration, was devised to serve propagandists, those members performing the function still most dear to the majority's aims. "The debates on this matter," wrote a participant, "were lengthy and very heated. But the villagers were still in power then. The prevailing mood of the society was strictly *narodnik*."[73] In anger, Osinskii left for Kiev. He had lost the battle but not the war.

Indeed, the central Land and Freedom core continued to be pressed toward change by individuals as well as by events. Osinskii had failed, but the issue remained. Shortly after he left, the *narodnik* members of Land and Freedom—watching uneasily from the capital city as violence accelerated—found themselves again under attack by one of their members who demanded that they review their strategies and revise their methods. This time the question concerned the nature of organization: of discipline, secrecy, and conspiracy as administrative principles, principles that, whether or not they were so recognized, were essential to the movement for "disorganization" and terrorism. This time, in the early summer of 1878, it was Aleksandr Mikhailov who demanded the restructuring of the society—that same Mikhailov who (as a close friend of Ol'ga Natanson) had participated in planning the original program and who had recently returned from propagandizing among schismatics in Saratov.

At a meeting (date unknown) of Land and Freedom members present in the capital city, Mikhailov demanded what one of his colleagues later called "radical changes of the constitution along the lines of centralization of revolutionary forces and a greater dependence of local groups upon the center."[74] He seems to have had a proposal in hand—or at least Soviet scholars date the draft of such a scheme from the months of April and May 1878.[75] Always impressed by the Bakunin-Nechaev "Catechism" that called for obedience and loyalty, secrecy and conspiracy within a revolutionary organization,[76] Mikhailov now urged members to tighten up their freewheeling, easygoing operation. By temperament he was a conspirator and even now keenly aware of the rising tide of violence. He argued that the decision of the majority should always hold sway over members of the organization, that members should pledge their obedience to the majority, and that following the center's dicta should be mandatory for all. The party simply must, he told one of his friends, "create a circle that would direct provincial actions, that such a structure of this circle was necessary to secure [ourselves] from spies."[77]

As with Osinskii's proposals, a heated argument ensued. Eventually Mikhailov had his way, and his opponents backed down.[78] The members present entrusted him to write a constitution along the lines he proposed and to delegate more authority to the party's central core, hereafter much more carefully defined, of which Mikhailov himself was becoming the leading member.

The Mikhailov constitution—at least in the draft form in which it has been preserved—set far more specific demands on the members of the organization not yet commonly known as Land and Freedom. Devised by Mikhailov himself and written with many corrections and strikeovers in the hand of Oboleshov, his closest friend, the statute never refers to any document it might be revising and seems likely, therefore, to represent the first written constitution that replaced the informal agreements entered into by the St. Petersburg circles the year before.

By the Mikhailov constitution of 1878, members are required to submit to the rulings of the organization's "basic circle." They must be willing to give their forces, money, sympathies, and even their lives for the cause, as the cause and its needs were defined by the majority, to whom the minority must always submit (articles 3, 7).[79] Although individuals were still granted the independence to choose the type of activity they preferred, the central circle could oblige any member to take up any activity when free volunteers were not forthcoming (article 17), a clause of which Mikhailov was frequently to take advantage. The "basic circle," located in St. Petersburg, was said to "control" the activity of "all groups and of each member separately."[80] "Full secrecy" was listed among "the basic principles of the organization," and provision was made for secret codes, passwords, and secret one-on-one meetings.[81] Members of the "basic circle" were encouraged to enter into local groups without revealing their identities as core leaders (article 29). Drawing on the famous "Catechism" devised by Nechaev with Bakunin's assistance, Mikhailov insisted that although any member might at any time leave the "basic circle," he might never reveal secrets or speak of his membership, and should he do so, "then the given member should be . . ."—but the document falters here, and the phrases "immediately killed" and thereafter "subjected to . . ." are crossed off and remain unreplaced, as if in disagreement between the composers (article 20).[82] Nevertheless "the ends," boldly proclaims the document, "justify the means" (article 9).[83]

Thus the statute of 1878—if indeed, as seems likely, Mikhailov's draft was adopted with only minor amendments—is that of a conspiratorial society, tightly linked and disciplined, highly centralized, and moving to abandon those live-and-let-live principles adopted the year before. The call for secrecy and obedience that found its way into the organizational principles of Land and Freedom served— whether by design or accident—to protect and encourage the perpetrators of the violence that was rising to formidable dimensions. The statute of 1878 anticipated the needs that arose the following year when Mikhailov embarked on his own campaign of terror and revenge. More importantly, as V. A. Tvardovskaia has pointed out, these constitutional revisions laid the basis for the conspiratorial structure that distinguished the later society, the People's Will.[84] Although the *narodniki* had denied Osinskii's request to increase the activity, authority, and financing of the terrorists, the members of Land and Freedom granted to Mikhailov the kind of organization that terrorism demanded.

Meanwhile, violence continued apace. One of the most spectacular of all "liberation" efforts occurred early in June 1878 outside the city of Kharkov and ended in a shoot-out between revolutionaries and police guards. Again instigation came from outside the Land and Freedom core, although many of its "disorganizers" took part, operating apparently as independent agents and not bound by the party's rules. This intricately planned liberation of the heroes of the trial of 193 occurred primarily at the instigation of one of their codefendants, Sof'ia Perovskaia, later regicide, but at the time a convinced *narodnik*. For the wellborn Perovskaia, whose own sufferings had been minimal and had not included any imprisonment before the trial, the dramatic speech of Ippolit Myshkin before the court served as an inspiration for what became an *idée fixe*.[85] Exonerated and released, she sought out friends in St. Petersburg and attempted to persuade them to help the propagandist leaders to escape, pressing her case to the point of becoming argumentative and irritating in her efforts. Remembering the successful efforts of Frolenko and Osinskii in Kiev a few months before, she sent her lover Lev Tikhomirov, later terrorist and writer, to enlist their aid, and when he returned without plans and results, she berated him severely and broke off their relationship.[86] Finally mounting a conspiracy, Perovskaia was greatly disappointed when Myshkin was secretly transferred to prison by freight train before plans for his escape could be activated. The attempt had to be limited to two other defendants—P. I. Voinaral'skii and S. S. Kovalik, who, like Myshkin, had been sentenced to ten years at hard labor.

No more intricate preparations were made in any conspiracy to murder a tsar. Fifteen or more people were eventually involved in the planning, among them Frolenko, who had recently so easily succeeded in bringing about the prison escape of Deich and his friends. Roles complete with disguises and false identification were assumed by such conspirators as Aleksandr Mikhailov, Perovskaia, Nikolai Morozov, Aleksandr Barannikov, Aleksandr Kviatkovskii, and others.[87] The conspirators were equipped with guns and dynamite, although they never seemed to have found a use for the latter. At a Kharkov apartment rented for headquarters, Mariia Nikolaevna Olovennikova/ Oshanina, terrorist, "Jacobin," and recently licensed paramedic, set up a field hospital to nurse potential wounded.[88]

Word was passed secretly about the scheduled transfer of the prisoners, but at the last minute the conspiracy failed. Fomin/ Medvedev lost his way en route to the crucial rendezvous; Barannikov fired for little reason at the coach, wounding a coachman and a horse; Kovalik was not in the carriage at all; and Voinaral'skii, whom the conspirators had omitted to forewarn, did not attempt to leap from the vehicle as they had hoped.[89] When the "liberators" reassembled at the conspiratorial apartment, it was to pack and flee. At the railroad station, Fomin/Medvedev was caught and arrested, but the others managed to escape.[90] Oshanina smuggled out the dynamite and guns in her luggage. Depressed by failure, Perovskaia slipped back into Kharkov for another attempt. This time, as with the successful Kiev manipulations, she hoped to plant a guard inside the prison walls. Frolenko helped for a while, but the project fell apart when he was called away and when the young designated spy/guard proved unreliable.[91] Even Perovskaia gave up, soon to manipulate her own escape from administrative exile and then to retreat to her studies and work as paramedic in Kharkov.

Undeterred by failure, the revolutionaries continued to dream of freeing their colleagues from imprisonment. Two attempts were made by unidentified radicals to liberate Fomin/Medvedev, but both of them proved abortive.[92] No more successful was Morozov's carefully planned and centrally sanctioned attempt to free Katarina Breshko-Breshkovskaia, who was to be transported to Siberian exile in early August 1878. Fully armed and eager to shoot, Morozov holed up in an inn in Nizhni-Novgorod, but Breshko-Breshkovskaia's escort guard chose another route and Morozov was forced to return to St. Petersburg empty-handed.[93] Meanwhile, Koval'skii, who had fired on approaching police in January, was sentenced to death by a military court in Odessa. At the demonstrations mounted by revolutionaries at the time of his execution, at least one man was killed, and Popko, the wealthy Dmitrii Lizogub (later hanged), and a revolutionary named Chubarov (pseudonym: Kaptan) were arrested.[94]

That summer the focus of terrorism shifted in locale to the capital city and in motivation to revenge with the daring murder of N. V. Mezentsev, head of the Third Section, the Russian secret police. There is no doubt that this assassination, executed by Sergei Kravchinskii on August 4, 1878, was inspired by Zasulich's deed and by Kravchinskii's own vision of himself as heroic avenger. A man of great strength, warmth, and ebullience, Kravchinskii had gone "to the people" in 1872, never participating in the "settlement" movement but for a time putting his muscle to test in a woodcutters' artel. Thereafter his activities led him abroad: he fought in the Balkan wars, wrote and translated in an Italian prison, and became a friend to leading revolutionaries in exile in Switzerland.[95] Zasulich's deed found him in Geneva where he was editing the revolutionary periodical *Obshchina* (The Commune) with his expatriate friends.

Kravchinskii poured his enthusiasm for Zasulich into an ecstatic editorial.

On the 24th of January in Petersburg, in the office of the city chief, there rang out a shot which was echoed in all Europe more loudly than all the Balkan cannons.

The world of egotism, calculation, self-interest, the world of banality and indifference was suddenly struck in the eye by an event of the most un-selfcentered selflessness, of the highest heroism.

A young girl fearlessly and in spite of all terrors entered the quarters of an outrageous despot in order not to leave unpunished an insult to a man whom she had never seen.

People fear heroism: it forces them to be too uncomfortably aware of their own banality. . . . But here the fact was too clear, too obvious. The wondrous form of the young avenger, flowing with radiance, has stamped itself upon the imagination of everyone. And the world bows before her.[96]

Adventurous, impulsive, and incautious, the challenged and excited Kravchinskii could not let himself be outdone in daring. In the spring of 1878, he returned secretly to St. Petersburg to his friends in Land and Freedom, filled with plans to become an assassin himself.[97]

Unfortunately, Kravchinskii was the least discreet of conspirators. His comrades were always alarmed and dismayed by his behavior. A gregarious and boisterous person, he attended secret meetings at Aleksandra Malinovskaia's without taking any precautions and even called attention to himself by exhorting his cabdriver to breakneck speeds on the way to the conspiratorial apartment. He spoke openly of his intentions and reported on his plans by letter to any number of absent comrades. In conjunction with his passion for elegance, he lived under the false documents of a Caucasian prince, dressed as a nobleman, and delighted in being called "Your Excellency" by his servants. He haunted shops and bought knickknacks for himself and his friends until he slipped into perennial debt and had to borrow money from everyone, including Oboleshov, then the treasurer of Land and Freedom.[98] Only by angry and eloquent insistence were his comrades able to persuade him to accept their aid and to plan an escape after accomplishing his daring feat, for he said he preferred to do his deed heroically alone (like Zasulich), facing arrest with courage and execution with aplomb.

On the fatal day, Kravchinskii stabbed Mezentsev on a public street in St. Petersburg. At the last minute, Zundelevich, who had just returned from abroad, was recruited as a signalman and was able to slip out of the square unobserved after performing his assigned task. Barannikov stood nearby, and it was he who shot and wounded Mezentsev's companion when the latter pursued the assassin. The escape carriage, drawn by the ubiquitous revolutionary stallion Varvar' and driven by Adrian Mikhailov, was waiting at the corner, but Varvar' was frightened by the shot and Mikhailov had trouble controlling him. Kravchinskii leaped into the carriage; Barannikov only made it by running behind, barely catching on. The conspirators escaped without a trace. Even Mezentsev's body guard was unable to identify them. Mezentsev himself died of stab woulds later in the day.[99]

To the horror of his friends, Kravchinskii refused to leave St. Petersburg. Instead, a few months later in a dramatic (some said "romantic") pamphlet entitled "A Death for a Death," he published the reasons for his action: the crimes of Mezentzev, against whom he credited the convictions of the 193, sundry exiles, mistreatment of prisoners at Petropavlovsk, and the hanging of Koval'skii, which had occurred in Kharkov on August 2 and which was actually long antedated by Kravchinskii's plot.[100]

Strangely, like Zasulich, Kravchinskii was no true terrorist. Having committed murder and explained it, he proceeded (in the pages of the first issue of the journal *Zemlia i Volia* [Land and Freedom], dated November 1, 1878), to urge others to abstain. "We must remember," he wrote,

that not by this route will we attain the liberation of the working masses. Terrorism has nothing in common with the struggle against the foundations of the existing order. Only a class can rise against a class, only the people themselves can destroy the system. Therefore the great bulk of our forces must work in the midst of the people. The terrorists—they are only a defensive detachment, the purpose of which is to protect these [village] workers from the traitorous blows of the enemy.... Directing all our forces towards the struggle with the government, we [would], of course, greatly expedite its fall. But then, having no roots in the people, we will not be in a position to follow through our triumph. It will be a Pyrrhic victory.... At the price of bloody battle and undoubtedly heavy losses, we will have gained nothing for our cause.[101]

This perhaps even now anachronistic *narodnik* stance set Kravchinskii at odds with many terrorists, including Nikolai Morozov, one of the other editors of *Land and Freedom*, who was already becoming fascinated with the thought of pure violence as the vehicle for revolutionary action. Morozov, however, held his tongue, and the quarrel did not yet develop to a climax, for later in November, arguing every inch of the way, Kravchinskii was persuaded by his worried friends to leave the country. The Land and Freedom leadership begged him to return to Europe to study how to manufacture dynamite.[102] They told him they needed his help, but secretly they wrote to Deich and Zasulich in Geneva and urged them to keep Kravchinskii there.[103] Kravchinskii fell for the plan, although he insisted that he would be back. Although he tried, he never made it; he never returned to his native land. Deich reports that he longed to be summoned by his friends, perhaps to some new grand heroic task.[104]

It is an irony of history that the two assassins that most inspired the Russian terrorists were individuals who on principle stood opposed to terror. For Kravchinskii's action, like that of Zasulich on whose example it was based, lent the movement new life, particularly as the proponents of violence found themselves forced to fight for their lives against a new police offensive.[105] In the St. Petersburg roundup that followed Mezentsev's death, the police, aided and abetted by a series of extraordinary anonymous letters (the author of which has never been identified),[106] were unable to lay their hands on or even to discover the identity of the murderer. Instead they settled for the arrest and detention of many revolutionaries who had not directly participated in the crime, or who were only peripherally concerned.

Thus early in October, following an anonymous tip, police located and arrested Aleksei Oboleshov/Saburov, Ol'ga Natanson (whose husband was already in exile), and Adrian Mikhailov, whose identity as the coachman in Mezentsev's murder was not established until much later.[107] Oboleshov's arrest revealed and destroyed the passport engraving enterprise that Land and Freedom had established in his rooms, and Adrian Mikhailov's detention was accompanied by the tracing of the revolutionary stallion Varvar', whose loss was a blow to the terrorist cause—from then on horses had to be leased from a professional stable.[108]

The discovery of the quarters occupied by Aleksandra Malinovskaia and her friend Fedorova/Zagorskaia/Kolenkina (Zasulich's one-time roommate) brought the matter even closer to home: one or both of them was rumored to be Kravchinskii's girlfriend and he had often visited there, along with such illegal revolutionaries as Sof'ia Perovskaia and Ol'ga Liubatovich, both recently escaped from exile. On the day the police closed in, Morozov, Liubatovich, and others had been invited to the apartment for a nameday celebration, but they had not yet arrived and received warning in time. During the police raid, Kolenkina pulled a gun out from under her pillow—she always carried a revolver—and shot twice at one of the policemen, but in standard revolutionary form she missed, and both women were taken into custody.[109]

The mysterious anonymous letter writer as well as trails picked up at the conspiratorial apartments led the police to many other individuals. A. F. Annenskii, his wife (the sister of the notorious P. N. Tkachev, who had already escaped abroad), and Tkachev's girl friend, A. N. Dement'eva, were picked up for questioning; although Dement'eva was released and soon permitted to move abroad to join her lover, Annenskii was eventually condemned by administrative order to a less pleasant fate in Siberia.[110] Violence reared again in December when V. A. Dubrovin and several companions resisted arrest; Dubrovin first shot at the invading police and then attacked one of them with a dagger, which (he told Popov) he always carried with him. Dubrovin's "testament," left in notes apparently discovered by the police, urged his revolutionary friends to acquire better revolvers and learn how to shoot.[111] Because he was an army officer, he was condemned by court martial and executed in April 1879. Meanwhile in the course of the same police campaign, Aleksandr Mikhailov, leader of the Land and Freedom St. Petersburg core, was arrested. The revolutionaries might have sustained a devastating loss, but Mikhailov struck the police officer with his own handcuffs and managed to escape.[112] In November 1878, a man named Sentianin (probably involved in the murder of the "spy" Nikonov) pulled a gun on the Kharkov police when they attempted to arrest him[113] and a month later Sergei Bobokhov, one-time student at the Medical-Surgical Academy, shot at a police officer who attempted to stop him as he was fleeing Archangel, to which he had been exiled for propagandizing.[114]

The St. Petersburg revolutionaries were unaware of the anonymous letters that had tipped off the police to their names and habitations, but they recognized the probability of some sort of organizational leak and took the usual violent action to plug it. Now Presniakov, recently escaped from prison, murdered the "spy" Zharkov, a deed almost certainly ordered by Aleksandr Mikhailov of the central Land and Freedom core. Its accomplishment was shortly announced in the St. Petersburg revolutionary press.[115]

Soon thereafter the revolutionaries' own spy, artfully planted in the offices of the Third Section,[116] reported another betrayal: a worker named N. V. Reinshtein, a trusted friend and colleague to Stepan Khalturin (soon to be bomber of the Winter Palace) in an organization called the North Russian Workers Union, was reporting all he knew direct to the secret police. Reinshtein had seemed a good friend to the revolutionaries: he made his quarters into a library of underground publications, he supplied the radicals with beautifully sealed false documents, and he was particularly adept in propagandizing the blue collar classes.[117] His murder was one of the more gruesome the revolutionaries accomplished. The crime occurred in a Moscow hotel room to which the unsuspecting victim had been dispatched on Workers Union business. The assailant met Reinshtein in his room, apparently by appointment, stabbed him repeatedly, and left the body to rot in its own blood. When the police discovered the corpse a week later, it was already in a state of decay. Propped against it was a note that read, "The traitor, the spy Nikolai Vasil'evich Reinshtein, has been condemned and executed by us, the Russian socialist-revolutionaries. Death to the Judas traitors!"[118]

The murderer was actually M. R. Popov, who had been summoned to St. Petersburg from a propagandizing odyssey in the countryside and who had committed the crime on orders from above. One wonders if the assignment was determined in the nature of a test, for Popov was always a devoted *narodnik* and repeatedly argued against assassination and terror. Having murdered Reinshtein, he was overcome with such an attack of asthma that he could barely breathe, and he had to leave the hotel, always in danger, to walk the streets until he recovered.[119] Later he abandoned the terrorist movement and joined the Black Repartition group, to serve in part as a go-between among various Kiev revolutionary circles. He was arrested in 1880 and in spite of long imprisonment lived to a ripe old age.

Violence continued in the South as well as in the North. At the end of January 1879, police investigations finally led them to Osinskii himself. To avoid a potential pitched battle, Osinskii was followed and arrested on the street, but even so, during his interrogation by G. D. Sudeikin, he pulled a gun, intending to kill his inquisitor on the spot. He was wrestled down.[120] When police located his residence, they were less lucky. Osinskii's live-in girl friend Sof'ia Leshern-fon-Gertsfel't (41 years old to Osinskii's 26) pulled a gun on the officers.[121] A month later in Kiev, a "real battle" broke out when Sudeikin himself led a raid on the conspiratorial quarters of Vladimir Debagorii-Mokrievich, Ludovic Brantner, and others; Sudeikin's life was saved by the bullet-proof vest he was wearing, but two of the revolutionaries died of wounds received.[122] Osinskii, Brantner, and their companion named Svidirenko were hanged; Leshern's death sentence was commuted to life imprisonment.[123] Degaborii-Mokreivich lived, for a time in exile, to write his fascinating memoirs of his revolutionary past. Having survived, Sudeikin continued his unique, successful undermining of the revolutionary movement until in 1883 he was killed by one of his own men, the double agent Sergei Degaev.

On February 9, 1879, Grigorii Gol'denberg, who had recently escaped from administrative exile in Archangel, murdered D. N. Kropotkin, the governor-general of Kharkov. Gol'denberg lay in ambush near the door of the governor-general's mansion, and when Kropotkin drove up late at night, he fired into the coach with a large-calibre revolver. He was able to slip away in the dark so rapidly as to avoid identification. Kropotkin (a relative of Prince Petr Kropotkin, the anarchist) died of his wounds the following day.[124] Although he seems to have acted primarily at his own instigation, Gol'denberg later admitted to the police that certain Kiev revolutionaries—particularly Osinskii—had helped him plan the assassination. One of them, a Pole named Ludwik Kobylanski, was probably with him at the time of the attack.[125]

Unlike many of the Southerners, Gol'denberg had maintained contact with the Land and Freedom organization in St. Petersburg. On its press on February 11 he printed his justification for his action, and in its journal on February 20 he published a similar statement about his deed.[126] Gol'denberg insisted that he had killed Kropotkin for the latter's "crimes," in part for suppressing student demonstrations and in part for forbidding prisoners in Kharkov to see their relatives and for ignoring the hunger strike they proclaimed thereafter.[127] Indeed, relatives' visits were the major source of contact between outside revolutionaries and their colleagues behind bars, so the prohibition of such visits took a severe toll of one facet of underground activities.

Eventually, Gol'denberg came to a striking end. He was arrested on November 13, 1879, at the railroad station at Elizavetgrad, where he was found carrying nitroglycerin for the attempt against the life of the tsar that took place along the Moscow-Kursk railway a few days later. Frightened, he soon began repenting his past and regaled the police with extraordinarily detailed and useful statements about a whole series of revolutionary deeds. He opened the door for dozens of arrests and investigations, and his depositions of 1879 featured in political trials for years thereafter.[128] He died a suicide in the Petropavlovsk fortress in 1880.

Only a few days after Kropotkin's death, a young Polish student named Leon Mirski attempted to assassinate A. R. Drentel'n, the replacement for Mezentsev as head of the secret police, in St. Petersburg. Mirski had been encouraged by Aleksandr Mikhailov, leader of Land and Freedom's central administrative core, and, despite certain deliberate mystification on Mikhailov's part, by Nikolai Morozov as well.[129] Before the assassination attempt, Mikhailov brought Mirski's plans to the attention of the council of Land and Freedom and proposed that aid be proffered to the young would-be murderer. The meeting to consider Mirski's attempt on Drentel'n was the occasion for vocal *narodnik* protest against terrorism, for Plekhanov strenuously questioned the wisdom of this and other similar efforts.[130] He was answered, he reported later, with a kind of act of accusation presented by Mikhailov: Drentel'n had engineered the police anti-terrorist campaign after the murder of his predecessor, he was a dangerous opponent, he had introduced Iakutsk into the political exile system. Plekhanov wrote later:

I do not say that this and many allegations of guilt seemed to me powerful and convincing enough. But of course my voice could not have had any meaning even then, for the sentence had already been pronounced by the entire membership of the council, except for one, who abstained from voting at all.[131]

The voice of protest went unheard, and Land and Freedom aided Mirski by providing him with a horse and offering its aid in selecting time and place for the attempt.

Mirski was nevertheless unsuccessful. He fired through a window into Drentel'n's carriage, but his horse was no Varvar'; frightened by the shot, the mount reared and sped off. Mirski managed to calm the horse enough to dismount, audaciously handed the reins to a nearby police officer, found a cab, and eventually disappeared into a tobacconist's shop—all in broad daylight.[132] The young Pole was readily identified by witnesses from police photographs taken when he had recently been released from Petropavlovsk fortress and admonished to stay away from radical activity among his fellow students at the Medical-Surgical Institute.

Members of Land and Freedom managed to conceal him in St. Petersburg and spirit him off to a village near Rostov-on-Don, where Popov's father (perhaps unwittingly) gave him shelter.[133] Their journal lauded Mirski's deed and deplored Drentel'n's easy escape.[134] Betrayed by a friend of the revolutionary he went to visit in Taganrog, Mirski was arrested in July in spite of his effort to shoot his way to freedom. He was tried in November and sentenced to death, but the governor-general of St. Petersburg commuted his sentence to life at hard labor, owing to his youth. He had acted under the influence of "women and literary figures" who had deliberately perverted his immature mind, the governor-general declared, and indeed Mikhailov's mysterious manipulations had apparently encouraged him.[135] In Petropavlovsk fortress, confined to the dreaded Alekseevskii ravelin, Mirski meticulously betrayed to the authorities the secret negotiations with prison guards undertaken by Sergei Nechaev in the hopes of arranging an escape.[136]

In these years of the escalation of violence—1877 to 1879—the propagandists in the countryside had taken no part in the murders and other illegal deeds, but they had borne their share of repercussions from the "disorganizing" movement. The government reacted to each revolutionary effort with an enhancement of police and judicial powers that in turn affected even those "villagers" remote from the centers of terrorism. Following the jury's exoneration of Zasulich, special police units were set up in the villages as well as in the cities, and among their duties was to "maintain surveillance over the actions of the regular village police" in such a manner as to put an end to any local camaraderie between police, peasants, and radical village employees.[137] After the Mezentsev murder, police were more heavily armed and were specifically authorized to use their revolvers in what the government called self-defense.[138] What the Soviet scholar P. A. Zaionchkovskii has termed the "transition from regular laws to emergency laws"[139] also included a careful review of the judicial system so as to avoid any repetition of Zasulich's escape;

in the future, jury trials were never authorized for political crimes, many such crimes were tried before military courts, and penalties increased in magnitude, a situation that affected (and frightened) propagandists as well as terrorists.[140] The exile system too was tightened in an effort to stem the tide of escapes, and literally hundreds of people were placed under police surveillance.[141] Sixteen revolutionaries were executed between April and December 1879, and arrests took place in locations from Saratov to Pskov.[142]

Intensive urban police roundups touched "villagers" too. In the investigations following major terrorist crimes, village propagandists who kept in touch with their urban friends were bound to be exposed. Examples have already been given. Thus Figner fled her first village assignment, betrayed by a letter from her radical sister in St. Petersburg, and soon a young messenger named Chepurnova was arrested and found to be carrying a number of letters addressed to Samara propagandists. Serebriakov blames Chepurnova's arrest with the breakup of the entire Samara settlement, for the letters spelled out the names of several revolutionaries.[143] The arrest of Malinovskaia and Kolenkina in the roundup following Mezentsev's murder frightened many villagers who had maintained contact with these St. Petersburg friends.[144] In Nizhegorod province, Kviatkovskii abandoned the butter production artel he had established when his quarters were searched; a telegram signed by him had been discovered by police in the quarters of an urban revolutionary friend.[145] Lev Gartman, district scribe in a village near Saratov, fled when he was traced through his urban connections and felt threatened with arrest.[146] Police reaction to the attempt on the life of Alexander II in the spring of 1879 was to prove even more devastating to the *narodniki*; at this time the Figner sisters fled the village where they had settled owing to their past association with the foiled assassin.[147]

Under the circumstances, many radicals in the provinces became unhappily aware that urban violence was threatening their situations and their work. "The farther [the violence went]," wrote Oshanina later, "the more clear it became that all other roots of activity were suffering from terrorism."[148] Such a dedicated terrorist as Lev Tikhomirov reported later that the "villagers" felt that terrorism was dangerous to their cause.[149] Mikhail Frolenko wrote that the *narodniki* were afraid that the series of assassinations would indirectly destroy their work among the people.[150]

In Europe, the respected circles of Deich, Zasulich, Stefanovich, and Kravchinskii deplored the violence in their homeland, fearing the government's retaliation against the propagandists in the countryside. Deich wrote that terrorism might lose for the "villagers" their carefully acquired sympathy and support.[151] From exile in Siberia, the old Chaikovets Sergei Sinegub wrote his friend Kravchinskii a warning before the latter's own exercise in assassination. Acts of terror, he said, would only alienate those whose sympathy the revolutionaries were trying to attract, and the movement would be ruined by the government's revenge, while murdered officials would only be replaced by someone else. At the time, Sinegub reported, Sof'ia Perovskaia agreed with him.[152]

Thus the ambivalence about escalating terrorism and the effects of corresponding police investigations upon their own work slowly brought about a reassessment of violence on the part of those *narodniki* who were working in the villages. After all, Land and Freedom had anticipated that violence would be confined to those instances in which the "villagers" needed support. Even the ultimate "blow to the center" was to be carefully coordinated with revolution from below. Instead, village work was threatened by police interference which was often caused by acts of terrorism. Of course, the government had little tolerance even for peaceful propagandizing, and the police might well have been able to isolate and arrest the "villagers" as time went on. But in 1879 propagandists were frequently traced through their urban comrades. When the terrorists of Land and Freedom later claimed that village work had been disrupted by police intervention, they might well have recognized how often such intervention had been inadvertently caused by themselves.

4

THE TERRORIST CONSPIRACY

During the winter of 1878–1879, violence followed violence, and the mystique of terrorism became ever more fascinating to the urban revolutionaries. Nourished by police campaigns and fed by judicial sternness, the terrorists called for more and more dramatic revenge against the government. It was the ultimate act of regicide, the proposed assassination of Alexander II, that brought to a boil the long-simmering division between terrorists and propagandists. The split in Land and Freedom began in St. Petersburg in the organization's core group, but it soon came to involve provincial workers and eventually caused the society's demise.

It is difficult not to credit one individual in particular for bringing about the crisis of 1879 through his constant addition of fuel to the terrorist flames. Aleksandr Dmitrievich Mikhailov had become the executive leader of the St. Petersburg center of Land and Freedom early in summer 1878 when he won the support of the organization for his program of conspiracy and discipline in revolutionary circles.[1] From that time until his arrest in the autumn of 1879, Mikhailov was the key figure in the terrorist movement. Nikholai Bukh described Mikhailov as a "watchful professor on the subject of conspiracy,"[2] and Figner called him

the inestimable watchdog of the whole organization, the type of master from whose vigil not a single detail of our public security escaped. He was, one can say, the all-seeing eye of the organization and the guardian of the discipline so necessary in revolutionary action; in his person [when he was arrested] we suffered a heavy and irredeemable loss. His elimination was a blow we remembered through all the unhappiness that struck us later.[3]

79

Mikhailov's role in encouraging terrorism has been neglected in many revolutionary chronicles because his arrest removed him from the scene a year and a half before the actual assassination of the tsar, but in the eyes of his colleagues, he provided the early leadership that made regicide possible.

In Mikhailov, the revolutionaries had found a perfect administrative leader. Not especially gifted with intellectual or theoretical abilities,[4] he was the kind of person that relished discipline, caution, watchfulness, secrecy, and that utter unquestioning obedience frequently demanded by conspiratorial activity. As revolutionary reading, he preferred the Bakunin-Nechaev "Catechism" to more theoretical treatises.[5] When as a gymnasium student from Kursk province he first made contact with Kiev radical circles in 1875, he considered them badly wanting in unity of organization and coordination of purpose; he actually founded a group dedicated to "subjugating" (his own word) the quarreling radicals under a single taut organization.[6] Unsuccessful in his aims, he transferred to St. Petersburg in the fall of 1876. There he became a devoted admirer of Ol'ga Natanson and participated in the discussions about setting forth a new revolutionary creed.

In 1877, Mikhailov went "to the people," opting to settle with a group of schismatics in the merchant quarter of Saratov. To gain their confidence, Mikhailov decided to pose as a schismatic himself and immersed himself in intricate study of their theology, to the point where he was able, finally, to debate details of Biblical interpretation in their public meetings.[7] Their theological minuteness and punctiliousness appealed to his temperament; when he returned to St. Petersburg, early in 1878, he came full of enthusiasm for his "profitable activity" among them.[8] His plan was to devote his own time to a careful study of religion, to found a special typography to publish works in the Old Church Slavic script, to recruit comrades to accompany him, and to return to his Saratov settlement.[9] He seemed a true *narodnik*, for a change.

But soon he had taken up his old cause of organizing, disciplining, and centralizing the loose-knit revolutionary groups, and it was not long before he began to look down on village propagandizing for its lack of discipline, its weakness, and its unstructured nature. He was determined to bring those members of Land and Freedom then located in the capital city into a more militant, conspiratorial organization. It was not an easy task, for on the whole the revolutionaries were outgoing, friendly, and gregarious. "In the characters, habits,

and morals of the most important members of our society," Mikhailov
wrote later,

there was much that was pernicious and harmful for the growth of a secret society; and a lack of constant caution, absentmindedness, and sometimes also
simply lack of willpower and awareness impeded any change, any reeducation of
the members' characters corresponding with the essence of [their] thinking. And
so [a colleague and I] began the most stubborn struggle against the broad Russian nature. One must give us our due: owing to our small forces, everything we
did could hardly be [expected to] succeed. What unpleasantnesses fell to our
lot, sometimes even mockery! Still in the long run, experience demanded recognition of the huge importance for the cause of our sometimes seemingly petty
instructions. We fought stubbornly for the principle of total commitment, discipline, and a certain centralization of the circle. Everyone now sees this as valid,
but in the circle then one's eyes could be scratched out, one could be called
Jacobin, general, dictator, and so on.[10]

It seemed to Mikhailov as it has often seemed to revolutionaries that
underground organizations must be disciplined, conspiratorial, and
secretive, in order to protect themselves from revelation to the police
by outside spies or even (whether consciously or not) by each other.

As we have noted, in early summer 1878 Mikhailov and a colleague
(probably Oboleshov) ardently pressed this disciplined vision of the
party on the members of the Land and Freedom council. During the
argument that ensued, Mikhailov insisted that members must agree to
fulfill any assignment imposed on them without exception. He could
not even understand the point of view of his opponents. He himself
was no poet, he pointed out, but he would gladly write poetry if the
organization asked him to.[11] He won the day, and Land and Freedom
reluctantly adopted discipline, secrecy, and obedience as organizational principles.[12] From then until his arrest, Mikhailov became the
society's acknowledged watchdog, leader, and commander.

To his credit, Mikhailov set his comrades an example in self-discip-
line and self-control.[13] Each night before he went to sleep, he wrote
out a list of problems for the next day, carefully memorized it, and
then destroyed it. The slogan he posted over his bed read "Never
forget your duties." He regularly arose early, planned his time, and
never wasted a moment.

For his colleagues, Mikhailov created a science of conspiracy
which he imposed on all party members. He occasionally secretly
followed them around to make sure they were obeying the code. On
the street, he would ask a colleague to read a poster, and if the man

could not do so from a distance, Mikhailov would demand that he buy eyeglasses for the revolutionary cause.[14] Arriving at an apartment, he meticulously checked corners, under beds, and in back rooms, even listening for suspicious activities next door before he sat down. It was he who set up the intricate signal system that saved many a revolutionary from capture at supposedly "safe" quarters invaded by police; Rosa Markovna Bograd, later Plekhanov's wife, remembered that Mikhailov insisted that she post a prearranged signal in the window of her room, so that from the street he could decide whether "everything was favorable."[15] Mikhailov demanded that his friends become acquainted with the appearance of the plainclothes detectives of the secret police, and he instructed them in ways to avoid "spies" who might be tailing them. He kept charts and maps of St. Petersburg and insisted that all revolutionaries know the city backwards and forwards, particularly the courtyards, small alleys, and potential backways of escape. Actually, he owed his own freedom to his knowledge of such byways and pass-throughs, for he had once used them himself in fleeing from a policeman.[16]

If Mikhailov's friends were reluctantly tolerant of most of his demands, they could not help but resent his efforts to restrict their communication with each other and their social activities in the capital city. Indeed, although Mikhailov was regarded as invaluable in his role of party administrator—he was enormously energetic, overseeing the press, the forging of passports, provincial correspondence, the allocation of funds, and many other matters[17]—he had few close personal friends in the organization. His own habits were never sociable; he regarded reading newspapers and sitting in cafes as a waste of time, and he seldom risked an appearance at the theater or a visit to a radical friend (except when necessary). His attitudes were particularly resented by his women colleagues. Perovskaia never liked him, nor did Sof'ia Ivanova, and the two of them deliberately attended the theater together, against Mikhailov's orders and to his annoyance.[18] Even Rosa Bograd, who called him her "mentor" and her "great teacher," was not above being annoyed. Once, she reported:

I met him at the theater, to my great surprise. They were performing the opera "The Life of the Tsar." When we came across each other in a corridor in the intermission, he suddenly informed me, "I am convinced that you are leading around a whole series of tails; coming to the theater, you have already lost track of them, and meanwhile one can follow after anyone one meets here more easily than anywhere else." Seized by the beauty of the music, enchanted with the charming melodies, I answered him smiling: "If you are so afraid of spies, then you had best stay home and not go to the theater yourself."[19]

Many of Mikhailov's male colleagues also regarded him as a "cold person with a mathematical mind."[20]

For Mikhailov, as Zheliabov once wrote, the organization Land and Freedom was everything—more dear than a heroic friend, more beloved than a woman for whose every happiness he might care.[21] On its behalf Mikhailov could become angry beyond his usual self-control, and the destruction of the central organization in the man-hunt following Mezentsev's murder roused him to a fury of hatred beyond the limits of logic.

As luck would have it, in September 1878, when Malinovskaia's conspiratorial quarters were invaded by the police, Mikhailov was away. He was traveling south to propagandize among troops in the Don area, where he was expected to meet with Plekhanov, a colleague he deeply admired. Through some fault in coordination, the two missed connections, for Plekhanov had already left for the capital city. In Kharkov, Plekhanov stopped to see Sof'ia Perovskaia, who directed him to Malinovskaia's in St. Petersburg as to safe conspiratorial quarters where he could find friends and gain information about the cause; Perovskaia had often been there, although Plekhanov had not. By pure freak, he did not go to the apartment—he realized at the last minute that he did not have enough change for a cab—and thus avoided the police ambush that had been put into effect after the raid. "Your poverty saved you from arrest!" cried a delighted friend later.

His narrow escape horrified Plekhanov, but when he checked out the situation, he was even more alarmed at the general devastation of the St. Petersburg Land and Freedom core.

As a consequence of the pogrom, I found matters in terrible disorder, as evidence of which one might cite the circumstances that comrades from the provinces, not informed about the Petersburg debacle, continued to direct people, including of course very illegal ones, to the apartment already in the hands of the police. I appealed to Kravchinskii and, discovering from him that no measures for warning provincial comrades about the debacle had been taken, set immediately to correct this negligence which we, the zemlevol'tsy [members of Land and Freedom], could pardon only in our dear Sergei, with his knightly character and desperate daring, distinguished by the most extreme lack of practicality.[22]

By telegram, Plekhanov summoned Mikhailov back. The leader hurried home from Rostov-on-Don.

Dumfounded by the disaster in the capital city, fearing for the ruin of his life's work, Mikhailov at once peremptorily summoned Land and Freedom members from the provinces, in at least one instance cancelling plans for a new settlement by commanding its propagandists to the capital instead.[23] Arriving there, the *narodniki* found their leader beside himself with rage. He demanded action, he called for revenge, he commanded violence on all levels. "All the power of his will and the force of his decisions poured out in the tone of his voice and in his eyes, which were shooting off sparks," wrote one of his colleagues.[24] Mikhailov demanded that they all fight with every means "for the very existence of a revolutionary party in Russia."[25]

The angry leader insisted on setting up what he called a terrorist fighting center, perhaps thus reinstituting the St. Petersburg branch of the old "disorganization" squad. He ordered the killing of Alexander Zharkov, supposedly a police spy.[26] He sent M. R. Popov, whom he had called back from the provinces, to murder Reinshtein, another "spy" whose testimony had apparently revealed much information about the operation and headquarters of the society.[27] He called for the assassination of Drentel'n, who had replaced the murdered Mezentsev as head of the secret police and was directing the campaign to capture the killers of his predecessor; the young Pole Mirski shortly attempted this deed, but failed.[28]

Mikhailov was so intent on revenge, so impassioned, and so full of hatred that Popov was convinced he had become irrational and that the broader ramifications of the actions he proposed had escaped him completely.

Without at all denying to A. D. his organizational capacities and that valuable quality of his talent whereby he was able, having mastered a new idea, to expend on it blood and sweat and make it into reality, I still think that had there not been in A. D. from the start that passion and almost narrowness of understanding of the actions to which current conditions were inevitably pushing the revolutionaries, the split in Land and Freedom would not have occurred.[29]

As Plekhanov clearly saw, the threat to the central core of Land and Freedom had converted Mikhailov to a path of violence once and for all.

From his arrival [from the South], matters became gradually set right, but he himself, under the influence of the Petersburg debacle, strongly changed his tactical viewpoints: Before, he stood unconditionally for agitation among the people, and now he began to demonstrate that we had not enough forces to perform [such agitation] and that we needed to concentrate on terror.[30]

Mikhailov's conversion to terrorism is a key event in the history of the Land and Freedom organization.

Indeed, in the months that followed, Mikhailov became the society's most influential proponent of violence. With his position of authority, he was able to gather around him the group of people who would later be responsible for forming the terrorist organization People's Will. They included young men like Aaron "Moishe" Zundelevich, an activist friend of the Natansons and currently Land and Freedom's foreign affairs ambassador; the student G. P. Isaev; N. I. Kibal'chich, a budding scientist who had recently been released after trial with the 193 and who became the organization's expert in the preparation of bombs; and Stepan Shiraiev from Saratov—one-time comrade of Plekhanov in propagandizing among the workers, later a servant of the revolutionaries as a manufacturer of dynamite.[31]

Among Mikhailov's most important converts in the spring of 1879 was Popov's dear friend Kviatkovskii, whom the leader had summoned back from the settlement at Voronezh. Once a "disorganizer" along with his friends Tiutchev and Presniakov, Kviatkovskii had become an equally ardent *narodnik* during his countryside odyssey with Popov. Now, to Popov's dismay, his comrade came full circle, and Mikhailov persuaded Kviatkovskii to terrorism so successfully that the one-time close friends found themselves in hostile and quarreling camps. "I left [St. Petersburg] in the beginning of January," Popov recorded later, and indeed this was the period of his "execution" of the "spy" Reinshtein in Moscow,

and in the second half of March I was again in Petersburg and found all my friends tilting on an inclined plane towards that activity which became later the path of the People's Will. And alas! Kviatkovskii, who so [emphatically] warned me not to become seduced by urban activity, should now have heeded his own advice himself.[32]

Indeed, such of Kviatkovskii's scattered notes as remain to us indicate that Mikhailov had persuaded him that "there is no faith" in village settlements, that "the Peter[sburg] affair," including publications, relations with "society," students, and workers, was far more important than any work among the peasantry.[33] "In order to become a tiger," Kviatkovskii wrote later, "it is not necessary to be one by nature. Under certain conditions, lambs will become [tigers]."[34] Mikhailov's angry zeal was more than his colleagues could resist.

During the spring of 1879, Mikhailov also used his influence to swing the balance on the editorial staff of the journal *Land and Freedom* in the direction of terrorism. The first issue of this journal had appeared in the autumn of 1878, and the original editorial board had consisted of Kravchinskii, Plekhanov, Dmitrii Klements, and Nikolai Morozov. Only the latter could be said to have espoused violence in the revolutionary cause, although it was Kravchinskii who had actually taken dagger in hand. From the start Morozov had chafed under the *narodnik* majority, contending that his colleagues unfairly refused publication of his own writings and arguing that the journal should change its title to *Za svet i svobodu* (For Light and Freedom; the Russian word *svet* also means "the world"), in order to avoid the populist connotations of the title that had been chosen.[35] He and Mikhailov shared their dislike of the journal's *narodnik* tone and especially of Kravchinskii's lead article in the first issue, wherein the recent murderer denied the efficacy of terrorism as a revolutionary method.[36]

When Kravchinskii, persuaded by his colleagues, left for Europe after the publication of the journal's first issue, Mikhailov tipped the balance toward terrorism by summoning Lev Tikhomirov to replace him. Although Tikhomirov may not have been an ardent terrorist when he was called from the South, he had moved to Kharkov after his release from prison (following the trial of 193), and there he was regularly in contact with the Ivichevich brothers and their circle. Having failed in his commission to plan an escape for the imprisoned 193-ers and thus having earned the scorn and anger of his previously beloved Perovskaia, he spent much of 1878 again in the South, this time in the Caucasus, where he did not participate in any radical activity.[37] Returning to St. Petersburg at Mikhailov's behest, he fulfilled some of his literary ambitions by writing for the legal journal *Delo* (The Cause) under an assumed name. Like other revolutionaries in the capital city, he became closely acquainted with N. K. Mikhailovskii, whom he later involved in the underground press.[38]

Tikhomirov was quiet and at first seemed reluctant to commit himself on matters of policy. Ol'ga Liubatovich, Morozov's beloved, refers to him as standing somewhere between the *narodnik* Plekhanov and her terrorist lover.[39] Nevertheless, in spite of his original timid role, Tikhomirov soon came to condone terrorist action, and with its second issue (appearing in December 1878), *Land and Freedom* endorsed violence, at least in what it called "self-defense."[40] Klements was arrested early in 1879, leaving only Plekhanov to defend the *narodnik* cause. As the spring progressed, Tikhomirov became ever more converted to terrorism, but Plekhanov's masterful and thoughtful articles continued to keep *Land and Freedom* from committing itself in the way Mikhailov and Morozov might have liked.[41] At the same time, Mikhailov's respect and affection for Plekhanov deterred him from making further editorial changes.

Mikhailov had another trick up his sleeve, and on March 12, 1879, there appeared the first copy of the four-page *Listok Zemli i voli* (Land and Freedom Leaflet), edited by Morozov alone and devoted exclusively to reporting on acts of violence, spies, arrests, and the like.[42] Gone were the theoretical articles on revolution, the speculation on the potential of the proletariat, the talk of ends and means. Instead, the *Leaflet*, published with Mikhailov's blessing, unhesitatingly incited to violence and revenge.

Comrades, how will we answer this crazy violence of police bloodhounds and gendarmerie butchers? How will we avenge our comrades who have been destroyed? Here is one of the most burning questions, [a question] which against our will shifts political events of recent times onto the front burner.[43]

As both Deich and Tikhomirov pointed out later, Morozov's publication thoroughly alienated Plekhanov and dramatically called attention to the fact that Land and Freedom was rapidly disintegrating into two quarreling factions, epitomized by the two hostile periodical publications.[44] Mikhailov seemed not to care.

In spite of his strong conviction of the necessity of violence, Mikhailov chose not to undercut the propagandist center of the Land and Freedom organization. Until the summer, he retained a conscientious personal commitment to the society's constitution and its premise of majority rule. Although he was not above acting in secret when the occasion demanded and although he was clearly gathering a terrorist core around him, he made no effort during the troubled winter of 1878–79 to break away from the Land and Freedom group. Perhaps it was a question of his faction's strength, for although the terrorists felt themselves gaining power in the party's central core, they were aware that they represented a minority in the party as a whole. Perhaps he hated to see Land and Freedom break apart.

Additionally, the proponents of violence were far from unified themselves. Morozov, Mikhailov, and Tikhomirov disagreed about the significance and potential consequences of terrorism. The two editors seem to have operated very much in their own milieu, but they did not much like each other. Neither felt much inclination to follow the leadership of the organizer and administrator. Tikhomirov regarded himself as an intellectual and devoted efforts to attracting intelligentsia support and to activities outside the immediate revolutionary organization. *Land and Freedom*, although it propounded violence in Tikhomirov's lead article for the fifth issue, probably published in March 1879, remained remote in tone and interests from the rabble-rousing demands of Morozov's *Land and Freedom Leaflet*, that during the same period was blatantly calling for "political murder."[45] Plekhanov had no particular affection for Morozov, and he admitted that his disagreements with this romantic terrorist became "significant" during the winter of 1878–1879, when both men were working together on the *Land and Freedom* editorial board.[46] At the same time, Mikhailov retained a deep and abiding admiration for Plekhanov as an intellect and a revolutionary. Next to Ol'ga Natanson, who had been arrested in the autumn and was soon to be released to her family to die, Plekhanov and Rosa Bograd, his future wife, were the only colleagues for whom Mikhailov felt a deep emotional attachment.[47] The organizer greatly respected the intellectual, and in spite of his increasingly terrorist stance, Mikhailov never asked Plekhanov to abandon his writing and editing. When Plekhanov did stop, in the spring of 1879, it was because of events within the terrorist movement, not owing to a request from its leader.

The event that caused the journal to collapse and led the terrorists to construct a secret organization of their own was the attempt on the life of the tsar by Aleksandr Konstantinovich Solov'ev in April 1879.

Solov'ev was a strange man and by all accounts not a balanced one. He had been brought up at a palace, his father having served one of the grand duchesses, and the Grand Duchess Elena Pavlovna had actually been young Aleksandr's benefactor during his brief tenure as a law student at St. Petersburg University.[48]

Never a great student—Solov'ev was uncommunicative and withdrawn, a small, undistinguished, uncertain man—he left the university in 1867 when he was 21, managed to get a teacher's certificate, and accepted a position as village teacher in Toropetsk district. Here he lived alone and, according to some witnesses, began to drink rather heavily.[49] At first he had been very religious; then he took up deism; then he gave that up too.[50]

In 1874, perhaps because of some conflict with the school administration, Solov'ev threw over his job to join the nearby commune directed by Nikolai Bogdanovich and his wife. For several years he lived at the commune and attempted to learn the blacksmith trade, but his physical weakness and a lung problem kept him from the heavier tasks at the smithy, and he never became a good smith at all. At the Bogdanovich ménage he met such leading revolutionary figures as Iurii Bogdanovich, Nikolai's brother; Dmitrii Klements, later an editor of *Land and Freedom*; and Adrian Mikhailov, the coachman in the Mezentsev assassination. Here he became acquainted with revolutionary literature and read some of the works of Karl Marx and even Tkachev's violence-preaching journal *Nabat* (The Tocsin).[51]

Solov'ev seems to have been deeply influenced by the strong Mariia Petrovna Bogdanovich, Nikolai's wife.[52] Guided and/or pressured by her, he married a village girl, whom he had once taught, and fathered a child born in 1877. His wife's vituperative attacks on him after his arrest may have been designed to save her own skin or motivated by an extraordinarily powerful hatred.[53] At any rate, shortly after their marriage, Solov'ev took his wife to St. Petersburg. There, in the autumn of 1876, his friend Iurii Bogdanovich, who had accompanied him from the smithy, introduced him to the Figner circle, and Solov'ev joined this so-called "separatist" group.

Figner gives us the most accurate description:

The narrow morose face—with its small grey eyes, its rather large, sharp nose, and its small light-brown pointed beard—was seldom lit by a smile. . . . He was completely unmoved in terms of material needs, and in terms of spiritual, never was a theoretician, did not enter into argument, always was extremely withdrawn and reserved. . . . In general conversations, Solov'ev was silent and was usually very sparing of words. He spoke jerkily and tonelessly. . . . He was a good man, and if a comparison is not superfluous, I would say that he was as good and gentle as a child.[54]

He was strangely awkward and eccentric, she reports. He would forget where he was living, or lose his way on the streets at night, or when challenged by a sentry "Who goes there?" he would answer, "The devil."[55] By the time Figner met him, he was 32 years old.

Like the other separatists, Solov'ev went to the countryside to propagandize in 1877. Unfortunately, his life among the people was not happy. In the first village, where he lived together with a Moscow worker named Vasilii Griaznov, the climate was unhealthy, and Solov'ev, never vigorous, left shortly. Thereafter he proved inadequate to his trade and drifted from one smithy to another, where jobs could be found. Once he served as a lathe-turner. Once after the Samara settlement had collapsed, Bogdanovich got him a job as a scribe. Once he applied for a job as a village teacher, but the inspector found him suspicious, and he quickly withdrew his application rather than suffer investigation, for he was traveling under a false passport.[56] Sometimes he was idle and unemployed; sometimes he moved around from place to place. Once he lost his papers. On several occasions his ill health forced him to return to St. Petersburg—not to his wife, but to his parents. He was convinced, rightly or wrongly, that he was constantly being pursued by the police.[57]

Understandably, Solov'ev was the first—and indeed one of the few—of the 1877–78 "villagers" to become discouraged with the results of his work and to become therefore dissatisfied with the entire settlement scheme. In the winter of 1878–79, he appeared in the village of Viaz'mino where the Figner sisters were working and told them that he was certain that propaganda among the people was to no avail, "for conditions of life among the peasants demonstrated to him the total impossibility of revolutionary activity among them."[58] He believed that only when the autocracy was destroyed would the radicals be able freely to work in the countryside, and to this purpose he planned to go to St. Petersburg and assassinate the tsar.

The startled Figners at first tried to dissuade him. Among other things, Vera pointed out, if he failed in his attempt, the village settlements might well all be destroyed by police investigation and retaliation.[59] Still Solov'ev's analyses did not fall on deaf ears, for by now the Figners too were suffering from the hostility of the village priest and the local scribe, and Evgeniia's school was feeling the ill effects of rumors that she was not properly teaching the Orthodox faith. The girls were obviously impressed with Solov'ev's argument although they were also frightened by his plan.

Their reaction did not deter Solov'ev. He arrived in St. Petersburg on December 31, 1878, thereafter living with his parents and plotting his deed. He was inspired by the example of Zasulich, to whom he later compared himself, and by Mirski's attempt to assassinate Drentel'n.[60]

Upon his return to St. Petersburg, Solov'ev made another representation of his reasoning to his friend E. P. Karpov. To Karpov he described what he considered the network of spies in the villages and the "open conditions" of village life, which provided "no place to hide."[61] Unlike the Figners, he had found the peasants impossible: depraved by drunkenness, held in bondage by local kulaks and inn-keepers, and steeped in ignorance that had no end to its depths. He was obviously, in Karpov's words,

deeply disappointed in the usefulness of his activity as a propagandist and also in the people themselves, of whom he once had spoken as bearers of justice, pre-servers by their very way of life of ideals, embedded in their souls, of the correct construction of the communal society.[62]

In the capital city in 1879, Solov'ev located his old friend Nikolai Bogdanovich, who had closed the smithy commune and moved to St. Petersburg. With him, the would-be assassin spent a number of even-ings, and probably through Nikolai or his brother, he contacted Aleksandr Mikhailov in the early spring. When he announced his regicidal intentions to the leader of Land and Freedom, Mikhailov sympathized and probably thoroughly approved. "At this time," Mikhailov later wrote, "I had not yet formulated a positive opinion on the question [of regicide], but my thoughts too were already moving in this direction."[63] Busy with Mirski's plot to assassinate Drentel'n, Mikhailov at first put Solov'ev off without discouraging him, but in March the assassination question was revived with the appearance of Gol'denberg, who arrived from the South where he had just murdered Kropotkin.

Gol'denberg claimed that he too wished to assassinate the tsar. Coincidentally, a third volunteer appeared: this was Gol'denberg's friend and probable assassination assistant, the Pole Ludwik Kobylan-ski, who had accompanied Gol'denberg from Kiev to Kharkov before the Kropotkin affair. With a touch of the macabre the three would-be assassins argued out their qualifications with Mikhailov, Kviatkovskii, and Zundelevich in a series of secret tavern meetings in mid-March.[64] It was finally resolved that Solov'ev was the more appropriate murderer because of Gol'denberg's and Kobylanski's background as members of ethnic minorities. "Only I satisfy all conditions," Solov'ev proclaimed. "I must go. This is my affair. Alexander II is mine, and I will not yield him to anybody."[65] The others fell silent and eventually agreed.

Having personally conveyed his blessing on Solov'ev's plan, Mikhai-lov brought the matter of regicide directly before Land and Free-dom's council, the body of all members currently present in the capital city. In a dramatic evening meeting on March 29, 1879, to which Solov'ev himself was not invited, Mikhailov informed the assembled members that a would-be tsarist assassin, whose name he refused to reveal, was seeking their support.[66]

The majority reacted in horror. Plekhanov, O. V. Aptekman, and V. N. Ignatov were bitter in their opposition; M. R. Popov, who had only the day before arrived in the city, was furious.[67] Although the assassination of the head of the secret police could be condoned, regicide was a vastly different matter, and the murder of a tsar was not be be tolerated.

"Anyone going so far as regicide . . . should be seized, bound, and driven out of Petersburg like a madman," one of the *narodniki* shouted, and another suggested that the unidentified assailant should be withheld from his deed by force if necessary.[68] Aptekman expressed his fear that terrorism would get out of hand, that the essence of the movement—propagandizing the people—would be "easily completely derailed." In the event of a failure, he predicted ominously, the government would react with further retaliations, which in turn would lead to "a second, a third—a whole series of attempts [at assassination] that the party will be obligated to take on itself, at its own risk and responsibility."[69] It is interesting that Aptekman privately concluded that the terrorists foresaw and desired exactly such a situation and commitment.[70] Plekhanov deplored the effect of terrorism on village work. "Under the influence of your adventures," he told Mikhailov and his friends, in his habitually scholarly tone, "our organization will have to abandon our old areas of activity one after another, as Rome abandoned its provinces one after another to the pressure of the barbarians."[71]

The stormy session got louder and louder and progressed almost to fisticuffs.[72] At one point Popov and Kviatkovskii, old comrades from "villager" days, ended by shouting at each other and harking back to Dmitrii Karakozov's attempt to assassinate Alexander in 1866 and to the peasant, named Komissarov, who (legend and deliberate publicity had it) saved the tsar's life.

Popov: Gentlemen, if Karakozovs are possible among us, how can you be certain that tomorrow there will not be a Komissarov in our midst—with his own intentions and with no concern about how the organization reacts to them?

Kviatkovskii: If you are a Komissarov, I will shoot you down too![73]

By Plekhanov's account (and this may be a variation on the above), one of the *narodniki* got so upset as to threaten to forewarn the potential victim by letter, so that he could take the precaution of avoiding public appearances. In answer:

One of the "disorganizers" [probably Kviatkovskii]: This is informing! We will deal with you as we deal with informers!

Popov: Well, then do you not want to kill us? If so, bear in mind that we can shoot as well as you![74]

When Mikhailov was requested to try to change Solov'ev's mind, he and his friends reported that the would-be assassin was adamant and would carry out his plans whether help was available or not. Years later Zundelevich ruefully reported that Mikhailov had exaggerated.

We then distorted [the matter] in spirit, depicting the situation as if Solov'ev would complete the attempt whether there would be help or not. I think that if we had ardently begged Solov'ev to change his intentions, he would have agreed not to make the attempt. But neither Mikhailov nor Kviatkovskii considered it necessary to dissuade Solov'ev. . . .[75]

When Plekhanov insisted, Mikhailov coolly pointed out that the mysterious murderer was a separatist and therefore not subject to Land and Freedom discipline. Plekhanov asked to meet the volunteer assassin; Mikhailov refused.[76]

The argument reached fever pitch. "I tried to calm Popov," Plekhanov averred later, "Several disorganizers pacified Kviatkovskii."[77] Things might have degenerated further had there not been a pealing of the doorbell.

"Gentlemen, the police!" cried Mikhailov. "Of course we will defend ourselves?" "Of course!" both the disorganizers and the narodniki answered with one voice. Each of those present pulled a revolver out of his pocket and cocked it, and Mikhailov slowly and calmly went to the hall to answer the door. Another minute and there would have been a volley, but the alarm was false: Mikhailov returned with the news that the doorman had rung and had simply come at an inopportune time on some sort of business.[78]

The interruption, in Plekhanov's words, "did us the service of putting an end to the heated scene." Mikhailov's proposal that the assassin be supplied with horse and coachman, as in the case of Kravchinskii the previous August and Prince Kropotkin in 1876, was voted down. But on the fallacious grounds that Solov'ev could not be dissuaded from his undertaking, those present reluctantly agreed that the society would not forbid individual members to aid the assassin as they saw fit.[79]

The angry encounter drew the lines between terrorist and *narodnik* as never before. Popov later denied the intensity of the clash and claimed that he and his opponents spent a friendly evening at the opera together after the meeting.[80] But the reports of fury from other participants do not seem exaggerated. As one of them later wrote:

The session came to be extremely tempestuous, and I was afraid that it would end with a split. . . . The opinions, as might be expected, were sharply divergent. . . . I do not remember such a stormy session as this. The "villagers" interspersed their objections with mass sarcasms and scorn. The terrorists maintained themselves with great restraint, although, obviously, they were strongly moved. . . . The administration [that is, Mikhailov] and the rest of our terrorists obviously basically wanted to sound out the "villagers" and to discover at least how much they could count on them in the sense of cooperating with their plans. In this regard, the administration's aim was fully achieved. In the council, two directly opposite courses were clearly expressed, and if this did not at the time lead to a split in the society, it was thanks to the fact that only a third of all members of the society were present in the council.[81]

The terrorists had finally come into the open and evoked their first major crisis. At this March meeting, battle lines heretofore blurred were openly drawn.

A few of the violent minority did indeed aid Solov'ev before the assassination. Mikhailov and Zundelevich agreed to follow the tsar's daily movements in an effort to enable Solov'ev to select an appropriate site for his attack, although Popov huffily refused their request for his help.[82] Someone aided Solov'ev in his futile efforts to ride a horse, soon abandoned as impractical for he could not learn, and to shoot a gun. Mikhailov eventually provided him with suicide poison, and Morozov gave him a large-calibre revolver that had once belonged to Dr. Orest Veimar. With ill grace, some of the *narodniki* helped to plan the composition and distribution of proclamations after the event.[83]

Then two days beforehand, having been carefully but mysteriously warned, most of the revolutionaries slipped out of town. Fearful of the coming roundup, Plekhanov went with them, abandoning his chores as propagandist among the workers and editor of the journal *Land and Freedom.* Although everyone probably anticipated that the journal's suspension would be temporary, *Land and Freedom* never appeared again. With its demise, the propagandists lost an important vehicle for expressing their views.

The fateful and unsuccessful attempt took place on April 2, 1879. Denied his horse and coachman, Solov'ev approached the tsar on foot as Alexander II strolled in the palace gardens. With his Smith and Wesson revolver, he shot point-blank five times—the first shot from approximately twelve paces and the next closer. As the tsar turned to run, Solov'ev pursued him, still firing. He was caught and toppled by several of the tsar's guards, with the aid (the police said) of an illiterate peasant—indeed a Komissarov—who grabbed his coat to slow him down.[84] Although he succeeded in popping the poison given him by Mikhailov into his mouth, he was immediately forced to vomit and thus to survive. Having traced the revolver—in spite of the fact that it had been passed from one revolutionary hand to another—the police were able to locate and arrest its original owner, Dr. Orest Veimar, also owner of the one-time revolutionary stallion Varvar' and shelterer the year before of Vera Zasulich before she escaped abroad; although he had nothing to do with Solov'ev's scheme, Veimar paid for the assassin's indiscretion with a long prison term.[85] Solov'ev himself confessed. He was tried, found guilty, and hanged on May 28.

The Solov'ev assassination attempt openly raised the question of regicide among the revolutionaries for the first time. His failure served to crystallize the hostility of the terrorists towards the propagandists in the Land and Freedom St. Petersburg center and caused the former to take clear action in opposition to the then party majority.

Morozov tells us that the day after the meeting to consider Solov'-ev's plan—and thus well before the assassination attempt itself—the Land and Freedom terrorists in the capital, frustrated in gaining organizational backing for regicide, arranged to meet secretly together. Although some members raised problems and objections, most agreed with Morozov's argument that if a split between terrorists and propagandists was inevitable, it was foolish to postpone its occurrence.[86]

Within weeks, the subgroup of terrorists devised a secret organizational base, separate from and unknown to the propagandist members of the society. Styling themselves dramatically *Svoboda ili smert'* (Freedom or Death), they set up a formal statute that called for the strict discipline, secrecy, and obedience that Mikhailov had taught them.[87] At first they met together in the woods of the suburb of

Lesna, but soon one of their new recruits donated the 20,000 rubles he had just received as his bride's dowry, and they were able to set up two conspiratorial apartments. Kviatkovskii and Sof'ia Ivanova presided over the quarters at Lesna.[88] In another apartment, Stepan Shiriaev lived with Anna Iakimova, the scientist Kibal'chich, and the student Isaev and studied "domestic preparation of nitroglycerine and dynamite," although they worked merely, as Iakimova primly insisted later, in experimentally small quantities.[89] Dynamite was a new weapon in the terrorists' arsenal, and they had a good deal of studying to do under less than ideal laboratory conditions. As Figner later described it:

In this primitively equipped, improvised laboratory, in constant danger of being discovered or of being blown into the air with the entire building, these daring comrades established several dynamite centers—[comrades] without any relevant training, experimenting as laymen, and facing death at any moment.[90]

It is impossible to believe that Mikhailov had not endorsed what his companions were doing, even though his moral commitment to Land and Freedom deterred him from taking active part in the conspiracy at this point. The private approval of this strong and dominant leader lent the secret subgroup Freedom or Death commitment and determination in its terrorist stance.

The terrorists could count on the continued support of the revolutionary press. Although *Land and Freedom* ceased publication after its fifth issue in March, Morozov's *Leaflet* appeared six times between March and June, its editor publishing with relish descriptions of terrorist deeds, police atrocities, and arrests, in addition to a series of mysterious warnings about traitors, actually supplied to him by N. V. Kletochnikov, the society's spy in the offices of the secret police. Throughout spring Morozov exhorted his readers to violence, even hinting that Solov'ev's efforts to assassinate the tsar should be repeated.

This insane arbitrariness that has deprived the socialists of any possibility of acting has turned them into revolutionaries, pulled them along the path of armed struggle, and tied their relationship with the government into such a knot that now all that remains to them is to say, "You or we, we or you, but we cannot exist together". . . . While the tsar is an unlimited despot, he is responsible to the conscience of the people for everything, for good and evil, responsible also for that situation in which we find ourselves now, and would be responsible even in the event that he did not directly take part in the most disgraceful manifestations of arbitrariness and reaction.[91]

Morozov's *Leaflet* served to make more clear the existence of a terrorist faction within the St. Petersburg core of Land and Freedom. By May, the split could hardly be ignored in the capital city, albeit many of the "villagers" in the countryside remained unaware of the intensity with which it was developing.

Sometime in May, both factions in the central organization agreed to the necessity of a formal membership meeting to reexamine Land and Freedom's statute and program and to hash out their priorities.[92] It is uncertain who first suggested such a plan, but all seem to have approved of it. Proponents of a full meeting of the society claimed that annual review of regulations was constitutionally required, and such a review had not ever occurred; even the Mikhailov constitution of 1878 was adopted by the St. Petersburg core rather than the society as a whole. A year had passed since then. The *narodniki* in St. Petersburg, bewildered and alarmed by the increasing stridency of the terrorist minority, could certainly judge from Morozov's writings that the terrorists had hardly retreated although they had gone underground. On the other hand, the terrorists, hoping to increase their numbers, funds, and facilities, had little objection to a meeting at which they might plead their cause or even attain their ends by manipulating their comrades. The time agreed upon was late June 1879, the site Tambov,[93] a town southeast of Moscow, the location of which would facilitate the attendance of Land and Freedom members working in the villages in the Saratov and Voronezh areas.

Thereafter events moved rapidly. Both terrorists and propagandists from the central Land and Freedom core began to marshall their forces for what would undoubtedly be a confrontation. Plekhanov and Popov, *narodniki* leaders, headed for the provinces to notify the "villagers" of the forthcoming congress.[94] The St. Petersburg terrorists knew they could count on considerable support in the South. But keenly aware of their minority position, they took the surprise step of communicating with the Russian colony in Geneva, whence they invited Vera Zasulich (whom they fallaciously assumed to be one of themselves) to return to Russia for the meetings.[95]

Then the supporters of violence took even more conspiratorial action by secretly scheduling a pre-conference meeting at Lipetsk, a venerable spa located not far from Tambov, so that they could quietly consider tactics and devise a plan to turn the majority of the Tambov congress in their own direction. They sent the arch-terrorist Frolenko (only recently summoned to St. Petersburg) out to the provinces to invite sympathizers to the secret meeting. Frolenko was ordered to find whatever support for terrorism he could locate, even among revolutionaries who were not legally members of Land and Freedom.[96] He was authorized freely to propose the assassination of the tsar as first order of the day. He left hurriedly, and within a short time, Mikhailov quietly followed to assist him.[97] The terrorists were eager to beard the enemy and establish themselves in revolutionary leadership.

With Frolenko's journey began the deliberate campaign on the part of the minority terrorists to convert to their point of view the propagandist majority inside and outside the Land and Freedom organization. By no means did the terrorists have a guarantee of success. Their strength always lay in the cities rather than in the villages, and those Southern urban circles where their forces were concentrated (in Odessa, Kharkov, and Kiev) had been decimated by arrests and executions over the previous year. Osinskii was gone, as well as Koval'skii and Vladimir Debagorii-Mokrievich.[98] Deich and Stefanovich had fled abroad.[99] Comrades and colleagues had been imprisoned or sent into exile. Among the villagers, few were supportive and many were opposed to escalating violence. The terrorists had no great record in influencing village habitués to abandon their projects. Several months before, in January 1879, Morozov and Mikhailov had made a concerted effort to persuade Vera Figner, who was visiting in St. Petersburg, to stay and join their "disorganization" work, but she had categorically refused.[100] Frolenko's assignment demanded the best of his efforts.

Frolenko, the "ambassador of regicide," went first to Orel, to contact Mariia Nikolaevna Olovennikova/Oshanina, who was living with her second husband, Aleksandr Barannikov, on her family estates. Oshanina, as she is most often called, was regarded by Frolenko as a strong potential supporter of terrorism.[101] She was not officially a member of Land and Freedom, but she had earlier participated in the attempt to free Voinaral'skii, and she was known to be a partisan of the militant conspiratorial ideas of P. G. Zaichnevskii and P. N. Tkachev. Frolenko found her delighted with his invitation to come to Lipetsk. She was terribly bored in Orel, she told him, and would be glad to get back to where the action was. It would be like sudden liberation from the Tatar yoke.[102] Barannikov readily agreed to come too. Frolenko wrote that although Barannikov had been strongly anti-terrorist in the past, "Now when I told him about the new direction and proposed to him that he take part in the elimination of Alexander II, he immediately agreed—undoubtedly the cry of society had reached out to him."[103] Frolenko had accurately analyzed the militant nature of his potential converts, and the pledge was sealed in a congenial evening of wine and song.

Frolenko did an even greater service in contacting Andrei Zheliabov, who was to become the leader of the regicides. When he first brought up Zheliabov's name as a possible supporter, his terrorist friends in St. Petersburg demurred—"a real *narodnik*," they called the future planner of the tsar's assassination.[104] But Frolenko knew better and judged Zheliabov not on the basis of ideology but on the basis of his strongly activist character—his willingness, as Frolenko knew from his well-told tales, to take on bulls, bullies, or police with equal courage and vigor.[105] Zundelevich also knew Zheliabov and had commended him to Mikhailov as a potential terrorist.[106] He and Frolenko proved to be right. In Odessa, where he was living on the land, Zheliabov agreed to aid in an assassination plot, although he refused to consider joining any permanent group of partisans of a "new direction," insisting that he would regard himself as a free agent once the regicide had been accomplished.[107] One of the advantages of the terrorist plan was that it adopted a limited aim that allowed adherents the possibility of resigning later; propagandizing, on the contrary, had always presumed a commitment of less definite duration.

On his tour of the South, Frolenko also invited Nikolai Kolodkovich, one of the Southern *buntari*, to attend the Lipetsk terrorist convocation.[108] It never occurred to him to invite Perovskaia, who was then in Kharkov, although he had come to know her well the previous year. She was at the time, as everyone understood, a dedicated *narodnik*, but what is more Frolenko saw her as a "timid rabbit," who was (from her sojourn in St. Petersburg in late 1877 and early 1878) rather antipathetic toward several leading Land and Freedom members, Mikhailov and Tikhomirov among them.[109] When Perovskaia later realized she had been left out, she was angry with Frolenko and berated him for it.[110]

Having accepted Frolenko's invitation, Kolodkevich in turn mentioned the Lipetsk meeting to Gol'denberg, later vociferous betrayer of the whole terrorist organization, and it was probably at Gol'denberg's own insistence that he was invited too.[111] In retrospect, Frolenko insisted that many leaders of the organization mistrusted

Gol'denberg and found him both unreliable and unintelligent. Mikhailov wrote that he was invited to Lipetsk "by accident, by error."[112] The truth is that this future "traitor" was at the time glowing with the prestige of his successful assassination of Governor-General Kropotkin just four months before. Some may have thought he talked too much about his deed and indiscriminately showed everyone the revolver with which it was accomplished,[113] but the terrorists were hardly being fussy about ardent supporters. Gol'denberg was one of the Southerners who, like Frolenko, had kept in close touch with the St. Petersburg core organization. Although later nobody wanted to take responsibility for his presence at the conspiratorial meeting, at the time his participation was not so "accidental" as it later seemed.

In the end, eleven conspirators attended the Lipetsk conference. From the South came Barannikov, Oshanina, Zheliabov, Kolodkevich, Gol'denberg, and Frolenko, who sprang from the Kiev *buntari* and considered the Ukraine his headquarters; from St. Petersburg, Aleksandr Mikhailov, Kviatkovskii, Morozov, Tikhomirov, and Stepan Shiriaev, the latter invited at the last minute just the day before.[114] This small group represented, as Morozov said, almost the entire force of the "fighting organization,"[115] such as it was. Inexplicably, Iakimova, Ivanova, Kibal'chich, and Isaev of the Freedom or Death dynamite manufactury were not there.

The Lipetsk meetings began on June 17, 1879.[116] Into the old spa, its healing waters known since the time of Peter the Great, the terrorists slipped in small, cautious groups, trying to assume the look of the ailing seeking cures. Barannikov and Oshanina, eager for action, had arrived almost a month early and were waiting for the others. The conspirators met casually at first, boating on the river, strolling in groups of two or three, and merging with the cure-seeking crowd. Shortly they located an idyllic spot for their more substantive discussions: an island of trees in the river's flood plain, where they were partially protected from outside view but were able to watch anyone who might think to approach. They all took horse-drawn taxis to the appointed spot. On the way, the exuberant Zheliabov could not resist showing off his strength; to the amazement of all, including coachman and horse, he single-handedly lifted the back axle of a carriage straight off the ground.[117] Once gathered, the conspirators spread blankets as if on a picnic, drank wine and beer, and nibbled snacks while they talked.

Their discussions went smoothly. There were few matters of principle on which they disagreed, and the St. Petersburg contingent had foresightedly set up an agenda for the meeting.

Morozov opened the first day's session with a short statement on the necessity of terrorism, a statement he had showed to Mikhailov and Kviatkovskii beforehand for their approval and suggestions.[118] Basically he argued that successful propagandizing among the peasantry was impossible without freedom of speech and movement, and that such freedoms were impossible under the tsarist regime. He exhorted his colleagues to "fight with the methods of Wilhelm Tell" (who was, along with Charlotte Corday, one of Morozov's immediate heroes)[119] until the repressive regime gave way to a government offering freedom of propagandizing and popular representation in some form.

What came to be called the "political" program—since it focused on political rather than social revolution—evoked little philosophical disagreement.[120] There were several minor additions to Morozov's remarks, including Zheliabov's practical contention that terrorism was justified because the revolutionaries did not have the strength to meet government troops head-on in the field.[121] One by one each participant rose to express similar ideas and to make his own speech.

The meeting might have lasted until nightfall had not Zheliabov intervened. Eventually only his energetic oratorical and organizational talents set things in order. Zheliabov not only guided and chaired the discussion that took place, but he spoke ardently for terrorism, surprising even Frolenko by the vehemence of his presentation.[122] At this Lipetsk conference, Zheliabov emerged as an impressive spokesman for the "new direction" and a leader of strength, potentially as great as Mikhailov himself.

On the third and last day of the meetings, Mikhailov rose to present a long "accusatory act" in judicial form against Alexander II, detailing what he contended were the crimes of the tsar's last years. "Should one for the sake of two good deeds in the beginning of his life forgive all the evil that he has done thereafter and will do in the future?" asked Mikhailov, and with fervor the group together shouted, "no!"[123] Although Mikhailov was not an easy, natural orator and tended to stutter under stress, his speech was "one of the most powerful speeches that I have ever come to hear in my life," according to Morozov's later judgment.[124] In the last session of the meetings, the Lipetsk conspirators unanimously adopted for first attention that project that had so disturbed their colleagues: They decided to concentrate their efforts on assassinating the tsar.[125] If the ultimate goals of the terrorists were nebulous, at least they knew what to do first.

More difficult than agreeing on their program was the problem of setting up a constitution for a new terrorist organization. Morozov apparently arrived at Lipetsk with a draft plan, but it provoked considerable debate.[126] Although the delegates agreed that terrorism demanded a secretive, conspiratorial organization run on a near-military basis—the principles advocated by Mikhailov for many years—several of those present were reluctant to commit themselves to the necessity for full obedience to a central core. (As Frolenko later wrote, "In general, as I have noticed, Russians acclimate to conspiracy, secrecy, the necessity to submit only slowly and with great unwillingness.")[127] On the whole, the provincial representatives were least willing of all, in that over the last several years they had enjoyed the greatest freedom of action, with no Mikhailov to tell them what to do. Zheliabov in particular—newly prestigious because of his contributions to the meeting's organization and operation—resented the idea of submission to centralized discipline.

Up until this time I personally did not see the need for a strong organization. Along with a number of other socialists, I considered it possible to act primarily on individual initiative, individual enterprise, individual cleverness. . . . The task was this: to understand the consciousness of the greatest possible number of persons among whom you are living. Organization was necessary only for receiving such resources as books and shipping them from abroad; printing them in Russia also [had to be] organized. Nothing else demanded special organization.[128]

But the Mikhailov/Morozov faction eventually had its way. The statute hammered out by the Lipetsk terrorists was based on Morozov's plan. It called for strong centralization. An "executive committee" was to coordinate the various sections of activity: literary-journalist, military, financial, etc. The "militant" section was to take the foremost role, and other area workers were always to act in its service. Within this dictate, each section could perform its own tasks independently, but each must always obey the center in its decisions about priorities, about the "necessity" and importance of various measures and undertakings. A general meeting might be called "infrequently" (Frolenko's word) to evaluate broad policy issues, but basically the central group remained tightly in control of policy execution. The statute provided for a three-person "administrative commission" and for a journal editorial board. All who entered the terrorist organization were to be termed "full members" or "agents" of various degrees, a measure for mystification of police and enemies that is reminiscent of the organization once designed by Petr Tkachev.[129] It is interesting that the Lipetsk statute survived to become the basis of the later People's Will organization, although Morozov huffily accused Tikhomirov of revising it beyond its original intent.[130]

On the second day of the meetings, the constitution was adopted after much amendment and debate. Frolenko, Mikhailov, and Tikhomirov ("whom many of us considered limp and impractical:" Morozov)[131] were elected to the administrative board. Morozov and Tikhomirov were named editors of the future terrorist journal. Upset with something in the balloting procedure, Mikhailov insisted that someone act as a keeper of records and secretary for the new organization, and Morozov was appointed, apparently by consensus and without a formal vote.[132] As the conference broke up, Shiriaev quietly approached Zheliabov and Kolodkevich about his needs for the dynamite manufactury; they approved of his projects and advanced him 500 rubles for future expenses.[133]

Although Frolenko later insisted that there was no spirit of separation at the Lipetsk meeting,[134] the truth is that the decisions taken make it perfectly clear that the terrorists were anticipating a new course and with it a new organization geared toward the new methods of struggle. The constitution as adopted made no provision for propagandists, neither among urban workers nor in the villages. The organizational structure (with its own executive, journal, and conspiratorial nature) left no room for the broad revolutionary aims of the old Land and Freedom, and the conspirators clearly named themselves as organizational chiefs and decision-makers. The Lipetsk terrorists must have sensed that their new society would seem anathema to most of their "villager" colleagues, especially with themselves set so firmly in control. It is true that in a later statement to the police, Shiriaev indicated that the terrorists had recognized several alternative arrangements in regard to their future association with the *narodniki.*

We found it appropriate to appear publicly under the name [Executive Committee] so that those members of the old *narodnik* organization who sympathized with our aims could enter into our society, or [so that] we could enter into the old organization, forming a separate group within it on a federative basis.[135]

Nevertheless, the Lipetsk decisions comprise a clear statement of independence, setting up as they did the framework for a totally new, terrorist-dominated organization.

Yet the Lipetsk conspirators did not take the final step of formally declaring that independence that their new statute virtually announced. They never, for instance, adopted a new name for their proposed organization. No memoirs reveal the exact nature of their debates, but one may surmise motives for their hesitation. Terrorists they may have been, but they were undoubtedly aware of the self-defeating nature of a split that divided the revolutionary movement. They cherished considerable personal friendship for their propagandist colleagues; some rather deep emotional ties had existed, such as Tikhomirov's one-time engagement to Perovskaia[136] or Morozov's infatuation with Figner.[137] Always conscientious, Mikhailov must have been aware that as recognized leader of Land and Freedom, he was betraying his own organization to the minority. More compelling was the concern for their own organizational future: if the partisans of violence withdrew categorically from Land and Freedom, they would lose what resources they had enjoyed as members, and they would have to start from scratch.

Under the circumstances, the Lipetsk conspirators decided to go to Tambov and confront their propagandist colleagues as planned. As Tikhomirov perceptively put it, they sought to seize the mother organization for themselves.[138] Anticipating winning some delegates to their point of view and losing some others, the conspirators hoped for a final showdown in their favor and the conversion of Land and Freedom into a primarily terrorist organization. Such a solution, if they could bring it about, would convey to terrorism the resources of the mother organization (its financial holdings, particularly the estate of Dmitrii Lizogub, now sentenced to death; its passport falsification equipment; its press; and not least of all its prestige) and perhaps even put the propagandists in the position of having to withdraw and accept responsibility for the organization's split.

The key to the conspirators' plan was to gain the majority at the Tambov meetings. Aware that they represented a minority in the society[139] and fearful that they would not through persuasion be able to win the necessary support, they devised a scheme to pack the meeting with proponents of terrorism. Before the sessions officially began, they decided to induce the propagandists of Land and Freedom to elect to official membership several terrorists who had never belonged to the party before. Once members, these terrorists would influence and swing, they hoped, the vote. Particularly important to the conspirators was Zheliabov, whose newly recognized talents made him a key leader and an ideal spokesman for the new direction. A dynamic orator, a powerful personality, and a great persuader, Zheliabov (like Gol'denberg, Kolodkevich, Figner, Oshanina, and many others) had never joined Land and Freedom and had no right to participate in the Tambov meetings at all. The plan reeked of deception and of conspiracy, but as things turned out, it worked.

With the Lipetsk conference at an end, the conspirators parted. Some of them went their ways, including Gol'denberg, whose presence (at least in hindsight) had never been entirely welcome.[140] Four went on to the Land and Freedom congress: these included the official members of that organization, namely, Morozov, Mikhailov, Tikhomirov, and Kviatkovskii. Several others remained in the old spa, awaiting word of their admission to membership so that they could attend the meetings too.

The Tambov conference loomed as a moment of crisis and perhaps a decisive battle in the turn from propaganda to violence. The conspirators approached it without confidence but with a plan. The "villagers" journeyed toward the meeting site with no inkling that their secretive comrades were attempting to manipulate the vote.

5

THE SCHISM

As it turned out, the events at the official meeting of Land and Freedom caught the terrorists by surprise and caused them, after considerable shuffling and realignment, to abandon their plans either to take over the mother organization or to found a new society of their own. What they anticipated as confrontation with their *narodnik* comrades emerged instead as compromise. The terrorists had felt themselves standing at a polar extremity from their propagandist comrades; instead, it turned out that the process of polarization had not engulfed the *narodniki* and that most of their colleagues were less stubbornly opposed to violence—or at least more determined to keep the party together—than they had imagined. Still in the long run, the reconciliation that occurred could only temporarily bridge the breach between the two factions. Terrorists remained frustrated about "wasting" Land and Freedom's limited resources on a propaganda campaign they regarded as fruitless; "villagers" remained uncertain about where political revolution accomplished without the peasantry's prompting might lead. Having patched itself together at its summer meeting, the society Land and Freedom tore itself apart in the months that followed. The final realignment of forces in terrorist and populist camps took place only after months of angry and frustrating argument, but at least both sides had opportunities to debate and to propound their viewpoints to those who were at first undecided.

At the last moment in June 1879, just as members of Land and Freedom were poised to converge on the provincial center of Tambov, the meeting place had to be changed. Popov, who (together with

Plekhanov) had been charged by the *narodniki* with making prelimin-
ary arrangements, had arrived in Tambov early and had contacted the
considerable contingent of revolutionaries already living there, a
group that included O. V. Aptekman and the recently arrived Figner
sisters.[1] Together they selected an appropriate spot for their confer-
ences: an area outside the city that one reached by traveling along
the river Tsen. One day shortly before the meetings were to begin,
the local revolutionaries hired two boats and set off to inspect the
site. In a feeling of camaraderie, warmth, and pleasure that Mikhailov
would have deplored, they begged Evgeniia Figner to sing the song
"Burnyi potok" ("The Wild Exile"), which all knew she did excel-
lently. Her singing attracted the attention of native Tambovists strolling along the riverbank paths, and a considerable group followed
along the shore to listen. They in turn attracted the attention of the
local police. When the boats finally landed, to Popov's great embarrassment, the police collected several of their passports—three to be
exact.[2] Since the identification was false—the product of the pass-
port-forging center of Land and Freedom in St. Petersburg—the three
revolutionaries found it necessary to leave town the next day, before
their illegal status was discovered. To avoid further arrests and to permit these threatened colleagues to attend the meeting, Popov was
forced to change its locale.

Because of its convenient location in the same general area—to the
south rather than east of Lipetsk—Popov and Vera Figner decided on
the city of Voronezh, where there was also a considerable revolutionary colony and where Popov had previously spent some time in his
own propagandist efforts.[3] They went there at once, and the two of
them rented an apartment together.[4] Thence they checked out and
approved a new location for the meetings, also in a forest on the edge
of town. Popov was saddled with the embarrassing task of explaining
to Petersburg what had happened and with the "unpleasantness" of
spending two days in the railroad center of Koslov, intercepting
those coming to the congress and informing them of the change in
locale.[5] Among the people he met were Perovskaia, arriving from the
South, and Frolenko, whose business had forced him to leave Lipetsk
early and who was returning to attend the full organization's meeting.[6]

To Voronezh—home of a famous monastery that was the object of
many pilgrimages and therefore a town accustomed to strangers—the
conspirators came on June 24, traveling as usual in groups of two or
three in order to avoid attracting attention. In the end they numbered

around 25 people, many of whom held proxies to vote for their friends who could not attend.[7]

Among the leaders of the propagandists were Lev Gartman (later a would-be assassin), Aptekman, Figner, Popov, Perovskaia, and above all Plekhanov—editor, writer, orator, propagandist, and the most articulate spokesman for the group. Plekhanov should have been able to count on the support of the provincial Land and Freedom members from Tambov, Saratov, and Voronezh—propagandists all. But years later he confessed that from the start he feared for the strength and unity of his faction.

For one thing, one of the strongest *narodnik* supporters had not come at all:

The late [A. I.] Preobrazhenskii was then an ardent *narodnik* and as such an opponent of terror. It was natural, therefore, for us to expect energetic support from him in our struggle with the "disorganizers" at the congress. However, he did not appear at the congress. Why? Because, he wrote us, he had begun an interesting transaction with the liberals, and he considered it necessary to continue it no matter what. You ask, what significance could liberals have for a man who, as an orthodox *narodnik*, denied terrorism exactly because it was one of the aspects of the political struggle? To this I answer that there is really not an atom of logic there.[8]

Waiting in Voronezh before the conspirators arrived, Plekhanov made an effort to consolidate the *narodnik* forces. He approached his old friend Nikolaev, nicknamed Egorych.

When I spoke with Nikolaev about our having to stand out against terrorism because terror threatened to engulf all our resources and forces and cause us to refrain from our agitational activity among the peasantry, he began ardently to reassure me. You are worried for nothing, he said. "How can we renounce our old tasks? *Vali valom* [we will go together] as before, that is all." And whenever I tried to demonstrate to him that the "disorganizers" were not disposed to "go together" as before, he lent a deaf ear. "This is how it seems to you," he said. I knew that not only did it seem so to me, but I also saw that we could not expect energetic and logical support from Nikolaev.[9]

Frustrated and worried, Plekhanov approached Perovskaia too, only to find that she was equally ambivalent. In principle, she told him,

she did not approve of terror, but once begun, the terrorist undertakings had to be finished. In vain I told her that we can only finish these undertakings by renouncing activity among the peasantry, but to the end of the congress she maintained her eclectic view. And so with almost everyone. Under such circumstances, could one count on victory?[10]

By the time the congress opened—or at least so Plekhanov said in later years—this most prestigious of the *narodniki* was anticipating defeat. "There could be no thought of carrying from Voronezh a decisive condemnation of terrorism," he wrote in retrospect. With some bitterness, Plekhanov blamed his comrades for "eclecticism" and a willingness to compromise—a lack of understanding, he insisted, that one must choose either agitation or terrorism, but that the two could not stand together. Among the *narodniki*, Plekhanov was probably the only one as adamantly convinced of his stand as the "disorganizers" were of theirs. His hope when the congress opened, he said, was to restrict the terrorists to the smallest possible share of resources and forces.[11]

But he had Mikhailov to deal with, and Mikhailov was an excellent organizer for the proponents of violence. Clearly, for all his astuteness in later analysis, Plekhanov remained in ignorance of the conspiracy that had been hatched at Lipetsk—that "Jacobin and Nechaev-like manoever by one-time comrades," as his friend Deich later termed it.[12] Plekhanov perhaps took heart when I. M. Tishchenko (nicknamed Titych) from Tambov was elected chairman of the meeting without an argument.[13] But he and the *narodniki* apparently had no suspicions when at the first session of the Voronezh meetings, Mikhailov requested that the members vote to admit three of his colleagues into the Land and Freedom organization. The request was granted unanimously, and Mikhailov's task had turned out to be simple. The leader of the terrorists straightaway sent to Lipetsk for his friends.

It is difficult to identify exactly who they were. Zheliabov was surely among them, but the identity of the others was never clearly recorded by conference participants. Almost certainly they included Kolodkevich. Shiriaev may have been added, although his own notes indicate that he returned to St. Petersburg after the Lipetsk meeting; he may have been admitted to Land and Freedom *in absentia* (as were several others) and his vote handled by proxy.[14] Evidence indicates that admission to Land and Freedom had been handled on a fairly casual basis and that membership records were poorly kept, especially as between the parent organization and sympathizers who often worked closely with its members. This informality accounts for the fact that Figner contended that Frolenko was a newcomer to the organization, although the latter insisted he had belonged since 1877,[15] and Frolenko included Perovskaia in his list of terrorists who were now admitted, although she was not yet a terrorist at all.[16] At any rate, the propagandists agreed to the expanded membership without (as Tikhomirov put it) suspecting a trap.[17] They later voted Deich, Stefanovich, and Zasulich the same privilege, but these three never had the opportunity to balance the influx of members by casting their votes for Plekhanov's faction, for they arrived in Russia too late and never attended the meetings at all.[18]

Luck was with the conspirators in another form, for at one of the early sessions of the Voronezh conference, the *narodniki* lost their leader and remained thereafter without his influence and aid. Perhaps Plekhanov saw no compelling reason to stay and fight since he could count on little support for his position. At what was probably the first session of the conference and directly following Morozov's reading of Osinskii's dramatic farewell address, Plekhanov rose, leaned against the trunk of a large tree, and asked Morozov to read an article on political murder that he had published in the *Leaflet*. Morozov was prepared and pulled it from his pocket, reading the words "with a firm voice, although trembling badly inside."[19] If Plekhanov, years later, remembered correctly, the article contained one of Morozov's favorite phrases: "Terror is revolution in action."[20]

This is our program? Plekhanov asked. Morozov reports that there was dead silence. Plekhanov remembers presenting a rebuttal, insisting that he and his comrades found the goals of revolutionary action to be far broader than the achievement of political freedom.

I retorted to Morozov that it seemed impossible to sanction the building of a parliament at the point of a dagger. I and several of my comrades hoped that we would succeed in extracting from Voronezh a resolution condemning such an extraordinarily narrow concept of revolutionary action.[21]

Frolenko broke the ensuing embarrassed silence by remarking on how well the article was written. According to Morozov, Plekhanov went white as a sheet and said with deep emotion, "Well, gentlemen, do you all think that?"[22]

There was more silence and further embarrassment. One of the *narodniki* from Saratov—we do not know who—pointed out that the Land and Freedom program of 1877 had made provision for violence ("disorganization") in the cities as well as propaganda in the countryside. To the astonishment of the terrorists, who had not expected a mood of compromise, a murmur of assent arose, and all but four members of the group agreed that this was true.[23] Plekhanov found himself isolated, abandoned by his friends and allies.

In spite of his statement that he had anticipated such a defeat, Plekhanov was (Morozov was sure) startled. He could only respond, "In that case, gentlemen, there is nothing for me to do here. Goodbye." Figner rose to call Plekhanov back, but Mikhailov prevented her: Better to let him go, Mikhailov told her.[24] Plekhanov's four supporters started to stand, but then they slipped back to their seats, whispered to each other for a time, and remained at the meeting.[25] As Plekhanov walked into the woods alone, even Morozov felt a pang: "We, expecting [our own] expulsion, suddenly without difficulty remained the victors, and he, considering himself all along the victor, became unexpectedly the defeated. Tears rose in my throat."[26] Plekhanov was by far the most articulate, able, and intelligent of the propagandists. Only he stood dogmatically for the total rejection of violence. Without him, as Morozov later said, the *narodniki* lost their "energy."[27] After his departure the group agreed by majority vote that (although he might apply for readmittance) he had relinquished his membership in Land and Freedom by walking out.

At the end of the day's inconclusive session, the group took a break for a day, probably at the instigation of the terrorists, who badly needed to confer about the surprisingly compromising tone their antagonists had adopted. Meeting quietly together after the official adjournment, the Lipetsk conspirators agreed to accept the compromise they felt they had been offered. Rather than attempt to take over Land and Freedom or to withdraw from it in protest, they would work within the organization as a recognized fraction, entitled to funds, other support, and a semi-independent position.[28]

At the same time, they took advantage of the adjournment to proselytize among their companions for support. Morozov desperately attempted to persuade Vera Figner to join the terrorist fraction,[29] while Zheliabov worked on many, including Perovskaia. The latter's stubbornness caused her pursuer to throw up his hands: "I can't do anything with that woman [*baba*]!" he was heard to complain.[30] He made an impression beyond his own awareness, for Figner sensed that Perovskaia was already greatly intrigued with him[31] —and later when she was converted to terrorism, they became lovers. Again, as before Lipetsk, the terrorists conducted a deliberate campaign to win support among their *narodnik* colleagues, to the point where the volume of private agreements (and arguments) greatly exceeded that at the formal meetings.

When they met again two days later in the woods, a modicum of peace had been negotiated, and all but Zheliabov and Mikhailov leaned over backward to avoid a split. Popov later wrote:

The mood of the congress was most peaceful. Both the right and the left of the assembled members of the organization Land and Freedom clearly expressed the hope not to push affairs to a split, in part because of faith in one another and because of comradely affections, but even more such a mood arose from the awareness of both sides that it was not so easy to create such an organization as Land and Freedom, at that time the only revolutionary organization that not only enjoyed authority in broad circles of revolutionaries but [enjoyed responsibility] for actions that all educated Russia followed with intense interest. In each of those attending the conference, the conscious wish to avoid the possibility of a split of the society gained supremacy to the extent that each tried to restrain himself, and if one or another orator got out of control and began imperceptibly to be carried away by himself, some one of his close friends immediately reminded him of this and with general assistance quieted the orator down.[32]

Zheliabov, the most enthusiastic of orators, was the hardest to control, for he apparently had believed a split between terrorists and *narodniki* was inevitable. Speaking ardently for terror—he was a constitutionalist and believed that violence could bring about an entirely new constitution, which would in turn permit legal propagandizing— Zheliabov was deliberately restrained by the terrorist Frolenko when on one occasion he spoke vehemently to the *narodnik* Popov.[33] Thereafter he maintained silence at the meetings but "occupied himself exclusively with private talks, trying to persuade individual people to his side."[34] Tikhomirov reports that the "majority" once quieted him too, fearful that he would foil the compromise solution.[35] When Mikhailov leaped to his feet to protest the nomination of a *narodnik* (the absent A. I. Preobrazhenskii, nicknamed Iurist) to the new administrative council, he was publicly berated by his co-conspirator Oshanina, who told him he was behaving badly.[36] In spite of tempers and impulses, the consensus was to hold.

At the third and last session of the Voronezh meetings, the compromise solution was adopted. In essence, the members of Land and Freedom reiterated their support of the program as it had existed since 1877—including its provisions for work among the intelligentsia, workers, and peasantry, and including specific support to be supplied to a terrorist or "fighting" organization—a newly invigorated "dis-organization squad."[37] Debating the potential murder of government agents, those present decided the issue in "the positive sense," as Popov put it later,[38] and they somewhat revised the program's word-ing to encompass attacks on leading government figures and policy makers in addition to lesser officials who directly threatened the revolutionary movement and the safety of its members. Popov claims that they spoke openly about the question of regicide, but if he is correct a decision was postponed.[39] To the list of permissible terror-ist acts, at Popov's request, they added agrarian terrorism in the countryside.[40]

Of the available funds of Land and Freedom, it was agreed that one-third would be made available to the terrorists and two-thirds preserved for use of the village propagandists. Popov was certain that the Lipetsk conspirators only agreed to this division of wealth in anticipation of winning over so many of the *narodniki* that the decimated work in the countryside would not cost much.[41] Fore-seeing trouble, those assembled decided that should there be dis-agreement about the use of funds or any other matter, Frolenko for the terrorists and Tishchenko for the propagandists would meet to negotiate a solution.

A three-man administrative committee was to be composed of Frolenko, Mikhailov, and Tishchenko. The journal *Land and Free-dom* would be edited by Morozov, Tikhomirov, and a third person uncertainly identified: either Tishchenko or Aptekman (replacing the expelled Plekhanov).[42] Morozov—or so he later claimed—was made record-keeper for the organization,[43] and at the last session the society admitted a number of new members: probably Vera Figner, who had already told Popov she intended to join; *in absentia* Deich, Stefanovich, Zasulich (assumed to be terrorists); and perhaps Pavel Aksel'rod.[44]

It was decided that the statute of Land and Freedom should be re-written to incorporate that measure of compromise won by the terrorists at Voronezh. Morozov subsequently recorded the new clause to be added.

Because the Russian populist-revolutionary party from its very origins and through all the time of its development has met an embittered enemy in the Rus-sian government, because in the last period the repressions of the government have attained their apogee, the congress finds it necessary to grant special en-hancement to the disorganization group in the area of struggle with the government, continuing at the same time as well work among the people in the sense of settlements and popular disorganization. Unanimous.[45]

The truth is, as Frolenko later pointed out, the Land and Freedom members had avoided extensive debate on those issues which divided them and had happily taken up practical issues of the day instead of substantive questions of tomorrow.[46] Thus the terrorists compromised, and Morozov's organizational plan for a strictly terrorist organization went back into the files, whence it emerged later, thoroughly debated and somewhat revised, to form the basis of the constitution of the People's Will.[47] The *narodniki* compromised, in that they agreed to turn additional resources toward projects for "disorganization." Impatient terrorists and hopeful propagandists agreed to a new start on the old basis.

The Voronezh meetings leave an epilogue to record. Depressed by defeat and saddened by the "defection" of his comrades, Plekhanov fled south—to Kiev and to the arms of Rosa Markovna Bograd, soon to become his wife and lifelong companion. The two had first met in St. Petersburg, where they probably made contact through Aleksandr Mikhailov, one of Bograd's early mentors in her revolutionary studies, through whose influence she had set up a circle of her own. Both men may have been rivals for her attention, but her affections settled on Plekhanov.[48] G. V., as Bograd called him, had been with her only a few days when, to her surprise, Aleksandr Mikhailov appeared. He had always admired Plekhanov in spite of their opposing points of view. Voronezh was to put an end to their comradeship, as the final split in Land and Freedom was to end many friendships.

Bograd later described their meeting:

Rapidly the conversation turned to the results of the congress, at which [point] G. V. passionately and sharply attacked its resolutions, which he called deviationist, a betrayal of the people's interests and of revolution. A. Mikhailov objected no less sharply and with quick temper. Yesterday's friends stood one against the other with glares of anger and hostile eyes. This was unbearably distressing. I finally intervened in the increasing passion of the argument and arranged with A. Mikhailov to meet him the next day in a park.[49]

Indeed, on the following day, Bograd and Mikhailov sat together— without Plekhanov—on a little bench for a quiet talk. Mikhailov, Bograd wrote, was convinced that his was the right path. He spoke of Plekhanov on this occasion with no bitterness—only, she reported, with love and kindness. There was no declaiming, just gentle and quiet conversation. "You know, Rosa," he said,

how I loved work among the people. I was ready to make any sacrifice available to me, but we were a handful, we were powerless to do anything under the autocracy; all our best forces were expended without result. There was only one alternative for our small strength: either completely to abandon revolutionary activity or to enter into one-on-one battle with the government. For the latter we had enough forces, heroism, and capacity for self-sacrifice.[50]

He began to try to persuade her to his way of thinking, but Bograd was deeply committed to Plekhanov. She wrote later:

I felt myself incapable of opposing his ardent, inspired words with any kind of banal expression. I did not say a word.
    "You are silent, Rosa Markovna? Your silence is more powerful than an attack."
    I with difficulty said, "Forgive me, I am not myself."[51]

On that sad note they parted, Mikhailov to tour the provinces explaining and advocating terror to revolutionary groups, Bograd to support her defeated, disturbed G. V.

But the status quo was not to last. Like many compromises, the decisions adopted at the Voronezh conference proved unsatisfactory to both opposing factions, and the solution did not endure. In spite of their suppression of their angers, their show of unity, and their agreement to work together, as before, in the organization Land and Freedom, the terrorist and *narodnik* groups found themselves at loggerheads almost at once. Within a few short weeks, points of difference had resurfaced and had proved to be insoluble after all.

In the first place, the terrorists did not slow the tempo of their efforts to recruit Land and Freedom members—as well as those from independent revolutionary groups—into their camp and to win them away from the "villager" point of view. Immediately after the Voronezh meetings, they sent Zheliabov to the South to agitate for "the new direction" among revolutionary circles of Kharkov, Kiev, and Odessa.[52] A remarkable orator, particularly before large groups, Zheliabov spoke enthusiastically, logically, and clearly. He had the gift of bringing his audience to an emotional peak. Traveling with him to Kharkov, Gol'denberg (who had not attended the Voronezh meetings at all) found him an effective missionary, in spite of the fact that many in his provincial audiences seemed puzzled about the schism and uncertain of what the fuss was all about.[53] Shortly Zheliabov was followed by Frolenko, who had even stronger ties with revolutionary groups in the Ukraine,[54] and thereafter by the terrorists Shiriaev and Barannikov,[55] all of them fervently exhorting to the cause of violence. Mikhailov too began proselytizing after his futile journey to Plekhanov.

In the capital city, other leaders continued their arguments and persuasions. The terrorists set up headquarters in the suburb of Lesna, where the fraction Freedom or Death had established a conspiratorial apartment. Here several of their comrades (including Anna Korba, newly recruited to the cause but an old friend to many)[56] took dachas for the summer season. Here Morozov finally persuaded the attractive and energetic Vera Figner to take up the cause of violence, and Kviatkovskii recruited young Nikolai Bukh, who had previously worked on the journal *Land and Freedom*.[57] Mikhailov soon returned here after his trip to the South, and Morozov and Tikhomirov, newly confirmed editors of a yet unestablished journal, contacted intelligentsia friends, while the former pursued his ardent love affair with Ol'ga Liubatovich, who had recently returned from abroad.[58] In the lush, green, summer fields the conspirators openly talked assassination and agreed that their first target should be the tsar. The dynamite manufactury of Freedom or Death—under the command of Shiriaev—quietly continued its experiments.

But now the battle was joined. Aware—perhaps for the first time— just what they were up against, the "villagers" began a campaign of their own. Their side was now blessed with the talents and reputations of Stefanovich, Deich, and Zasulich, who, with the aid of the terrorist Zundelevich,[59] had returned to Russia from Switzerland too late to attend the Voronezh meetings but who had all (according to most sources) been admitted to Land and Freedom *in absentia* by that congress.

The support of these expatriate revolutionary heroes—and especially of the notorious Zasulich—greatly abetted the *narodnik* cause. Zasulich and Deich had both been responsible for terrorist attacks in the past, yet neither of them actually supported terrorism as a principle, and all three returned exiles were to draw ever closer to Plekhanov in the next few years. Stefanovich and Deich remained in St. Petersburg for several weeks to recruit propagandists among the revolutionaries in the capital and then along with Aptekman traveled south in the same cause. Zasulich they left in St. Petersburg, where she lived in Lesna too; she was in constant danger of attracting police attention, since the Senate had called for her retrial for the Trepov crime.[60]

The activities of the returned expatriates particularly annoyed the terrorists, who had invited the emigré clique to the meetings at Voronezh under the mistaken impression that the three were proponents of violence. Instead all three turned out to be ardent supporters of the opposing faction. Morozov was particularly disappointed in the stance of Zasulich. "We invited her to the Lipetsk [but he may have meant Voronezh] congress in the firm conviction that she would be a partisan of the new method of struggle," he wrote. Instead, the terrorists discovered this founder of terrorism to be

extremely friendly with Stefanovich and Deich, and together with them, switching over [to the side of] our opponents, thus suddenly surrounding [the *narodniki*] with a halo in the eyes of the young students, who worshipped [Zasulich].[61]

These *narodnik* leaders did well for their faction, for they assured the adherence of such Land and Freedom members as M. R. Popov, A. I. Preobrazhenskii,[62] and M. K. Krylova (who had charge of the Land and Freedom printing press)[63] to the propagandists' cause.

But the terrorists were even more annoyed at the turn of good luck that the *narodniki* enjoyed at the end of August when Plekhanov rejoined them in St. Petersburg. For two months G. V. had lived with his Rosa in Kiev and despaired. At first he held himself in "complete isolation" from his comrades and could only ask himself sadly what was left for him to do.[64] His parting with Mikhailov was a blow, and Bograd was sure that in spite of their quarrel with each other, they would take their mutual love to the grave.[65] But Plekhanov was a strong man and could not long endure without action or hope. Gradually he became convinced that "one in the field is not the war."

In her reminiscence about this year's events, Bograd describes how he argued with himself. After all, the propagandist group party still existed. It could count on Aptekman in spite of his fetish about party unity; Popov would never whole-heartedly join the terrorists; Perovskaia was still hesitating and at any rate had promised to return to the "villagers" once the terrorists' major mission was complete.[66] In August, Plekhanov slipped south to meet Popov and returned to Bograd in a more optimistic mood. Then came word that Deich, Stefanovich, and Zasulich had arrived in the capital city. Plekhanov hurried there and found, as he suspected, that they "agreed with me in almost all questions of revolutionary theory and practice."[67]

In St. Petersburg, possessed of his old vigor again, Plekhanov thus resumed his position as leading *narodnik* agitator. The terrorists raged; to them, his involvement was tantamount to transgression. After all, he had left the meeting at Voronezh and by majority vote had been presumed to have sacrificed his membership in Land and Freedom. Under the circumstances, he had no right, as Morozov bitterly pointed out, to participate in any of the organization's negotiations. The propagandists who "communicated to him all the secret actions of the society" were behaving strictly in opposition to the Land and Freedom statute, recently reaffirmed.[68]

Not unexpectedly, the sharpest conflicts between the two factions arose in connection with the resources of Land and Freedom, particularly its money and its press. The original decision to allocate one-third of the society's financial holdings to the terrorists was soon openly deplored by that group. The partisans of violence felt that the "villagers" had no pressing need for funds and that they could wait, while terrorism's plots demanded immediate and substantial monetary support. In late summer, when it became apparent that the society would have a hard time getting its hands on the estate unofficially left to it by the revolutionary Dmitrii Lizogub (executed early in August),[69] the problem became even more acute. With their Lizogub hopes disappearing in smoke, the terrorists claimed more from the common funds. They pointed out that several members of the *narodnik* faction (notably V. N. Ignatov and E. P. Durnovo in Moscow) had control of considerable estates that might be tapped by the propagandists in compensation.

An even more violent argument arose about the printing press facilities. In 1877, after it had been purchased in Berlin by Zundelevich and shipped illegally to St. Petersburg, the secret press of Land and Freedom was reassembled with some difficulty in quarters just off the Nevskii Prospect on Nikolaevskii street. Here Nikolai Bukh and M. K. Krylova lived as man and wife, with a "servant" (M. V. Griaznova) and her lover, a typesetter nicknamed Ptitsa.[70] Kept in deep secrecy (Tikhomirov, who was an editor of *Land and Freedom*, never saw the press until after the arrest of his senior colleague Klements),[71] the typography survived even the raids following the Mezentsev assassination. In April 1879—the month of Solov'ev's attempt on the tsar—the last edition of the society's official journal, was printed on it, but Morozov's terrorist *Leaflet* continued publication through May and June. Over the summer, during the months of the schism, the presses fell temporarily into disuse.

It was a bad blow to the terrorists when Krylova suddenly announced her allegiance to the *narodnik* point of view, especially since her colleague Nikolai Bukh had apparently moved away from the quarters to be in Lesna near his terrorist friends and left her in full command. One day she simply told Morozov, who was technically co-editor of the journal, that she would print no more terrorist-oriented *Leaflets* because, as she said, "Political freedom will encourage the development of the bourgeoisie and thus inflict injury on the working people."[72] Recognizing her phrases as part of the rhetoric of Plekhanov and Stefanovich, Morozov frantically tried to argue her out of them. His efforts to change her were in vain and led only to stubborn reassertion and finally hysterics: "At the end of all conversations with her, I simply had to run for cold water to pacify her somewhat," he wrote.[73] Tikhomirov and Mikhailov had no better luck. "She cried, but refused to work," Frolenko wrote.[74] Krylova threatened to defend her presses at point of arms, although even Plekhanov and his friends apparently felt she was going too far. In the end, rather than surrender the presses, she packed their components into two large trunks and hid them with an elderly lady known to Mariia Koval'skaia, one of her *narodnik* friends.[75]

By late August, when many of the proselytizers returned from the South, it was apparent to most participants that a split in the organization was inevitable. Zheliabov and the terrorists were sure of it, and only a few of the *narodniki* (Perovskaia, who came to St. Petersburg this month; Stefanovich, who also returned then) still hoped to hold Land and Freedom together.[76] In the final days of summer, ties broke, wrote Morozov, "like a spiderweb," whenever opposing factions got together.[77] "Yesterday's comrades," Liubatovich said later, "became alienated from one another like strangers."[78] Koval'skaia described her meeting with her old friend Perovskaia.

She [Perovskaia] joyfully embraced me in greeting; but after a few phrases we both felt as if some sort of impenetrable wall stood between us. We continued our insignificant conversation, but somehow it went sluggishly, not as of old. [When Plekhanov arrived and began to joke] in his usual pert tone . . . we were not in the mood for these jokes. It was difficult to go through the split of the party and everything accompanying this split. Perovskaia silently threw a reproachful look at Plekhanov, lowered her eyes, and took up her book.[79]

Perovskaia's expression reminded Koval'skaia of the old "distrustful" look that she had sometimes shown in the past. When Zheliabov arrived at the meeting, he and Plekhanov exchanged a few diplomatic phrases and then "rushed into battle."[80] As the most articulate spokesman for the *narodniki*, Plekhanov got into heated arguments with his good friend Milhailov too.[81]

For Mikhail Popov, it was the most difficult time in his life as a revolutionary. Particularly impressed with the arguments of Stefanovich and Deich, who convinced him that work among the peasantry of the Chigirin district might still bring profitable results,[82] he eventually broke with his old terrorist friends. Tikhomirov tried to persuade him to stay: "You too, Rodionich, though you feel sorry about the split! Yet we will all remain the very same as we were and differ only in evaluating the present situation."[83] To which Popov replied, with foresight, "Once the wheel has spun to one side, it will be difficult to return it to the other." When Popov came to say goodbye to his friends before he left for Kiev, Mariia Oshanina took his hands. "Stay with us, Rodionich," she begged, but he would not do so.[84] Morozov was less pleasant in parting, and the coolness between the two outlasted their many years in prison and exile.[85]

By the time Frolenko returned from the South late in summer, the strain of the conflict was more than any of them could bear. Better to split rather than go through this hell, Mikhailov told him with tears in his eyes.[86] By now only Aptekman had any hope of unity. Returning to St. Petersburg from the provinces, probably in late August, he was horrified to find the society in a more antagonistically disunited state than at the Voronezh meetings. "I protested then as energetically as I knew how," he wrote later,

I said that it was very unreasonable, imprudent to break apart at a time when our party was still insufficiently strong, when we had still not succeeded in organizing among the people a sufficiently solid militant party, when the very situation of things—the constant and untiring battle with the government, in one form or another—demanded from us great concentration of forces and energy. . . . I wanted at least to save the journal. I thought that if *Land and Freedom* were to print the same program that was worked out at the congress in Voronezh, then both fractions would be satisfied. There was no point, of course, in demolishing our material and literary forces; there was no point in giving the government occasion for pleasure; there was no point, in a word, in upsetting the youth, workers, and society. I told my concerns to this side and that, and proposed to publish a *common* organ under the *same* title *Land and Freedom* . . . The negotiations remained futile.[87]

Even Aptekman had to give up. Nothing could be done. Finally each faction appointed delegates to work out details of a final separation;

from the *narodniki*—Stefanovich, Popov, and probably Preobrazhen-skii; from the terrorists—Mikhailov, Tikhomirov, and Zundelevich.[88]

It took months to hammer out an agreement, but by October the deed was done. The terrorists were to have the central typography and to get what they could from Dmitrii Lizogub's estate—and although the bulk of the estate was eventually awarded elsewhere, they benefited from the use of 8,000 rubles that remained in a secret fund that Lizogub had set aside for terrorist activity even before his arrest.[89] The *narodniki* were to rely on other sources of wealth. They also agreed to make use of the press that one of their members had farsightedly acquired the previous spring and had stored in hiding with a sympathizer in Smolensk. Each group would run its own journal, but each promised not to attack the other—a promise soon broken on both sides.[90]

Neither faction was to use the old name, Land and Freedom. Instead, the terrorists took the title the People's Will. The constitution they adopted was based on their Lipetsk decisions, and soon (as they had anticipated) they threw all their efforts into assassinating the tsar. The Plekhanovites took the name *Chernyi peredel'* (Black Repartition)—the peasant term for a complete redistribution of land. The immediate fate of their organization was less lucky than that of their rivals'. In spite of the strengths of the propagandists still in the countryside, they never succeeded in setting up even such coordination as had existed under the Land and Freedom group. By 1880, police action in St. Petersburg had caused Plekhanov, Deich, Zasulich, Stefanovich, and many others to flee the capital city and resettle in Switzerland.

Old friendships had been broken, and old ties had disappeared. Koval'skaia reports that Perovskaia made one further effort to persuade her old friend into the ranks of the terrorists, although Perovskaia at the time (autumn 1879) still thought of herself as an independent supporter of regicide and had not permanently joined the organization People's Will. Meeting in a St. Petersburg restaurant at an appointed time, the two young women miserably argued with each other.

> Perovskaia: I want very much to persuade you to join us. You have nothing realistic. We have vigorous action ahead.
>
> Koval'skaia: All my militant nature strives towards you. I am in favor of terrorism, but in your program the political side takes precedence over the socialist.

Having torn yourself from the people, you will complete a political overthrow but not a socialist revolution. . . .

Perovskaia [finally]: Know that if there was an immediate cause of vitality among you, I would have come with you, but I do not see that you have such a cause.[91]

Their parting was a sad moment for both old friends. It was the last time they met; they never spoke to each other again.

6

THE MYSTIQUE
OF TERRORISM

It is not surprising that Land and Freedom split. From the beginning—from the very initiation of a "disorganization squad"—the society had divided its activities into two phases: village propaganda and urban violence. Pledged at first to cooperation, the participants in each found themselves drifting further and further apart. The late summer of 1879 saw a break, complete with personal quarrels and miseries.

In the end, the terrorists were able to attract into their organization considerable numbers of the once-dedicated *narodniki*. We must ask ourselves how, under the circumstances, they succeeded. Why did the People's Will, with its dedication to political violence and assassination, win the day over its rival, propagandist organization? Why did so many of the most articulate and able members of Land and Freedom—some of whom had argued ardently against terrorism—become converted to a cause they had previously deplored? The questions are not easy to answer.

For the split was deep and real. By 1879 observers indicate that the *narodniki* of the countryside had little in common with the terrorists of the cities. Many of the urban revolutionaries had never gone "to the people," as Deich points out.[1] Those who had (like Aleksandr Mikhailov, Mikhail Frolenko, Morozov, and Deich himself), once returned to their city circles, rapidly came to feel remote from their country cousins. For a while, established ties still kept them in contact. Until the terrorist conspiracy of spring 1879, country workers still made occasional trips to St. Petersburg, perhaps more out of a need for camaraderie and a break in routine than to report on pro-

125

gress or request aid: witness Figner during the Christmas season of 1878. Members of the central core made periodic forays into the countryside, where they contacted *narodniki* for local information and assistance; thus Plekhanov sought out Sof'ia Perovskaia in Kharkov in the autumn of 1878 because he knew she would have information on "safe" quarters both there and in St. Petersburg. At the central core of Land and Freedom, Mikhailov had probably helped set plans for a new "settlement" at Voronezh in 1878; when he needed the help of the "settlers" after the successful police raids that autumn, he had no hesitation in peremptorily summoning them back from the countryside, and they came, loyally, without questioning.[2] The network remained intact. Yet witnesses indicate that during 1879, bonds were actually disintegrating.

By the time of the Voronezh conference, the terrorists had come to feel alienated from the propagandists of the countryside. To them, it seemed that they stood in the center of action, that the path to revolution lay through violence alone. Between city and country, as Figner wrote:

A moral estrangement took place. In Petersburg, a battle was going on that required the constant dedication of all forces and also had an unprecedented agitational effect. Intoxicated with success, embittered by failure, one looked down with surprise and scorn upon the Saratov and Tambov villages, where the sojourn of dozens of comrades revealed no sign of active battle, no [visible] results. This irritated the Petersburgers the most. Every members who remained among the peasants seemed to them to have withdrawn from the zealous battle to which they were sacrificing body and soul.[3]

In the view of urban terrorists, the "villagers" had virtually disappeared from the active revolutionary stage. If their country activities demanded both caution and isolation, events in the cities brought the urban revolutionaries into ever more constant contact. With every major terrorist deed and every strong government reprisal, the St. Petersburg center was drawn more closely together, united in common approbation or hostility. By such events country cousins were by no means unaffected, but their reactions had to be kept secret and isolated, and even the information often came to them well after the fact. In regard to the trial of 193, Shiraiev observed:

Circumstances pressured the urban group more and more . . . joining and uniting them ever more closely to each other and setting them apart from the village groups. Indeed, all the terrorist enterprises—the staging of demonstrations, the operation of the presses, etc.—not only gave the participants an occasion to get to know each other better, to draw closer together, but also separated them from the others [in the countryside], by the simple fact that each given undertaking was kept secret in detail from all who did not personally participate in it and often was initiated by individual groups at their own risk without the knowledge of the majority.[4]

The demand for secrecy that united the conspirators tended to place the "villagers" farther out in the cold.

From the point of view of the propagandists, the terrorists seemed ever more to be withdrawing from the real cause of importance: agitation among the peasantry about peasant rights and economic/administrative evils, with the aim of eventually summoning the peasants to make revolution for themselves. This was the cause that the "villagers" had undertaken with the new program of 1876, and three years later they had accumulated a good number of complaints, not the least of which had to do with the attitudes of their urban colleagues.

For one thing, the leadership of the central core of Land and Freedom had fallen to a terrorist, in the person of Aleksandr Mikhailov. By 1878, Mikhailov's commitment to violence was clear and obvious, even before the conspiracies of the spring of 1879 and the withdrawal of Plekhanov from the editorship of *Land and Freedom.* The funds that had once supported the organization's journal were shortly diverted to Morozov's strictly terrorist enterprise, the *Land and Freedom Leaflet.* "Villagers" began to resent many aspects of the central policy in regard to financial resources. They disliked the focus of the Petersburgers on their own needs and interests (particularly after the government raids of autumn 1878) to the detriment of those of the country workers. A sympathizer with terrorism at the time, even Tikhomirov was aware that

the activity of the Petersburg members was in no way directed to the aid of those in the villages. With [villagers] they undertook correspondence, but its content was totally foreign to [their real] interests. They sent money to the villagers, but little and unwillingly. All their attention and forces, willy-nilly, were focused on their own activities: the press, agitation in society, agitation among students, the terrorist group, and finally the worker movements—this is what absorbed all forces and resources.[5]

In vain "the villager petitioned . . . for more money, for more people, books, for the organization necessary for village coordination, etc."[6]

Murders cost money, and violence was the focus of the terrorist creed.

Around violence "villager" objections came to be centered, not only for the time and money it consumed but particularly because it became apparent that the police, aroused by terrorist acts and in possession of documents that linked the *narodniki* with their urban colleagues, were beginning to threaten village activities. From the countryside, propagandists complained that the terrorists were destroying that work which the organization Land and Freedom, including its "disorganization group," had been established to abet and protect.[7] In St. Petersburg Plekhanov, whose presence there and whose work on the journal *Land and Freedom* placed him in closer proximity to urban than to village colleagues, protested the policies of the city terrorists on similar grounds.[8]

Indeed, to the propagandist, the terrorist had become a superfluous show-off, caught up in his own glamor and feeding his own ego by near-frivolous acts of daring that endangered the entire movement. He had lost track of the revolutionaries' fundamental goals. As Figner put it:

The "villagers" in the countryside believed that the urban Land and Freedom [members] were shooting off fireworks whose glitter distracted youth from real work and from the people, who were in such need of [our] strength. The slaying of generals and gendarmerie heads was in their eyes less productive, less necessary work than agrarian terrorism in the countryside.[9]

In the long run, such conflicting views on the importance of violence and of propaganda caused alienation of the one group from the other until the essential unity of Land and Freedom came in jeopardy. The country was so far from the city. Life-styles altered; interests became more focused. Tikhomirov described an imaginary meeting:

When after a long absence the previous comrades met—one from the village, another from the city—it was apparent that they were dissatisfied with each other. The villagers already had a somewhat strange provincial manner, were not interested in any world events, talked only about certain details of popular life. He [the villager] had obviously become derevolutionized from the point of view of the city man. The Petersburger did not seem to the villager to be liberal; he dressed well and spoke of politics and attacked not the kulak or the lord, but the government. . . . Thus mutual displeasure grew and ripened into a full break.[10]

"Mutual displeasures" and lack of common interests were only exacerbated by terrorist manipulations and conspiracies in the spring of 1879. By the time of the congress at Voronezh, many city revolutionaries and village propagandists had drifted apart in convictions, outlook, interests, and priorities, and the ultimate goals they shared seemed inadequate to pull them back together.

More challenging than the problem of the schism itself is the question of how a handful of terrorists, during and after the spring of 1879, were able to convert many previously dedicated *narodniki* to their point of view. Of course many propagandists stood by their guns. Of the thirteen propagandists that we know attended the congress at Voronezh, eight remained true to their original program; the figure includes Aptekman, Plekhanov, and Popov, who continued to protest the schism in their arguments with the terrorist contingent, and five others, who slipped quietly back to the countryside to continue their work with or without organizational support.[11] Nevertheless, although history has exaggerated the movement into the organization People's Will, the assassination project drew together several dozen activists, from within and without the Land and Freedom organization, among whom many who became leaders in the assassination project had seemed particularly devoted to their village assignments. The triumph of the People's Will in this regard is particularly startling when compared to the pale success of Plekhanov and his friends in attracting members to their organization Black Repartition.[12] An analysis of these conversions is vital to an understanding of the movement toward terrorism in 1879 and thereafter.

The swing toward violence after Voronezh is the more difficult to interpret because the participants who described it later were keenly aware of their failure to accomplish their aims through the successful assassination of Alexander II in 1881. Unwilling to admit that terrorism was a mistake, that the penalties paid in executions, imprisonments, and increased police diligence were all for nothing, the assassins—often lamely—attempted to justify their deed in their memoir literature of later years. They did so by claiming in retrospect that their *narodnik* stance had been misguided, hopeless, foolish, and wrong; that the police had persecuted them into failure in the countryside; that they then had no alternative but to turn to terror. In retrospect, they contended that it was not the assassination but the propaganda that had been out of joint.

Thus years later, "villagers" contended that the peasantry had been unresponsive to their propaganda and unhappy with their presence in the village. "For three years," wrote Figner in retrospect, "the members of Land and Freedom of the North and the *buntari* of the South sought to reach the heart of the people. All was in vain: The people were silent, the village slept."[13]

There is no denying that in many instances she was right. Sometimes the situation of a whole village made it impossible to propagandize; Figner herself had found it so when, as a paramedic, she coped day and night with those so ill as to have no hope, and Ivanchin-Pisarev reported that he could do nothing in a village known for its drunkenness. If some peasants were too miserable to respond to the revolutionary dream, others were too prosperous to wish to do so; Lev Deich found the Molokany so, and deemed them improper subjects for any radical propaganda at all.[14] One might argue that it was among the middle ground—those neither too rich nor too poor—that the *narodniki* found their friends. The significance of such carefully selective propagandizing as a successful stimulus for broad social revolution is debatable, but that is another story.

Among some propagandists, the inability to arouse peasant response caused a bitterness that may well have led them to abandon their country positions. Although one might well evoke his own restlessness and ineptitude, Solov'ev assessed blame clearly on the peasants among whose villages he had roamed. He found them steeped in drunkenness and ignorance beyond repair, and Figner was warping his words when she later claimed he remained true to the *narodnik* creed.[15] N. I. Sergeev (although he admitted he had won sympathy from a number of individuals in the village) found the peasantry on the whole irredeemable and reported that

The people were deaf to my propaganda. . . . Peasant indifferentism and the lack among [the peasants] of any wish even to know about whether there is some way of exchanging their bitter fate for a better one left me completely at a loss and filled me with extreme indignation.[16]

These reactions led Lenin to assert that the *narodniki* had lost faith in the peasantry, and his analysis has been echoed by many scholars, Western and Soviet, including the careful investigator V. A. Tvardovskaia.[17]

But is their analysis valid? Certainly it is only partially so. There is no doubt that many of the propagandists inspired interest and evoked support. We have cited above the most notable and articulate examples from those memoirs that treat of life "among the people" in the greatest detail. Of those who stuck it out, few found the peasants unresponsive to demonstrations of friendship and offers of aid. Figner, Deich, Mikhailov, Ivanchin-Pisarev, Kviatkovskii, Popov, and many others were not met with hostility and rejection. Even the laughter accorded the city girl who could not drive the team of oxen was not bitter but amused.[18] Rarely did those propagandists who abandoned the "flying" approach—and Solov'ev might well be considered a "flying" *narodnik*—find themselves rejected in anger or fear. They never, of course, roused the peasants to rebel, but according to their program, they had not intended to. From their own accounts—accounts that leave the reader with a sense of the intimacy and warmth of their relationships in the village—they had made friends and set examples. Their later contention that their efforts were frustrated is understandable only as a reassessment in terms of different, broader, and unattainable goals. Only after they turned to terrorism did these *narodniki* decide they had failed. V. N. Ginev assessed the situation thus:

The future members of People's Will, leaving the village for the city, were not disappointed in the people. It seemed to them that the people understood them, and if it were not for police hindrances, activity in the village in the spirit of the program of "Land and Freedom" would have been perfectly possible.[19]

Ginev's analysis brings up a further point—another commonly cited reason for leaving the countryside and moving to the city. Often reluctant to blame the peasants for their "failure" in propagandizing and eager to justify hands-on combat with government officials, the newly-born terrorists of 1879 frequently argued that government repression had put the *narodniki* out of business.

Oddly enough, this rejection of the possibility of work in the villages because of the watchful and punitive eye of tsarism arose first among revolutionaries in the cities, where police activities were actually concentrated. Thus A. V. Iakimova, who had never gone "to the people," later wrote:

The unproductive activity among the people . . . from 1873 and after, and also the settlement of members of the party "Land and Freedom" in the villages as scribes, paramedics, teachers, and others, clearly demonstrated the necessity of attaining political freedom, not as a goal but as a method for removing the obstacles separating the revolutionaries from the masses, and thus opening to the masses a broad path for their own development and for unleashing their own will. The unlimited monarchical government, the autocratic tsar must bear responsibility for everything, in both the economic and political spheres of government activity.[20]

Morozov wrote boldly (although with precarious accuracy, since he had not worked in the countryside since 1874) that terrorism "was the result of the persecutions of the government, which made propaganda extremely difficult if not impossible."[21] Anna Korba, never herself a "villager" and late in joining the revolutionary movement, described the arguments adduced by the terrorists when, probably in early 1879, she journeyed to Finland to make the acquaintance of Morozov and his friends who were staying there.

They had recognized the necessity of destroying the autocracy as a consequence of the insurmountable obstacles which were set in the path of the propaganda of socialism and even the simple spreading of knowledge in the village. The cruelties and inhumanities with which the government attacked the socialists pushed them along the road to political struggle.[22]

From St. Petersburg the dynamite manufacturer Stepan Shiriaev wrote that the "red terror" of the revolutionaries was only a response to the "white."[23] And Sof'ia Ivanova, friend to Perovskaia and later her biographer, stated that after several years,

the majority of the party came to the conclusion that under given conditions, socialist propaganda among the people was impossible and that therefore a struggle for political freedom was necessary, [a struggle] in which terrorism emerged as one of the methods. They considered it essential to achieve such a state of affairs under which their propaganda of socialist ideas—both in the city and in the village—would be possible.[24]

Once they had turned to terrorism, this argument about government persecution was taken up almost universally by the village workers. After all, it not only justified their rejection of their propaganda in the countryside, but it commanded the destruction of governors-general, gendarmerie chiefs, secret police leaders, and eventually the tsar himself.

But were they right? Were they correct in asserting that they had been driven from the villages by the tsarist police? A careful reading of the literature actually indicates that only a handful of arrests had taken place in the villages themselves.[25] In most of those instances, "villagers" were unwittingly betrayed through the activities, apprehension, and police investigation of their urban comrades. Police struck down provincial urban centers like Saratov; they attacked would-be terrorist quarters in St. Petersburg and Kharkov; they confiscated indiscreet correspondence and followed naive messengers from urban centers. But their actions against "villagers" were generally confined to follow-through on other, primarily urban investigations. The claims of some "villagers" to have been pursued helter-skelter by police seem either exaggerated out of their own fears, derived from their own restlessness, or justified only in result of their inadvertent betrayal to police by terrorist acquaintances.

Solov'ev may stand as the primary example. Having roamed from village to village, having abandoned one job after another, he told the Figner sisters that he had been pursued hither and yon by police intent on his apprehension. Yet in the police file accumulated at the time of Solov'ev's arrest for attempted regicide and carefully published in three long articles in *Byloe* (The Past), there is no single indication that Solov'ev was known to the police at all before his assassination attempt.[26] As a heavy-drinking schoolteacher, as a member of the Bogdanovich communal artel, as a roaming blacksmith and scribe seeking to propagandize among the peasantry, Solov'ev seems to have escaped all notice by the gendarmerie, for no single report by any government investigator was ever discovered to add to his dossier. There is every indication that his roamings resulted from restlessness and incompetence at his profession and that consciously or unconsciously he claimed police persecution in order to avoid facing the truth.

On the other side stand the Figner sisters. Figner's report on her work in the village with her sister Evgeniia abounds in enthusiasm and excitement; it has been cited previously. Nevertheless, the sisters ran into trouble, particularly in terms of hostility from local officials and clergy. To the court that was trying her in 1882 for terrorist activity, Figner reported her growing frustrations and anxieties.

Within a very short time, a whole league was set up against me, at the head of which stood the marshal of the nobility and the district policeman, at the tail the village policeman, the scribe, and so on. They circulated all possible rumors about me: that I had no passport . . . that my diploma was false, and others. When the peasants did not want to enter into some unprofitable bargain with a landowner, they said that Filippova [Figner] was to blame, and when the district assembly lowered the scribe's pay, they said that the paramedic [Figner] was responsible for it. Open and secret inquiries occurred; the district policeman came; several peasants were arrested, and my name figured in their interro-

gation; there were two denunciations to the provincial governor, and only because of the trouble the president of the court took upon himself was I left in
peace. Around me a police-spy atmosphere developed. People began to be afraid
of me. The peasants sneaked around back yards to come to me at home. . . .
Thus I was deprived of the possibility of simple physical closeness with the people and not only could not do anything but could not even communicate with
them about the most ordinary goals.[27]

The truth is that such hostility was annoying and perhaps frightening, but it could easily have been anticipated. Nobody claimed that
work among the peasantry was sweetness and light or that one could
take up the peasants' cause without arousing suspicion and irritation
on the part of conservative local officials. Figner's own description
does not include claims of pursuit by the tsarist police, although
twice she was endangered by the arrest of a city comrade. Speciously,
she later insisted that she and Evgeniia had failed in their mission
because of government repressions. Speaking of their reaction to
Solov'ev's argument for terrorism Figner wrote:

We saw clearly that our previous work was in vain. The revolutionary party had
again suffered a setback through our efforts. It was not because of the inexperi-
ence of its members [and here she seems to be referring to the failures of the
"crazy summer" propagandists] nor because of the ignorance of the propagandists of their work nor even because of exaggerated hopes for the strength and
readiness of the masses. No and again no: We had to withdraw from the [village]
arena with the awareness that our program was truly alive and its claims rooted
in the people, the sole ground of failure being lack of political freedom.[28]

Yet the Figner sisters stayed in their village. Police threatened only
after Solov'ev shot at the tsar; thereupon his movements were traced
and his visit to Vera and Evgeniia of a few months before was revealed. Even then the police did not locate Ivanchin-Pisarev, with
whom Solov'ev had stayed shortly before descending on the Figners
and whom he recklessly came to see again in St. Petersburg, just two
days before his assassination attempt. By then many of the propagandists had left the villages where they had been working. For many of
them, the threat of investigation and revelation as revolutionaries
arose when police arrested their urban comrades, raided city centers,
or intercepted letters sent to them from St. Petersburg headquarters.[29]
Urban terrorism and revolutionary settlements evoked constant
police attention, but villages were generally left alone unless urban
gendarmes commanded their investigation. The Figner sisters finally

abandoned their village when Solov'ev was apprehended and they foresaw that the police would trace his movements to themselves. At that, they were not ready to quit.

The truth is that neither police persecutions nor peasant indifference disturbed the most dedicated *narodniki*, and those who stuck out their jobs were convinced that they were indeed on the right track—a track that some day, perhaps in the far future, would lead to peasant revolution. When the Figner sisters left their positions in the village, they were still optimistic about working among the people, no matter what Vera wrote later about police harrassment and the need for civil rights. She and Evgeniia journeyed to the settlement at Tambov, not to the Petersburg terrorists, intending not to quit but to find new positions and begin again.[30] Aleksandr Mikhailov was full of enthusiasm when he left the schismatics at Saratov, and his plans to return do not indicate any sense of defeat nor depression about his work.[31] Popov and Kviatkovskii would have settled in Voronezh; it was neither the police nor the peasants that chased them away, but Mikhailov's urgent summons to St. Petersburg—a summons based on arrests in the city, not in the countryside. Years later Popov—who refused to join the People's Will and was not pursued by a need to justify the assassination—argued that village work had been perfectly possible under such political conditions as existed; that the peasantry was susceptible to propaganda; and that it was the urban revolutionaries, through their renunciation of village work, who spoiled the game.[32] Thirty years later, returning to his native district after decades in custody, Popov heard tales from the peasantry that caused him "without any self-delusion" to aver "that our activity left traces among the people."[33] In 1879, little evidence speaks to defeatism among him and his colleagues.

No wonder, then, that many of the *narodniki* were slow and reluctant to abandon their village projects for violence.

How difficult it was for the revolutionary-propagandists of the seventies to renounce their long-lived hopes, how difficult it was for them to transfer to the lonely, titanic struggle with the government, [a struggle] that was uprooting them from the people,[34]

wrote Ol'ga Liubatovich (never a "villager") in her later memoirs. Propagandists left their posts "laboriously, guiltily, feeling ill," rejecting a mission that "a short time ago had filled their whole existence."[35] They were, as Serebriakov reported, sick at heart.[36]

Memoir literature upholds this judgment. After the Voronezh conference, when Aptekman was summoned to St. Petersburg, he expressed his misery at leaving the countryside for what he sensed would be the last time. "I left the village," he wrote, "with a heavy heart. I would never again return."[37] Several of his comrades from Tambov refused to accompany him because of their village commitments.

Others had similar doubts even while they succumbed to terrorist pressures to move to the city. Speaking of the Voronezh meetings, Figner wrote of herself and Perovskaia that they

had just torn ourselves away from the village; with all the forces of our souls [we both] were still tied to it. They invited us to participate in the political struggle, [they] called us to the city, but we felt that the village had need of us, that without us it would be darker there. Reason said that it was necessary to set forth on that same path on which our comrades, the political terrorists, had already embarked, flushed with battle and challenged by success. But emotion told us otherwise; our mood was different. . . . However, when at the Voronezh congress smiling comrades said of us that we were sitting between two chairs, that after certain medication we would conquer our emotion, our mood, then having renounced the moral satisfaction that life among the people afforded, we firmly took our stand with our comrades.[38]

Anna Korba wrote something similar about the attitude of Nikolai Alekseevich Sablin, who committed suicide two days after the assassination just as police were approaching the apartment he shared with Ges'ia Gel'fman.

By conviction and inclination, Sablin was a propagandist-*narodnik*. His love for the peasantry and all toiling people was deep and sincere. He possessed the capacity to merge with the peasantry and influence it. . . . The impending People's Will activity inevitably drew its members away from work in the village and in the factory. To these conditions Nikolai Alekseevich reconciled himself with difficulty. In the depths of his feelings, he preserved an affinity for the village, and the outcome of the struggle of the young party seemed to him problematic and its goal attainable merely in the far-off future. Thus hesitations, full of drama, whether to join the People's Will or not.[39]

But the classic example of reluctance to abandon propaganda for terror remains Perovskaia herself. At Voronezh, she had stubbornly argued the *narodnik* cause even against Zheliabov, who impressed her deeply on this first meeting. Thereafter she returned to her work as a paramedic, but shortly (probably in late July or early August 1879) she appeared in St. Petersburg, still not convinced but apparently ready to listen. She was unhappy with the choice in front of her; according to her friend Ivanova, she "seemed to retreat into herself" and refused to join either the People's Will or its rival propagandist revolutionary group.[40] By autumn, she had made up her mind, but although she participated in one of the assassination attempts of November 1879, she did so as a free agent, more or less on temporary contract to the Executive Committee, and insisted that she would enter into such contracts only for the duration of individual projects, as circumstances dictated. After the November failures, Perovskaia announced that she would return to her Kharkov hospital and had to be convinced all over again.[41] She did not officially join the People's Will until December 1879.

Not only were they reluctant to abandon their village mission but, as Frolenko pointed out, the new recruits to terrorism did not lose hope of returning to the countryside they preferred, and they worked out new, idealistic plans for propaganda even while terrorism was luring them away.[42] As late as 1880, Perovskaia talked of going back to the village as soon as the tsar was dead.[43] Zheliabov said the same; to Oshanina, early in 1881, he seemed to express the wish that terrorism would go away and leave him at peace. "We were enterrorized," he wrote. "Now it is necessary for us to work on the organization of revolutionary forces in the countryside, but meanwhile we cannot retreat without finishing what we have begun."[44]

Just before his arrest in 1880, Popov, who had retreated the autumn before to Kiev to work for the *narodnik* cause, received a letter from his friend Barannikov, who had joined the People's Will in St. Petersburg. Barannikov was tired of the agonies of terrorism and hoped it would soon all be over. He told Popov, "Only one thing holds me here: I do not want to stay once the matter we have started is finished. As soon as the affair [the murder of Alexander II] is over, we must go back to establishing the Voronezh settlements again."[45] Things did not work out as he hoped.

Given their devotion to their jobs and their conviction that they were gaining the respect of the peasantry, these *narodniki*, as the evidence shows, were not easily convinced that the village should be abandoned and that the assassination of the tsar should become the task of highest priority. Therefore in the summer of 1879, beginning at Voronezh and continuing in a series of near-formal debates held at Lesna, the terrorists launched a concerted campaign to win their country cousins over to violence. In ardent and zealous declarations, they emphasized the promise of terrorism, insisting that the assassination of the tsar would have positive results for the propagandists' village work. In retrospect, many of their arguments seem specious or muddy, but they are worth repeating in that they influenced some *narodnik* decisions and they demonstrate how far the terrorists had come from those days in 1878 when they had argued that murder was necessary only in self-defense or desirable only as an act of revenge.

What was the terrorist plan? What did they think the murder of Alexander would accomplish? The trouble was that the terrorists themselves never systematically agreed on what to expect after the tsar lay dead. Too many, in the words of Samuel Baron, "thought little about the significance of what they advocated."[46] Too many were, as Degaborii-Mokrievich wrote in indignation when he returned from exile early in 1881 to find the atmosphere changed beyond belief, "people of action, and not people of ideology."[47]

For some—and Tikhomirov called them "pure terrorists"[48] —terrorism was a method of dramatic action, designed to demonstrate hatred and to epitomize though not necessarily evoke revolution. In his long accolade to terror, published in England in 1880, Morozov argued that among the vast seas of Russian peasantry, the droplets of influence scattered by the limited number of propagandists could never succeed in bringing about that social revolution that was the *narodniki*'s eventual aim—an argument not easily refuted. Morozov wrote:

At the present time on the limitless plains of Russia, with its scattered villages and relatively insignificant factory cities, where the dispersion of the peasant population impedes the organization of a great village uprising and the insignificance of the city proletariat does not up to now present a serious danger for the government, the growing revolution is taking a completely unique form. Deprived of the possibility of appearing in village or urban uprising, it is expressed in the "terrorist movement" of educated youth.[49]

Morozov saw terrorism as a heroic method of struggle, without which struggle might come to an end. Although he occasionally expressed more specific aims (the disorganization, demoralization, and weakening of the government), he tended to see violence as a creed, an inspiration, a spark, a constant reinvigoration of the revolutionary faith.

The goal of the terrorist movement in our country must not consist merely in one-time restraint of Russian despotism; it must make its methods of struggle popular, historical, traditional. It should introduce them into life, so that in the future the better elements of the population, a new group of individuals, will advance against each new appearance of tyranny, will destroy power by means of political murders.[50]

Morozov compares the dedication and heroism of the assassin with that of the early Christian martyr. The mystique of violence and bloodshed creates heroes, and heroes can rise above any adversity.

Although one may suppose that Liubatovich felt sympathy for her lover's views, such a blatantly romantic definition of assassination never appealed to most of his colleagues, and Morozov usually found himself isolated among them.[51] Both Zheliabov[52] and Tikhomirov,[53] influential figures in the terrorist movement, renounced Morozov's views and averred their outright opposition to his interpretation of the new violence. To them he probably maintained something of the old romantic flavor of Bakuninist anarchism and something of the irrational vision of the fanatic; they seem to have treated him on occasion with a certain condescension, as if he were too young to understand. Nevertheless, the heroic vision of the terrorist mystique hung like an aura over young enthusiasts and in the long run may have brought about more conversions than some of the less emotional arguments.

Somewhat more specific than Morozov's ideal—but perhaps equally unrealistic—was Iakimova's conviction that terrorism would bring about social revolution: that the masses would recognize, once the tsar was dead, that the tyrant had feet of clay, and that this knowledge of the government's weakness would spur the peasantry to violence with pitchfork and with axe.

By means of active political struggle with the government, [the terrorists] hoped to destroy the somnolent tsardom; to undermine tsarist authority and [end] the awe of governmental power; to destroy the fatalism, the absolute bowing to destiny ("Nothing started, nothing ended," as one often hears from the peasant one is propagandizing); to demonstrate the possibility of organized struggle; to rouse a spirit of action and [evoke] the people's faith in success of the struggle; by means of propaganda and agitation through action to popularize the methods of the People's Will to the greatest possible degree in Russia and outside her boundaries.[54]

In short, Iakimova proposed to accomplish the aims of the *narodniki* through the method of assassination.

The argument was not unpopular among terrorist zealots. It had the advantage of maintaining long-sought goals and avoiding the soubriquet *politiki*, which reeked of abandoning social revolution achieved by the people themselves. The hopes for an aroused peasantry were expressed concisely by Nikolai Bukh, converted to terrorism by Kviatkovskii in the summer of 1879, who was convinced that "Terrorism . . . will stir up the masses, force the people out of their age-old sleep, show them clearly that there exists a force which is fighting against their enemies and protecting their interests."[55]

Many revolutionaries echoed Bukh's and Iakimova's views. On his way to Siberia in autumn 1881, V. G. Korolenko compared notes with the other political exiles who were his traveling companions and concluded that many *narodniki* had indeed been "dreaming not of a constitution but of a general cataclysm which would overturn the entire order."[56] Korolenko describes the evening when Aaron Zundelevich related (to Dmitrii Rogachev, early propagandist and Chaikovets; Ippolit Myshkin, heroic orator of the trial of 193; and himself) the decisions of the terrorists at the Lipetsk meeting—a meeting not attended by Zundelevich (who was abroad, arranging for the return of several Russian radicals from Switzerland), but apparently reported to him by his friends. Zundelevich described Mikhailov's impassioned speech—the accusatory act—that ended with the question set to the terrorists: "Should we forgive the tsar for all the evil that he has done and that which he will do in the future?" In Korolenko's account:

They all said no.

When amid deep silence Zundelevich finished his report, the *narodnik* point of view was expressed by Rogachev.

"Tell me, Zundelevich," he asked, "what you had in mind in making an attempt on the life of the tsar, whom all the people still recognize as their liberator."

At this point-blank question Zundelevich became somewhat confused. It was obvious that he had no ready answer.

"We thought," he answered, "that this would produce a powerful stimulus which would free the creative forces inherent in the people and serve as a basis for social revolution."

"Well, but suppose this did not occur and the people did not foment social revolution—as actually happened. What then?"

Zundelevich pondered as if in uncertainty, and then answered: "Then . . . then we thought . . . to compel."

Rogachev guffawed so sincerely and clearly that I unwittingly remembered his laughter at the Volga wharf at the peasant project to solve the land question by murdering a landowner. For me there came clear once again what I had realized already in a conversation with Iurii Bogdanovich at Perm: The blow was inflicted in despair, technically accurately, but totally blindly. The *narodniki* were right: Assassination of the tsar did not serve as a stimulus to further action, and Russia was still living through a long period of reaction—perhaps a longer period than would otherwise have occurred.[57]

Although these cynical reactions of the old propagandists were conditioned by hindsight, very probably the argument for spontaneous peasant rebellion upon the assassination of the tsar was met with some uncertainty even in 1879. The experience of the Chigirin revolutionaries, who managed to arouse some of the peasantry only by evoking the tsar's name; the ambivalence of Bakunin's arguments about pro-tsar peasant loyalties; the experience of those who had come to know the peasants best must have made this argument seem specious to many.

Among the debaters when Land and Freedom split, a small group argued that after the assassination of the tsar, the assassins owed it to the people to seize the reins of government and enact legally the socialism of which they dreamed. If others supported the views of Lavrov and/or Bakunin, these "Jacobins" may be said to reflect the speculations of Petr Tkachev, who had lost faith in the peasant's "instinct" for revolution and who, writing in his journal *Tocsin* in the freer air of Switzerland, found conspiratorial seizure of power to be the only effective substitute for that popular action on which no one could rely.

Among the terrorists of 1879, Maria Olovennikova/Oshanina/Barannikova/Polonskaia (the latter the name she adopted during her life abroad after 1881) was the strongest sympathizer with this "Jacobin" view. Oshanina had grown up in Orel, where she (along with a number of other young women) had been caught up by the ideas and personality of P. N. Zaichnevskii, probably author of the notorious and violent-espousing proclamation "Young Russia" that was distributed throughout the St. Petersburg underground in 1862. Like Tkachev, Zaichnevskii had lost faith in peasant social revolution and centered his hopes on a conspiratorial seizure of power, after which the conspirators could deliberately revise society in their revolutionary image.[58] Oshanina worked for a short time as a propagandist, but soon she abandoned this *narodnik* stance to serve as one of the leaders in the attempt to liberate—by violence—the heroes of the trial of 193. At Lipetsk, she appeared with her husband Barannikov, and their position as terrorists was confirmed.

Indications are that Oshanina found little support for her contention that the terrorists should attempt to seize the reins of government.[59] Always less philosopher than activist, she has left us little material on her own arguments or actions, beyond the series of explicit answers to questions put to her by the historian Serebriakov shortly before her death.[60] One witness claims that her arguments were often less logical than colorful and frequently enhanced by her own considerable personal charm.[61] She had a few close friends among the terrorists—namely, E. D. Sergeeva, also from Zaichnevskii's circle, who soon became pregnant and dropped out of the movement, and Tikhomirov, Sergeeva's spouse, who was perhaps influenced by his wife but who was never a dedicated "Jacobin."[62] In 1879, Oshanina's voice was scarcely heeded, and it is uncertain how fervently—if at all—she pleaded the Jacobin cause. Not until after the assassination did the decimated Executive Committee (under her influence and perhaps Tikhomirov's) endorse the conspiratorial seizure of power,[63] and by then it was far too late.

Most of the terrorists, to one degree or another, took a middle line. Unable to condone or even imagine the seizure of power, they were also unable to convince themselves that they could rely on peasant rebellion. Instead they hoped and believed that the assassination of the tsar would cause the government, disrupted by murder and terrified about its own future, to grant concessions to its subjects. They hoped that Alexander III, who as heir to the throne had been fallaciously rumored to be a liberal,[64] might give in and grant a constitutional assembly, with concurrent guarantees of Western-style liberties: freedom of press, meetings, propaganda, and expression. Under such a revised government, propaganda among the peasants might easily be conducted with the aim of provoking social reform or socialist revolution. In the summer of 1879, this hope was probably eagerly snatched at by those *narodniki* whose greatest desire remained the possibility of resuming their posts in the villages.

Very probably such demands for political reform—and the soubriquet *politiki* was derived from these aims—had first arisen among the Southerners. A leading scholar of the revolutionary movement suggests that the call for constitutional rights was inherited by radical

Kiev students from a group of Ukrainian liberals and zemstvo officials led by I. I. Petrunkevich—a group whose aims were "distinguished by much greater realism when compared with the utopianism of the active *narodniki*."[65] If V. Bogucharskii is right in his speculation, then leading Southern *buntari* (including most specifically Popko, who murdered Governor-General Geiking out of revenge, not in hopes of political concessions) adopted the platform of political freedom and constitutionalism even before Osinskii endorsed it, apparently in 1878.[66] Others among the revolutionaries credited Osinskii with originating the demands for civil rights and with maintaining close ties to the Ukrainian liberals.[67]

Zheliabov, a Southerner, endorsed the calling of a constitutional assembly as the first aim of the assassins, and Kolodkevich (also from the Ukraine) lent his strong support.[68] Zheliabov's oratorical and persuasive talents gave him as much influence as anyone in the terrorist movement, and he put them to good use. Guarantees of freedom of speech, assembly, and press would put an end to ubiquitous police "terror," he argued, thus clearing the way to propagandize the peasantry into socialism.[69] He sought a specific form of government, and he said: "We are not anarchists. We stand for the principle of federal structure of the state, [and] as a means of attaining this structure, we recommend very specific institutions."[70] Facing the court that was about to condemn him to death for his role in the assassination, Zheliabov made a strong statement for popular representation. In the first session of the trial, he insisted that only the people could set up a truly legal system of justice and a legitimate tribunal.

I consider the government one of the interested parties in this matter, and I propose that as a judge between us—the party of revolutionaries and the government—there is only one possible [mediator]: an all-people's court, either chosen by the direct vote of the people or in the form of its lawful representatives to a constitutional assembly.[71]

The unexpected dynastic ability to survive shattered his hopes.

The call for a constitution as a concession from a government harried and harassed by assassins found important support in Aleksandr Mikhailov's endorsement. Although Mikhailov was removed from the scene by arrest in the fall of 1880, and although his expressed support of the "political" program dates from the time of his trial in 1882, one may presume that he (whose first furious demand for violence had grown out of anger at police action and insistence on revenge) had endorsed the constitutional program in his earlier years as well. At his trial, Mikhailov referred to the summer of 1879:

Here [at Lipetsk] first of all it was decided to secure that popular administration necessary for progress, happiness, and welfare in Russia, and a path was sought to promote the transfer of power from the hands of the current government to the hands of the people.[72]

Such hopes for political reforms inaugurated by a government under siege were shared by many of the *narodniki* in 1879. Even Morozov, whose romantic visions of heroism sometimes clouded his logic, later wrote that the terrorists primarily sought "freedom of speech, press, and public activity for all transitional political and social parties," although he continued to insist that political reform must be accomplished by the methods of Charlotte Corday and Wilhelm Tell.[73]

The call for political revolution with limited aims rather than social revolution with the broad goal of overturning contemporary mores and institutions has caused certain Soviet scholars to argue that Morozov and his friends were reactionaries, setting the revolutionary movement on a restricted, one-way track.[74] Yet it seems clear that the limited hope of achieving political freedom appealed to the *narodniki* exactly because of the restricted nature of the goal. Once the aims were achieved, supposedly through assassination of the tsar, the assassins themselves could move back to their mission among the peasantry. Zheliabov, Perovskaia, Barannikov and others (as has been mentioned above) considered themselves to be free once the deed was accomplished and often dreamed of that moment. Once the tsar was gone, once the constitution was adopted, work would be easy, happy, and profitable. Propaganda and education would cause the peasant to choose socialism, even through violent revolution. As Nikolai Bukh remembered explaining to his colleagues:

Living among the people, you will be in a position to point out to them this growing force [of revolutionaries], to arouse them to the revolutionary road. This will increase the productivity of your revolutionary work, will build a strong foundation under it. Lacking this foundation, almost all our village settlements have collapsed.[75]

To the promise of peace to come, of propaganda to be made, some of the *narodniki* were undoubtedly attracted, and it remained a drawing card in terrorist proselytizing.

From this association of terrorism with constitutionalism the
politiki drew their soubriquet and their special cast. Strange combi-
nation: the establishment of legality by murder, as the historian
Bogucharskii has remarked: "The conditions of life were such that
healthy principles led to unhealthy methods of bringing them to life;
in the eyes of the revolutionaries, political activity became almost a
synonym of terrorist activity."[76]

Aleksandr Mikhailov too was aware of the strangeness of these
"bedfellows," and he tried to explain their congruity to the court.

When [the participants at the Voronezh congress—but it seems he was really
referring to Lipetsk] decided thus in favor of the necessity of a transfer of
power [to the people], then naturally the question arose about methods by
which the party should move towards this [goal]. Above all, of course, we
passed to the consideration as to whether there were no peaceful, legal means
by which this could be accomplished, and after multifold consideration of this
question, we were forced to answer it negatively: such methods did not exist.
Only then did [we] recognize the necessity of a revolutionary path, during the
period when a legal path, a path of conviction, might not yet be possible, that is,
while we could not attain any great freedom; it was decided to act by force of
the party and organization to help all of society and to all possible extent also
gain the aid of the people . . . The assassination of the tsar stood among other
methods.[77]

As it turned out, of course, the *politiki* were fantasizing in their
hopes of governmental collapse once Alexander was dead. Even the
hoped-for concessions in terms of freedoms and constitutionalism
were never forthcoming. Indeed, it is difficult to imagine whence
they drew their hopes. The dynasty had survived worse crises before,
even when the line of succession to the throne was far weaker than in
1881. Momentary confusion in the government was followed not by
liberty but by oppression.

In the debates on the fields at Lesna in the summer of 1879, the
propagandists—particularly Plekhanov and Stefanovich—responded to
their antagonists with a series of sophisticated and historically based
arguments. Already a reader and student of Marx, Stefanovich, who
had returned with his emigrant friends from Switzerland, argued that
political freedom would bring no benefits to the lower classes. Civil
rights, Stefanovich told Krylova, would only open the door to the
power of the bourgeoisie, and the influx of capitalistic practices and
institutions would not only further repress the peasantry but would
work to destroy that peasant socialism, represented by the commune,

on which the *narodniki* had laid such great hopes.[78] If the memory of a member of the Saratov circle is correct, the argument that political freedom could only benefit the bourgeoisie and would thus lead only to the economic enslavement of the people had been advanced by other *narodniki* too.[79] Plekhanov was probably among them, although we have no exact record of what he said.

The argument from historical development here begins to touch on the question of the coming of capitalism to Russia. The revolutionaries considered themselves socialists, and there is little doubt that they viewed capitalism as evil. Future Marxists among them (like Plekhanov) may well have accepted the postulate that associated "bourgeois freedoms" with capitalism. Yet it is unlikely that any of the *narodniki* envisioned the coming of capitalism to Russia as a dictum of historical determinism and, so far as can be judged by their debates, they all still seem to have believed that capitalism could be avoided in their native land. What A. Walicki has called the "controversy over capitalism" was reserved primarily for later years; after all, Zasulich (and she was there) did not write her famous letter to Marx until 1881.[80] Although (as Walicki nicely demonstrates) much *narodnik* thinking about the evils of Western capitalism was probably based on a reading of *Capital* or other similar analyses, the acceptance of Marx's historical determinism was later in coming.[81] The argument proffered by Stefanovich and Plekhanov in 1879 simply contended that bourgeois traditions, established when the bourgeoisie attained freedom of operation, would harm rather than benefit the peasantry.

Although other arguments of the Plekhanov faction have unfortunately not been reported to us, surely the propagandists would have seized on the transfer from social to political revolution as a matter to be deplored. The political-social dichotomy in Russian revolutionary thought has been emphasized by several scholars—with special thoroughness by the Soviet philosopher R. Blium. Walicki contends that the emphasis on social revolution as compared to political was a hallmark of the early populist movement.[82] Political revolution was clearly disliked by such *narodniki* as Ivanchin-Pisarev, Debagorii-Mokrievich and others. It represented the abandonment of the cherished principle that the people should make revolution for themselves—a principle that lay at the heart of the whole new program of 1876.[83] Such arguments were Tkachevian at best, and Tkachev had never been a favorite of these revolutionary populists. To all of these *narodnik* arguments, the terrorists found answers. After all, political revolution was basically a method by which the government could be forced to such concessions as would make social revolution possible to attain. After all, the old program anticipated a long period of work among the peasantry before revolution would occur, and the potential arrival of capitalism in Russia (as suggested by the propagandist faction itself) lent revolution a sense of urgency that had been remarked but not truly answered by the program of 1876.

Nevertheless, it is not easy to assess the effect of these terrorist arguments upon the distressed young propagandists during this grand debate in the fields and dachas of Lesna. One can cite only Krylova as a specific convert, for she clearly opted to join the Black Repartition, Plekhanov's group, on the basis of Stefanovnich's arguments, however she interpreted them. Further evidence is lacking. It is impossible to tell whether Popov, Preobrazhenskii, and others were influenced by the debates or whether they had long since made their anti-terrorist commitments. Plekhanov was a powerful orator—more articulate, more erudite, more intellectual than any of the others. Once Zheliabov, himself a fine speaker with strong emotional appeal, was moved to admit admiringly to his rival, "I am impassioned, but you can exceed me. In you there dwells a Tatar."[84] Deich wrote later that

in setting forth his views, Plekhanov used all direct methods: He argued, proved, appealed to logic, gave citations from history, etc., but [and here he was referring specifically to debates over the Solov'ev affair] he never resorted to "military manoevers," to intrigues, even unimportant ones, which unfortunately it is impossible to say of his opponents.[85]

It is possible that the remotely erudite, intellectual arguments of the Plekhanov faction did not evoke quite the same fiery response as the heroic call of its terrorist rivals.

One can imagine the intensity of the grand debate in 1879—propagandist pitted against terrorist, friend pitted against friend, young people congenitally ardent and zealous, devastated by long hours of contention, bitterness, and distress. At Lesna, old antagonists met: Morozov argued with Popov, Plekhanov met face to face with Zheliabov, and newer individuals in the movements—persons like Anna Korba or young Nikolai Bukh, one of the proprietors of the Land and Freedom press—were courted individually by each side in turn, during long walks along the grassy paths. The occasion was deeply emotional, according to all participants, and the tension lasted not days but weeks. Under the circumstances, it is likely that responses were emotional too, and all indications are that the decisions made in this time of stress were based at least as much on emotional reactions as on logical acumen. One might argue that here the terrorists had the advantage, for acts of violence were distinguished less by logic than by daring, and "disorganizers" moved through "direct actions, without concerns about consequences," as the biographer of one of them wrote later.

Such is the psychology of every revolutionary deed. The moment therein of direct action dominates any thought of responsibility. Only he who puts into this act all of his will and, striving towards the defined goal, [all of] his decision and decisiveness, only he can be a real revolutionary capable of great deeds.[86]

Terrorism offered many emotional satisfactions. To begin with, it was propagandizing in the village and not violence in the cities that called for more difficult, more enduring, more frustrating commitment from its participants. Russian village life had never been congenial. Rather it was tough and demanding, in spite of the rewards and satisfactions that it occasionally offered. It was not so much physical vigor that the countryside required of its settlers, for most of the "villagers" had opted for intellectual labors. Rather it was the emotional strain, the frustrations, the tedium, the loneliness they had endured that caused the propagandists constant suffering in their work. Tiny, isolated hamlets were a far cry from the cities where most of the revolutionaries had been born, raised, or educated. Camaraderie with illiterate peasants could not replace bull sessions with educated friends. Work in the village was frequently routine, filled with petty tribulations, small frustrations, and evening exhaustion. Impatient young men and women were not suited to such small deeds, and the revolutionary temperament was by definition an impatient one.

For some of the revolutionaries, life among the people was impossible even to contemplate, and many of them were wise enough to know so. Valer'ian Osinskii, for example, never tried to go to the peasantry; in Deich's description this dynamic, restless, imaginative, and impatient man "did not have the slightest aptitude for activity among the people, [activity] that called for self-control, patience, and tranquility."[87] Although he spent considerable time at the Saratov settlement, where he indulged in the more congenial work of contacting intellectuals and teaching factory workers, Plekhanov, a dedicated *narodnik*, was never suited for village work; his lack of contacts in the countryside was a major factor later in the inability of the Black Repartition to build a successful propagandist organization.[88] The same was true of such "disorganizers" as Presniakov and Tiutchev, whose biographer later wrote that he was a "villager" by conviction only and always remote from the village.

As a member of Land and Freedom and as a *narodnik*, Tiutchev was in these years a philosophical supporter of the village, ideologically a "villager," as it was then termed. But over and above this, in all his makeup, in his lifestyle, and mostly in his revolutionary activity, he was a typical city man. Not the village but the city caught his attention as a practicing revolutionary; to work in a village was for him out of the question . . . although by conviction he was a *narodnik-buntar'*.[89]

Many of these terrorists had never really chosen to attempt village propaganda, to the extent that even Zheliabov later expressed his disgust with them.[90] Others went, stayed for a time, and then returned to their city life with an enthusiasm that increased with time. A Solov'ev, clearly unsuited to the routine of village work, roamed restlessly through peasant settlements in the Volga region, always discontent, always seeking some action more grandiose, always unable to settle down. Kviatkovskii, a one-time village enthusiast, later reported to Morozov that he would never go back. "The village is not for me," he wrote. "There purely instructional work is necessary. One must explain, interpret. What kind of a teacher am I? I want to fight for freedom, not preach in someone's ear in a whisper."[91] Even the most successful of the propagandists suffered frustrations and uncertainties. Had Figner's sister not been with her, she might well have left her post earlier than she did. Village life was tedious and boring, Iakov Stefanovich complained,[92] and many of the propagandists could not help but agree with him.

Morozov and Aleksander Mikhailov provide interesting examples. In the summer of 1874, as a youth of twenty, Morozov spent a number of weeks at a small village smithy, not entirely out of touch because of its proximity to Ivanchin-Pisarev's estate, where many of Morozov's comrades were in residence. He worked hard and attempted to convert his coworkers to socialism and revolution, an effort for which he paid (after a brief sojourn abroad) with arrest and trial with the 193 propagandists. When he returned to the village after his release in 1878, Morozov was soon bored and irritated. He found the country infinitely dull. He had followed Vera Figner, for he was caught up in his infatuation for her and ready to serve as she served; it is interesting that he was soon convinced that Iurii Bogdanovich and Solov'ev, who were there too, had come for the same reason.[93] No one of them found an immediate assignment.

Soon Morozov lost his patience. He never even saw a newspaper, he complained. When word reached this small commune in Saratov province of Zasulich's exoneration for her attempt on Trepov's life, even his comrades agreed that Morozov was not suited to village propagandizing, and they carefully voted him the position of their representative in St. Petersburg.[94] By the summer of 1878, Morozov was already doubting the ability of the "villagers" to stick it out, for, as he wrote later, "they have in their imaginations a totally idyllic vision of working among the peasantry in the guise of simple people."[95] Morozov himself had tried it once, achieved what he evaluated as some success, but refused to go it again.

The same was true of Mikhailov. In 1877 he had left his work among the schismatics of Saratov with the firm expectation of returning. But as the months in St. Petersburg passed, as he became accustomed to the excitement and challenge of life as a revolutionary in the capital city, he changed his mind. By the end of summer 1878, when he met Morozov at a student protest meeting in Moscow, Mikhailov was beginning to realize what sacrifices his propagandizing had demanded of him. In Morozov's description, which may not be completely accurate:

Mikhailov: You cannot imagine how divorced from the whole world you feel when living in the backwoods in the guise of a common man. You do not have a chance to get newspapers or journals; it is impossible to read books, except for cheap popular ones, or to receive many letters from friends, or to meet often with comrades and the local intelligentsia. After the first days of novelty, you little by little acquire the sensation of your total hopelessness, complete loneliness, the more so because they are arresting your city comrades every month, one after another, and the new ones do not even know you. Every day you feel as though you ever more and more remain without any link with people who think like yourself, as if you exist alone in the world, among backward people, who are strange to you in spirit.

Morozov: Yes, I know from my own experience in the past. And when news began to reach me about street demonstrations in the cities and about the beginning of the struggle for freedom that I had long awaited, I could no longer be patient. My comrades noticed this and sent me away.[96]

Indeed, life in the city meant danger, excitement, and tension, but it was in many ways easier, as Popov pointed out, than the loneliness, tedium, and isolation of village work. Popov thought the urban workers had nothing to complain about.

. . . I, for instance do not at all understand how Aleksandr Mikhailov, Tikhomirov, and Kviatkovskii could be upset when not only were they not in an isolated situation, but [they were] actually much better off than their antagonists, the villagers. Somewhere in the villages were scattered some two score persons, completely ripped off from the world of culture and linked with it only by Aleksandr Mikhailov, Tikhomirov, and the others who made up the central office of the organization at this time.[97]

In St. Petersburg, life was dangerous but never dreary. It offered opera, theater, newspapers, books, and universities—high culture compared with the desolation of the Russian countryside.

But it was not just "culture" that the "villagers" missed. Primarily they missed each other. Of course, among them were individuals who had the inner strength to go it alone: witness Perovskaia, who was stubborn and determined in her Kharkov hospital, and Solov'ev, a natural loner who more easily than not operated nomadically—though even he sometimes sought out friends. But Figner alone was miserable, and only when her sister Evgeniia joined her did she make the most of her village experience. Ivanchin-Pisarev called Mariia Pavlovna Leshern-fon-Gertsfel't to work with him at Baltai, and he and Bogdanovich were never far apart. Reference has already been made to the role of provincial quarters as communal centers; Morozov long remembered the pleasure of meeting his friends and hearing their tales at the Saratov settlement. These young people—as Figner's circle had realized in its commitment to warmth and camaraderie—had a need for each other. Their desire for communication and closeness derived in part from their sharing of dangers, of common experiences and goals. It included but was not limited to a sense of loyalty to the group. Deeper drives and stronger needs caused them to close ranks against the world and to seek each other out.

No wonder, then, that young radicals returning to the capital city routinely ignored Mikhailov's strictures and happily appeared in public together at operas and plays. No wonder Malinovskaia's quarters were crowded with friends, in spite of the dangers of such meetings: Kravchinskii, who had recently murdered Mezentsev, was a frequent visitor there in 1878, and so were the recently escaped exile Ol'ga

Liubatovich and her lover Morozov, all of them sought by the tsarist police. Here at Malinovskaia's the revolutionaries gathered joyously to welcome Deich and Stefanovich, successful escapees from Kiev prison, and Kravchinskii roared out his approval. When the police finally zeroed in on the apartment and captured Malinovskaia and her roommate Kolenkina, the revolutionaries barely survived, for they had planned a name-day celebration for the following evening and several of them nearly walked into the ambush the police had set.[98]

Here in the capital city they gathered to dance on Figner's name day too—she was the beauty, the "Venus of the revolution," as one tsarist official later wrote,[99] and her lively personality was attractive to them all. Dressed in their finest frockcoats and gowns, they celebrated with food and dance the wedding of Tikhomirov (who had to marry under an assumed name) to Kat'ia Sergeeva, both soon members of the central terrorist circle.[100] No wonder the assassins of the tsar long afterwards vividly recalled their last wonderful New Year's celebration—the warmth and friendship, the wine and song, the toasts and dancing, the pleasure they derived from being together.[101] Isolated from the rest of the world, the revolutionaries needed each other. From each other, they gleaned strength and reinforcement. In the village, strength had to be summoned up from their own individual inner resources, for only the peasants were nearby.

One could argue that, in spite of the propagandists' reluctance, the time was ripe for the terrorist recruitment campaign. By 1879, the isolated village *narodniki* had already been subject to a series of pressures that made their remoteness seem more severe. For example, many young propagandists watched as their colleagues marched off to the Balkan war, an event Tikhomirov believed stood at the root of the militant response, the call for violence. Figner had actually tried to enlist but had been refused by the authorities in 1877.[102]

The release of many imprisoned colleagues after the trial of 193 also reminded "villagers" of the suffering their comrades had endured and undoubtedly increased their sense of isolation from the mainstream of revolutionary action. The effect of such imprisonment is a matter still to be carefully explored, and Soviet scholars often exaggerate the militancy that prison produced. But whatever its effects on the prisoners (many of whom suffered lengthened sentences and more severe punishment owing to Zasulich's attempt on Trepov), the publicity and heroism of the imprisoned could not help but act on the "villagers." Perovskaia actually left her Kharkov hospital to organize a rescue of Myshkin, the hero of the trial, and Morozov, strained to a breaking point by the tedium of life in the countryside, abandoned village work forever to return to more challenging efforts in the city.

But most potent of all in its effect on the observers was the fearless example set by urban colleagues in their series of violent deeds. Watching in concern lest their own mission be shattered, "villagers" still could not help but admire and envy their colleagues—for the heroism of the Zasulich attempt, for Kravchinskii's daring murder of Mezentsev, for Solov'ev's shot at Alexander himself. Figner was admiring, although she did not completely approve.[103] Shiriaev, who was in St. Petersburg at the time of Solov'ev's attempt, wrote that the "deed produced an extraordinarily powerful impression on me" and caused him to seek "something new, some stronger measures."[104] Sof'ia Perovskaia admitted that she joined the terrorists because their cause had "vitality."[105]

Popov later described this new "revolutionary mood" and spoke perceptively of the difficulty of resisting it:

People with militant temperaments could not remain satisfied with the humble, not to say colorless activity which until then was being conducted in the villages, but it was impossible to achieve any [change] by merely calling a halt to such activity. The mood on the whole had to set its own direction. Such a mood could only be channeled in a particular direction by creating something powerful in the village. . . . Those of [the villagers] who did not agree with the opinion that it was essential to be concerned only with terrorist activity . . . were clearly conscious at any rate of the need to create something strong, something powerful in the village to satisfy the current revolutionary mood.[106]

For Popov, that "something" was what he called "agrarian terrorism,"[107] but for others even violence in the countryside proved not to be challenging enough.

In 1879, in their recruitment of *narodniki* to the terrorist cause, the partisans of violence demonstrated a keen understanding of the frustrations of village life and of how the activist, revolutionary personality might react to them.

Thus Frolenko, traveling the countryside to invite friends of terror to the conspiratorial meeting at Lipetsk, sought out those whose temperaments were least suited to the village work they were doing, whose dynamics might most easily cause them to move from the niggling to the heroic mode. He looked up Zheliabov in spite of the advice of his colleagues because he knew Zheliabov to be "lively,

articulate," and more of a *buntar'* than many acknowledged *buntari*—
Frolenko was so convinced not on the basis of Zheliabov's stated
philosophy but because he knew this future terrorist had once attacked an enraged bull with a pitchfork.[108] He sought out Barannikov, who had a "direct, militant nature," and Mariia Oshanina,
who was "active, capable of conspiracy" and above all bored with
life on her family estate. He ignored Perovskaia, who seemed to
him a "timid rabbit" although she had already participated in the
attempt to free Voinaral'skii at gunpoint; he apparently under-
estimated her determination and was probably surprised when later,
"as a lively and active person"[109] she joined the People's Will.
Everything indicates that Frolenko hardly argued principles at all. He
knew that terrorism was where the action was and that a need for
action to replace quietude was a more potent element in his campaign than was any theoretical argument about political rather than
social approach.

In their call to action when the forces of both factions were assembled at Voronezh, the terrorists took off their gloves. They were
not always kind. Here Tikhomirov called the propagandists *kul'turniki*
to their faces,[110] insulting them by insinuating that they had abandoned the goal of revolution (which they had never set as their
immediate goal to begin with) in favor of simply bringing education
to the peasantry. He knew what he was doing; he later wrote that the
strongest argument for terrorism was to tell a propagandist that
propagandists were not revolutionary at all, for the cult of revolution
had come to be the lifeblood of these zealous radicals and out of
their absolute faith in "revolution," whatever that turned out to be,
they could easily be caused to leap from one measure to another.[111]
Even the term "villager" (*derevenshchik*), applied by the propagandists to themselves, came to be used pejoratively by their urban colleagues.[112] Tikhomirov was echoed by his friends. Kviatkovskii later
accused the "villagers" of working only with petty legal problems
and avoiding the illegal *bunty* that he thought they should have been
organizing.[113]

Soviet scholars have supported this view: The *narodniki* became
kul'turniki instead of revolutionaries, writes one,[114] and another
insists that they were "useful cultural workers, but the social and
revolutionary content in their work was lacking."[115]

Derogatory labels, designed to undermine, must have accentuated
the *narodnik* plight and torn the "villagers" apart. Years later Aptekman protested:

This was not simple cultural work, as some very naively described it; this was preparatory-revolutionary work because, I repeat, *revolution* was the highest principle of our varied cultural activity: the liberation of the people by the people themselves. This was invisible work, not remarked by the naked eye, but [work] that drop by drop hollowed out a fissure and cracks in the then still inert mass of the peasantry. Through these cracks and fissures, revolutionary thought, emotion, and will incessantly permeated deep down. And together with "the objective process of history," our underground work in the long run created in the people a certain atmosphere of *discontent, anxiety*, and *displeasure*.[116]

History was deaf to Aptekman's protest. He was speaking of a program adopted in 1876 but set violently aside three years later.

Reading the later memoirs of the young converts to violence and bearing in mind the lure of urban culture as against village backwardness, of comradeship as against loneliness, of action as against tedium, one finds it impossible to avoid the conclusion that the new militant mood excited enthusiasm on the basis of emotional as much as intellectual reaction. It is unlikely that the intensive and reasoned debates of 1879—especially considering the uncertain promise of terrorism adduced by the *politiki*—were themselves ultimately responsible for many conversions. Even an ardent terrorist like Frolenko came to admit that reasoning counted for little.[117] A later astute observer of Russian patterns wrote that these young people, who lacked knowledge of men, who knew little of political institutions, and who were often naive in their analyses, easily substituted wild-eyed enthusiasm for sober judgment.[118] Subjected now to a concerted campaign in which they were ardently urged to rejoin their friends, the crusaders who had spent frustrating months in the villages found themselves caught up in their "need to do something"—*any*thing—in the active, revolutionary spirit.[119]

Many of the participants in the debates of summer 1879 realized even at the time that the claim of terrorism was as much emotional as intellectual. Thus Liubatovich, who had favored violence from the time of her escape from exile in 1878, was convinced that the split in Land and Freedom was based on temperament rather than on principle, for she could never isolate any valid justification for the terrorists' methodical demolition of that organization.[120] Deich wrote that the daring acts of murder grew not out of an intellectual commitment to terrorism's goals but out of what he called "taste."[121] Tikhomirov, who was one of the most sensitive and thoughtful of the revolutionaries, later wrote that deeds of violence began first, and only later did the revolutionaries attempt to justify them in principle and systematize them in goal,[122] an opinion which, oddly enough, was echoed by a high official of the tsarist government in his history of Russian terrorism:

Encouraged by the success of the first terrorist outbreaks, the devotees of anarchism from then on considered the principle of "terror" as the most propitious mode of action and the most rational slogan for their plots and their agitations. They busied themselves with creating "theories" and "systems," seeking to convince the government and the public of the legitimacy of their crimes. The origin of the terrorist principles is thus explained more logically by consideration of an opportunistic character.[123]

Typical of the terrorists was, for Popov, his one-time friend Kviatkovskii, who was so driven by his emotions that he "did not himself see the difference between those actions to which he was attracted by temperament and those [ideological] convictions that were embedded in his soul.[124] "The *mood* of youth was stronger than its *thinking*," Aptekman was to write. "The members of People's Will rushed into the fire, lay down their lives in the struggle for liberation of the country. Youth saw this and, enchanted, followed after the fighters."[125]

Indeed, what ardent revolutionary, what isolated "villager" could ignore the call to heroism alongside of his comrades in the revolutionary cause? "The aristocratic revolutionary," wrote Thomas Masaryk later, "aspired to distinguish himself by deeds of personal heroism."[126] "It was difficult, even impossible, to think about the village," Frolenko reported later, "about the slow work there."[127]

The dagger made the plow seem pale.

The means of pacific propaganda, often even disguised in legal forms, were no longer sufficient; the hour had therefore come to revolutionize the country with dagger in hand, with revolver, and with dynamite. Grand would be the personal glory of the heroes of this struggle in the bosom of the party as in the annals of revolution; this was a subterfuge to create men of action, to astonish the world by high deeds of a new kind, as well as by the atrocity of the plots. As for methods—all were valid in achieving the end; and this end, above all, consisted in proving to the Russian world while persuading ourselves as well that revolutionary action was not falling fallow, that the party was not dispersed, annihilated, or extinguished, that it was still strong and imbued with principles of vengeance against the slightest retaliations of the government.[128]

In Masaryk's descriptive words, "The horror of crime, the horror of assassination had a deliriant influence upon these young minds, made them drunken with death, and in proportion as it did this, it unfitted them for any very detailed work."[129] From the free air of Switzerland, the pamphleteer P. F. Alisov raved that "the dagger was the only logical weapon of liberation," but he was not thinking of logic at all.[130]

In the memoir literature, it is remarkable how often the revolutionaries insisted that they were drawn to terrorism in spite of themselves, by something like an irresistible force. It became desirable euphemistically to blame "life itself" for the commitment that they knew was based less on intellectual analysis than on emotional reactions—the commitment that ended in such undeniable failure. So Tikhomirov said that the move towards terrorism was "irrepressible."[131] Morozov wrote that "life itself fatally led our organization to change to a new path."[132] Frolenko likewise insisted that he could prove "how life itself, history itself instigated [the terror], in spite of the fact that certain theorists with all their power tried to resist this phenomenon."[133] Serebriakov was sure that once violence started, "there was no turning back."[134] Terrorism, wrote Frolenko dramatically, was "in the air."

Over the city there hangs a murky cloud. It is felt by everyone, a heavy nightmare bears down on everyone. Not quietly but thundering comes the urgent cry that it is impossible to live thus, there must be a way out; [the cry] resounds and echoes everywhere. People who earlier scarcely, barely heard and little interested themselves in the revolutionary movement now come to seek out the radicals, to show them the way out, to propose themselves as activists, setting assassination as the best, the only method to write an end to such asphyxia. . . . Living in such an atmosphere, breathing the air, saturated with the expectation of something special, and hearing constantly the cries and demands for deliverance, they demanded that one seek the way out at once, at that exact moment; the clue to method was carried on the air.[135]

Nobody listened to Aptekman when he suggested that "the fatal logic of events" was hardly a reasonable argument.[136] Instead, friend followed friend to St. Petersburg and into the violent stream. Tikhomirov was not far wrong when he called terrorism a "mass, herd movement among the revolutionary intelligentsia."[137] In the call to heroic deeds issued by their comrades, few wished to be left behind.

On March 1, 1881, having reasoned that it was better to do something grandiose and have done with it than to continue their unspectacular chores, the terrorists succeeded in assassinating Alexander

II. To a great extent, this final deed was an act of desperation. A spurt of dramatic activity in the winter of 1879-80—a period in which five unsuccessful attempts were made on the life of the tsar—was followed by months of routine work (mostly propagandizing and publishing) in St. Petersburg and by increasingly desultory planning. Perovskaia admitted to a friend that she felt suicidal;[138] Zheliabov seemed frequently exhausted and depressed.[139] Called to a special conference to debate future efforts, Oshanina (who had been living in Moscow) found her colleagues changed and enervated.[140] Members of the Executive Committee of the People's Will were talking of the countryside again.

Meanwhile, police pursuit intensified. By early 1880, the conspirators had lost Kviatkovskii and Zundelevich to arrest. In January 1881, the press was raided and seized by the police. In the months immediately before the assassination, a host of leaders was taken, including Aleksandr Mikhailov, Kletochnikov, Kolodkevich, Trigoni, and (with the latter on February 27) Zheliabov himself. The government was gaining ground and closing in on its prey. Zheliabov's arrest provoked the desperate decision to act at once before all was lost.

As for attaining their other aims, long debated in the summer of 1879—the calling of a constituent assembly, the establishment of civil rights for all Russians, the inspiring of immediate peasant revolt—the revolutionaries can only be judged to have failed. History, having driven them to their deeds, presented them ironically with Alexander III.

Meanwhile, we have few statistics on those who turned quietly aside. Such Land and Freedom stalwarts as Moshchenko and Tishchenko, Aptekman's friends, never even attended the debates on the fields of Lesna; after the Voronezh meetings, they simply went back to their work among the peasantry near Tambov. V. N. Ignatov and Popov slipped back to the provinces too, the latter to be arrested early in 1880 in Kiev, where he was working for the Black Repartition.[141] The fate of Plekhanov and his friends lay elsewhere, for by 1880 their organization collapsed and they all emigrated abroad to find their fame as the first generation of Russian Marxists.

But there are insufficient data on the men and women who, rejecting terrorism, chose to work as before: to devote themselves, patient but often frustrated, to building schools, to vaccinating the poor, or to seeking legal redress for those peasants wronged. Writing later, Stefanovich recognized their existence: They were not vocal, he said, but they were there, they were educating and propagandizing.[142]

Some of these men and women had been members of Land and Freedom or of its offshoot organizations. They may be said to represent the first wave, the early professionals in local activism. By the 1890s, they were joined by others—scribes, teachers, nurses, paramedics employed by local government assemblies—many of whom felt an affinity for the socialist revolutionary cause. History demonstrates that these men and women in the countryside came to be respected, trusted, and even beloved by the people they served with "small deeds."

7

RETROSPECTIVE

Given the memoirs and data available, it is impossible to conclude that the Russian propagandists of 1878 eventually entered the terrorist camp out of their conviction that their countryside labors were in vain. Evidence indicates, on the contrary, that they were proud of their village accomplishments, that they believed they were winning friends and gaining support, and that they felt themselves to be operating within the schedule and principles of the new Land and Freedom program, in spite of all impediments. In this new, fresh movement toward the people, only a few of the participants actually involved came to see themselves as failures.

The position of the "villagers" in regard to violence had been ambivalent from the start. True, they agreed to the fatal inclusion of a "disorganization" group within the Land and Freedom structure, but this murder squad was never intended to assume more initiative than necessary in its support of their own efforts to win over the peasantry. As terrorist acts accelerated, the "villagers" could not help but admire the heroism of their colleagues who assassinated police chiefs and tortured "spies," but from the start they were also concerned about the effects of violence on their own work in the countryside.

For violence seemed to be of no particular help to the *narodniki* at all. Violence bred police investigation, and prying gendarmes were bound to seek out village propagandists through their organizational and comradely ties with urban terrorists. The *narodniki* justifiably feared that the peasants, steeped in conservative tradition, might misunderstand the supposed need for violence and might actually deplore terrorist deeds, particularly those directed against the person of the tsar. Much as they admired the courage of a Zasulich or the daring of a Kravchinskii, they could see little but trouble ahead. The winning of the village, to which they had devoted months of their young lives, might remain indeed an empty and fleeting victory.

But violence continued apace. Distinguished at first by individual actions and reactions—the pulling of a gun when the police approached, the murder of persons known to be acting as police spies—the terrorist monster called constantly for more. It became a matter of pride to carry a weapon, to practice target shooting, to sleep with a gun under one's pillow. Political prisoners in jail or exile were liberated daringly at gunpoint. But soon "self-defense," as the revolutionaries termed it, did not satisfy the intensity of the violent mode. Led both by the North (where Zasulich and Kravchinskii inadvertently provided terrorist models) and by the South (where a series of Ukrainians took upon themselves the execution of governors-general and others), the terrorists demanded revenge—revenge for "crimes" against political prisoners or police campaigns that had destroyed their illegal urban presses and conspiratorial quarters. The line between "self-defense" and "revenge" was never clearly drawn—not even in the constitution of Land and Freedom—and caught up in the fervor of their drive toward violence, the revolutionaries were unable or unwilling to make a distinction. Their insistence that individual government servants were responsible for the laws and actions that they deplored led them eventually to the most responsible official of all—the tsar himself.

All of this was watched uneasily by the "villagers." The gulf between village and city was already making itself felt; we have the testimony of participants on both sides as to the growing alienation of the *narodniki* from the "disorganizers." Yet there was something intriguing in terror: it offered an opportunity for action, a chance for heroism, an exaltation of self that could never be found in the mud lanes of a tiny backwater town. Village work demanded a kind of patience and dedication that many of the young revolutionaries did not possess—as witness the frequent changes of employment and locale, the restlessness that one senses in the career of a Solov'ev among the peasantry of Central Russia.

By 1879 the terrorists were becoming frustrated too: frustrated by police actions directed against their urban centers, frustrated by their inability to defeat their government opponents, and frustrated even by the seeming lack of concern for their martyrdom on the part of their isolated village comrades, who thought of them as shooting off dramatic, symbolic, dangerous "fireworks." By 1879 the terrorists were demanding ever more resources in order to replace the police-destroyed urban centers (the passport manufactury in St. Petersburg, for example), to produce that dynamite to the drama of which they were turning, to sponsor increasing numbers of efforts to eliminate government officials. They needed the press on which to describe their feats and explain the "crimes" of their victims. They needed colleagues who would aid them in future attacks, especially the attempts on the life of Alexander II.

The year 1879 was crucial, and in this year the proponents of violence proved their mettle. By deliberate manipulation, they destroyed Land and Freedom, the organizational link with their colleagues, and gained most of its financial resources for themselves. By argument often specious and by promise often overdramatized, they campaigned to attract village colleagues to their plots, drawing particularly on the increasing restlessness that they wisely sensed.

Terrorism was too often a state of mind. It grew from feeding on its own danger, daring, and heroics. It was never fully justified by the arguments adduced by its proponents—not even by those terrorists from the Ukraine whose hopes for civil and constitutional rights were based on the delusion of a decrepit government cowering in fear and a new tsar concessionist in character. A man named Plekhanov could argue from more realistic and more intellectual premises—so, perhaps, could Tikhomirov, although he seems not to have tried. Too many of the others were dominated by their emotional reactions to the magnetism of violence: by their need to act, their drives to become heroes, a strange attraction to martyrdom, their feelings for each other, their fervor about something that was "contagious" or "in the air" or "inevitable." Few of them, according to their memoirs, did much careful analyzing at all, beyond the intricate planning of the next, ever more spectacular and gruesome, terrorist deed.

Their ultimate failure to attain their goal—for however muddily they expressed themselves, their goal lay in social and political improvement—became a personal tragedy for many of them—Tikhomirov, for example. For others, like Morozov (although he languished in prison while Tikhomirov moved forward to fame and fortune), the deed of assassination justified itself, and failure to achieve revolution was outweighed by success in achieving the death of the tsar. This convoluted reasoning left the terrorists celebrating an event even while losing track of its significance, not just in Russian history but in the attainment of goals they sought.

To a great extent, this manuscript has raised more questions than it has answered. The basic cause of terrorism remains a matter for thoughtful investigation, speculation, and debate. If we have concluded that violence was not easily accepted among the Russian propagandists and that terrorism was at first confined to a small urban group that later persuaded others to join it, we have to a great extent still begged the issue. All young people—even impatient ones—are not prone to commit violence and assassination. Did the lure of drama and heroism act more strongly upon personality types or upon individuals of particular backgrounds? Was violence as a solution (given the hypothesis that it was never adopted out of logical determination of its results) really inevitable, really "in the air?" And if so, is there, after all, any hope for avoiding terror in the future? Must one indeed end with the agonizing conclusion that violence pursues society in cycles, in certain cultures, at certain periods of time, and that society itself must live through these episodes of terrorist excesses without any recourse before them?

The example of the Russian terrorists—fomenting violence from defense, revenge, or some deep emotional commitment; persuading impressionable colleagues to join them; failing logically to anticipate the results of their ultimate violent deed—may with further investigation prove instructive not just for our history but for our future.

NOTES

INTRODUCTION

1. On Nechaev, see Philip Pomper, *Sergei Nechaev* (New Brunswick: Rutgers University Press, 1979).

2. "Avtobiograficheskaia zapiska i pis'ma S. Shiriaeva (s predisloviem R. M. Kantora)," *Krasnyi arkhiv*, 7 (1924): 81–82.

3. Adam Ulam, *In the Name of the People: Prophets and Conspirators in Pre-revolutionary Russia* (New York: Viking Press, 1977).

4. B. P. Koz'min, in his epilogue to N. A. Morozov, *Povesti moei zhizni* (Moscow: [Akademiia nauk], 1961), II: 660. The same author in "K istorii 'Zemli i voli' 70-kh godov (Programma tambovskogo poseleniia zemlevol'tsev)," *Krasnyi arkhiv*, 19 (1926): 170, asserts that many propagandists switched to terrorism because they were "dissatisfied with their activity and convinced of the impossibility of making revolutionary propaganda among the people."

5. P. S. Tkachenko, *Revoliutsionnaia narodnicheskaia organizatsiia 'Zemlia i volia' (1876–1879 gg.)* (Moscow: Izd. Vysshaia shkola, 1961), p. 264.

6. L. Berman, "Kievskii protsess 21-go v 1880 g.," *Katorga i ssylka*, 81/82 (1931): 72.

7. Franco Venturi, *Roots of Revolution: A History of the Populist and Socialist Movements in Nineteenth-century Russia* (New York: Alfred A. Knopf, 1960), pp. 576, 577.

8. Avrahm Yarmolinsky, *Road to Revolution: A Century of Russian Radicalism* (New York: Macmillan, 1959), p. 217.

9. Samuel H. Baron, *Plekhanov: The Father of Russian Marxism* (Stanford: Stanford University Press, 1963), p. 32.

10. Philip Pomper, *The Russian Revolutionary Intelligentsia* (New York: Thomas Y. Crowell, 1970), p. 133.

11. Ronald Seth, *The Russian Terrorists* (London: Barrie and Rockliff, 1966), p. 60.

CHAPTER 1: THE NEW POPULIST PROGRAM

1. All the surveys of the revolutionary movement in Russia and many personal accounts tell of 1874's summer activities; see also V. N. Ginev, "Revoliutsionnaia deiatel'nost' narodnikov 70-kh godov sredi krest'ian i rabochikh srednogo povolzh'ia," *Istoricheskie zapiski*, 74 (1963): 220–44; B. S. Itenberg, "Nachalo massovogo 'khozhdeniia v narod,'" *Istoricheskie zapiski*, 69 (1961): 142–76.

2. See S. F. Kovalik, *Revoliutsionnoe dvizhenie semidesiatykh godov i protsess 193-kh* (Moscow: Politkatorzhan, 1928), combining the series of articles written by the author under the pseudonym Starik in the journal *Byloe* in 1906 (Nos. 10, 11, and 12); V. Kallasha, ed., *Protsess 193-kh* (Moscow, 1906); Ippolit Myshkin, *Rech' na sude* (Geneva, 1903); A. Iakimova, "'Bol'shoi protsess ili 'protsess 193-kh:' O revoliutsionnoi propagande v imperii," *Katorga i ssylka*, 37 (1927): 7–31; and N. A. Troitskii, "Protsess 193-kh," in *Obshchestvennoe dvizhenie v poslereformennoi Rossii* (Moscow: Nauka, 1965), pp. 314–35.

3. Vera Figner, "Mark Andreevich Natanson," *Polnoe sobranie sochinenii* (Moscow: Izd, V.O.P., 1932), V: 205; this collection of works is hereinafter cited as Figner, *PSS*.

4. "Iz avtobiografii Very Figner," *Byloe*, 1917, No. 2 (August), p. 171. For Figner's autobiography, first printed here but later published in Russian as *Zapechatlennyi trud*, in *PSS*, Vols. I and II, and in many other languages this author has also used *Nacht über Russland* (Berlin: Malik Verlag, 1926), the earliest complete edition easily available to me. This work is hereinafter cited as Figner, *Nacht*.

5. Figner, "Iz avtobiografii," *Byloe*, 1917, No. 2, pp. 170–71.

6. Ibid., p. 171.

7. Details are drawn from Figner, "Iz avtobiografii," and from "Ocherki avtobiograficheskie," *PSS*, V: 143–51.

8. See *Protsess piatidesiati, suzhdennykh za sotsial'no-revoliutsionnuiu propagandu v Ivanovo-Voznesenske, Tule, Kieve, i Moskve* (London: Nabornia Vpered, 1877); Figner's account, "Protsess '50-ti,' 1877," *Katorga i ssylka*, No. 33 (1927), pp. 7–20; and the recent biography of one of the accused, Marie Claude Burnet-Vigniel, "Bardina: Itinéraire d'une populiste," *Cahiers du monde russe et sovietique*, XVI, (1975): 321–52.

9. Figner, "Iz avtobiografii," *Byloe*, 1917, No. 2, pp. 172–73.

10. Figner, "Ocherki avtobiograficheskie," *PSS*, V: 143–44.

11. Ibid., pp. 148–51.

12. See details later in this chapter.

13. Figner, "Iz avtobiografii," *Byloe*, 1917, No. 2, p. 171.

14. Itenberg, "Nachalo," pp. 155–57.

15. Figner, "Natanson," *PSS*, V: 207.

16. Deposition of Iurii Bogdanovich, 1881, "Iz narodovol'cheskikh avtobiograficheskikh dokumentov," *Krasnyi arkhiv*, 20 (1972): 213.

17. Figner, "Natanson," *PSS*, V: 207.

18. Figner, "Iz avtobiografii," *Byloe*, 1917, No. 2, p. 171.

19. For biographical material on the young Natanson, see Figner's sketch, *PSS*, V: 204–216.

20. Ibid., pp. 204–5.

21. Ibid., p. 207.

22. On this episode, see Boris Sapir, ed., *Vpered! 1873–1877* (Dordrecht: D. Reidel, 1970), I: 337–46.

23. Lavrov to G. Lopatin, [London], 14 January [1876], in Boris Sapir, ed., *Lavrov: Gody emigratsii* (Dordrecht and Boston: D. Reidel, c. 1974), I: 350.

24. A. S. Buturlin (Taksis) to Lavrov, Moscow, 22 April 1876, in Sapir, *Vpered!*, II: 304.

25. L. Deich, "Valer'ian Osinskii (k 50-letiiu so dnia kazni)," *Katorga i ssylka*, 54 (1929): 12. Deich called Natanson a "typical opportunist and eclectic."

26. Ibid., pp. 10–13; O. V. Aptekman, *Obshchestvo "Zemlia i volia" 70-kh godov; po lichnym vospominaniiam* (Petrograd: Kolos, 1924), pp. 185–87; Figner, "Natanson," *PSS*, V: 206.

27. Deich, "Osinskii," pp. 11–13.

28. Figner, "Natanson," *PSS*, V: 212.

29. Ibid., p. 211.

30. See Kropotkin's account in *Memoirs of a Revolutionist* (Boston and New York: Houghton, Mifflin, 1899), pp. 352–77; also S. M. Kravchinskii/Stepniak, *Underground Russia* (London: Smith-Elder, 1883), pp. 161–71; A. I. Ivanchin-Pisarev, "Pobeg kn. P. A. Kropotkina," *Byloe*, 1907, No. 13, pp. 37–42; and Martin A. Miller, *Kropotkin* (Chicago and London: University of Chicago Press, 1976), pp. 122–29.

31. Figner, "Natanson," *PSS*, V: 207; Deich, "Osinskii," pp. 10–11.

32. Figner, "Ocherki avtobiograficheskie," *PSS*, V: 159–62.

33. Figner, "N. I. Drago," *PSS*, V: 301.

34. Vladimir Debagorii-Mokrievich, *Vospominaniia* (Paris: J. Allemane, 1894–98), II: 113.

35. Iakimova, "'Bol'shoi protsess,'" p. 9.

36. Quoted in E. A. Serebriakov, *Obshchestvo Zemlia i volia* (London: Tip. Zhizni, 1902), pp. 29–30. See also Itenberg, "Nachalo," p. 149.

37. Itenberg, "Nachalo," pp. 153–57, contrasts the ideas of O. V. Aptekman, who thought they were fairly well organized, with those of Vladimir Debagorii-Mokrievich, who thought they were not.

38. Quoted in Serebriakov, *Obshchestvo*, pp. 29–30.

39. N. A. Golovina-Iurgenson, "Moi vospominaniia (Iz revoliutsionnoi deiatel'-nosti 70–80-kh godov)," *Katorga i ssylka*, 6 (1923): 33; see also Serebriakov, *Obshchestvo*, pp. 5–7.

40. Ginev, "Revoliutsionnaia deiatel'nost'," p. 228.

41. Aptekman, *Obshchestvo*, pp. 49–50; Itenberg, "Nachalo," p. 148.

42. "Bookish" and "doctrinaire" are the exact words of Andrei Zheliabov in his description of this movement to the court that was about to convict him of assassinating the tsar: *Delo pervogo marta 1881 g. Protsess Zheliabova, Perovskoi i dr. Pravitel'stvennyi otchet* (St. Petersburg: Tip. V. Ia. Mil'shteina, 1906), pp. 338–39.

43. Figner, "Iz avtobiografii," *Byloe*, 1917, No. 2, p. 180.

44. This was true of many of the women and even of Dmitrii Klements, a man of "sensitivity and delicacy," to whom the rough exterior of the peasant

was difficult and even distasteful to assume. See E. Dubenskaia, "D. A. Klements," *Katorga i ssylka*, 66 (1930): 173.

45. A fine collection of these pamphlets, many of which were written in an approximation of peasant dialect, has been preserved in the library of the International Institute of Social History in Amsterdam.

46. L. Barrive, *Osvobozhditel'noe dvizhenie v tsarstvovanie Aleksandra vtorogo* (Moscow: Tip. russkogo tovarishchestva, 1909), pp. 124-25.

47. Ginev, "Revoliutsionnaia deiatel'nost'," p. 224; Kovalik, *Revoliutsionnoe dvizhenie*, pp. 137-38.

48. Morozov, *Povesti*, I: 190.

49. Ibid.

50. Leonid Shishko, *Sergei Mikhailovich Kravchinskii i Kruzhok chaikovstev; iz vospominanii i zametok starogo narodnika* (St. Petersburg: Izd. Vl. Raspopa, 1906), pp. 32-35, contains a good description of this episode in the countryside; there is a short biography of Rogachev in Deich, *Za polveka* (Berlin: Izd. "Grani," 1923; reprint Cambridge: Oriental Research Partners, 1975), II: 194-203. M. F. Frolenko, "Khozhdenie v narod v 1874 godu," *Katorga i ssylka* 11 (1924): 10-11, attests to the reception of these two heroes in Moscow.

51. Deich, *Za polveka*, chapter entitled "Kak my v narod khodili."

52. David Footman, *Red Prelude: The Life of the Russian Terrorist Zhelyabov* (New Haven: Yale University Press, 1945), pp. 52-53; see also [L. A. Tikhomirov], *Andrei Ivanovich Zheliabov* (London: Vol'naia russkaia tip., 1882 and other editions), p. 11.

53. This period of Perovskaia's life, when she was not in St. Petersburg, is best portrayed by the people who knew her in the provinces: thus "Sof'ia Perovskaia v Stavropole: Vospominaniia M. S. Karpovoi. . . ," *Katorga i ssylka*, 15 (1925): 231-34, and V. L. Perovskii, "Moi vospominaniia," as published in the same journal in 1925, particularly the third installment, *Katorga i ssylka*, 17 (1925): 63-79.

54. Itenberg, "Nachalo," p. 161.

55. Ibid., p. 171; Ginev, "Revoliutsionnaia deiatel'nost'," pp. 224-25.

56. See "Pokushenie A. K. Solov'eva na tsareubiistvo, 2 aprelia 1879 goda," *Byloe*, 1918, particularly part III in No. 9, pp. 184-91.

57. Deposition of Iurii Bogdanovich, September 1882, "Iz narodovol'cheskikh avtobiograficheskikh dokumentov," *Krasnyi arkhiv*, 20 (1927): 212.

58. Itenberg, "Nachalo," pp. 159-61; A. I. Ivanchin-Pisarev, *Khozhdenie v narod* (Moscow: Molodaia gvardiia, 1929), pp. 11-14.

59. Morozov, *Povesti*, I: 188-90.

60. Figner, "Ocherki avtobiograficheskie," *PSS*, V: 152.

61. Aptekman, *Obshchestvo*, p. 182.

62. Ibid., pp. 182-83; Serebriakov, *Obshchestvo*, p. 8; Figner, "A. I. Ivanchin-Pisarev," *PSS*, V: 201.

63. L. Deich, "G. V. Plekhanov v 'Zemle i voli,'" *Gruppa "Osvobozhdenie truda"* (Moscow: Gosizdat, 1923-28), III: 44-45; Figner, "Iz avtobiografii," *Byloe*, 1917, No. 2, p. 177. See also Dmitrii Kuz'min, "Kazanskaia demonstratsiia 1876 g. i G. V. Plekhanov," *Katorga i ssylka*, 42 (1928): 7-40, and "G. V. Plekhanov i demonstratsiia na Kazanskoi ploshchadi, 6 dekabria 1876 g.," *Proletarskaia revoliutsiia*, 1924, No. 4, pp. 254-58.

64. O. V. Aptekman, "Dve dorogie teni," *Byloe*, 1921, No. 16, p. 11.

65. Figner, "Natanson," *PSS*, V: 209, and "Iz avtobiografii," *Byloe*, 1917, No. 2, p. 176.

66. S. N. Valk, *et al*, eds., in *Revoliutsionnoe narodnichestvo 70-kh godov XIX veka* (Moscow: Nauka, 1964), II: 27–34 and 367, note 1, present two versions of this program, one of which is clearly dated May 1878 and is regarded by them as the final version of a very similar document that remains undated. Thereby Valk *et al.* reject a document that was earlier believed to represent the first 1877 version of the program (see *Arkhiv "Zemli i voli" i "Narodnoi voli"* [Moscow: Politkatorzhan, 1932]) and instead follow the conclusion of G. M. Lifshits and K. G. Liashenko, "Kak sozdavalas' programma vtoroi 'Zemli i voli'," *Voprosy istorii*, 1965, No. 9, pp. 36–50, that this earlier-recognized "program" was really a series of notes composed for the benefit of P. A. Kropotkin in August 1877. The "program" presented by Serebriakov, *Obshchestvo*, pp. 9–12, is of later date. The version presented by Aptekman, *Obshchestvo*, pp. 193–198, although in rough form, corresponds to the documents offered by Valk *et al.*

67. Valk *et al.*, *Revoliutsionnoe narodnichestvo*, II: 27.

68. Ibid.

69. Aptekman, *Obshchestvo*, pp. 192–93; Shiriaev's later statement in "Avtobiograficheskaia zapiska i pis'ma S. Shiriaeva," p. 85.

70. Figner, "Iz avtobiografii," *Byloe*, 1917, No. 2, pp. 174–75.

71. Shiriaev, "Avtobiograficheskaia zapiska S. Shiriaeva," p. 85.

72. "K istorii 'Zemli i voli' 70-kh godov (Programma tambovskogo poseleniia zemlevol'tsev)," *Krasnyi arkhiv*, 19 (1926): 170.

73. Deposition of A. A. Kviatkovskii, June 23, 1880, "Avtobiograficheskoe zaiavlenie A. A. Kviatkovskogo," *Krasnyi arkhiv*, 14 (1926): 160.

74. Deposition of Iurii Bogdanovich, September 22, 1882, in "Iz narodovol'cheskikh avtobiograficheskikh dokumentov," p. 215. Cf. "Avtobiograficheskaia pokazaniia M. F. Grachevskogo," *Krasnyi arkhiv*, 18 (1926): 160.

75. This was the lead article in *Zemlia i volia*, No. 5 (dated 8 February 1879), as republished in B. Bazilevskii, ed., *Revoliutsionnaia zhurnalistika semidesiatykh godov* (Paris: Societé nouvelle de librairie et d'éditions, 1905), p. 237.

76. Zheliabov to the court, *Delo pervogo marta 1881 g.*, p. 339. Many others expressed similar awareness of the new revolutionary methods.

77. Valk *et al.*, *Revoliutsionnoe narodnichestvo*, II: 27–28.

78. Ibid., p. 28.

79. Ibid.

80. The long discussion of the moment the society adopted this name, as presented by Tkachenko, *Revoliutsionnaia narodnicheskaia organizatsiia*, pp. 52–73, seems hardly worthy of repetition here.

81. Valk *et al.*, *Revoliutsionnoe narodnichestvo*, II: 28.

82. Ibid.

83. Figner, *Nacht*, p. 67.

84. Ibid.

85. Kviatkovskii's speech to the court, in G. A. Kuklin, *Itogi revoliutsionnogo dvizhenii v Rossii za sorok let (1862-1902 gg.): Sbornik program. . .* (Geneva: Izd. G. A. Kuklina, 1903), in the addenda, p. 25.

86. Serebriakov, *Obshchestvo*, p. 17.

87. Trades are listed by Figner, "Iz avtobiografii," *Byloe*, 1917, No. 2, p. 167; Frolenko, "Khozhdenie v narod," pp. 14–15; Iakob Stefanovich, *Zloba dnia: Deistvuiushchim i gotovym deistvovat' sotovarishcham moim, moe druzhee [sic] poslanie* (n.p., 1880), p. 259, and elsewhere.

88. See Valk *et al.*, *Revoliutsionnoe narodnichestvo*, II: 367, note 2.

89. Figner's discussion, in "Iz avtobiografii," *Byloe*, 1917, No. 2, pp. 173–75, follows the 1877 "program" closely, both in organization and in phraseology. Aptekman's notes, *Obshchestvo*, pp. 188–98, seem also to refer to the written program, specifically to the document published by Valk *et al.*, *Revoliutsionnoe narodnichestvo*, II: 34–42.

90. Valk *et al.*, *Revoliutsionnoe narodnichestvo*, II: 34–42. For a discussion of this constitution and its adoption, see chapter 4.

91. Figner, "Iz avtobiografii," *Byloe*, 1917, No. 3 (September), pp. 267–68; Morozov, *Povesti*, II: 252. Aptekman, *Obshchestvo*, p. 273, reports that no "villager" could get along without these centers, for without them the propagandists became an army without a general. He might better have said an army with a USO.

92. Figner, "Natanson," *PSS*, V: 209.

93. Aptekman, *Obshchestvo*, pp. 191–93.

94. Aptekman, "Dve dorogie teni," p. 11.

95. B. P. Koz'min, in "K istorii 'Zemli i voli' 70-kh godov," p. 170.

96. [Tikhomirov], *Zheliabov*, p. 15.

97. Figner, *Nacht*, p. 64.

98. Zheliabov to the court, *Delo pervogo marta 1881 g.*, p. 339.

99. Kuklin, *Itogi*, Addendum, p. 24.

100. Deposition of Bogdanovich, "Iz narodovol'cheskikh avtobiograficheskikh dokumentov," p. 212.

CHAPTER 2: THE VILLAGERS AT WORK

1. Figner, "Natanson," *PSS*, V: 210.

2. See "Iz zhizni saratovskikh kruzhkov (Iz materialov O. i I. Markovykh)," *Byloe* (London), No. 4 (May 1903), especially pp. 3–10.

3. Ibid., pp. 9–10.

4. Aptekman, *Obshchestvo*, p. 265, tells us that Plekhanov took with him three factory workers from among his St. Petersburg converts, but none of them proved successful as village propagandist. On Plekhanov's activities, see "Iz zhizni saratovskikh kruzhkov," pp. 8–9, and L. Deich, "O bylom i nebylitsakh: Iz literaturnogo nasledstva G. V. Plekhanova s dopolneniiami L. Deicha," *Proletarskaia revoliutsiia*, 1923, No. 3(15), pp. 31–32; this article reports Plekhanov's answers to Deich's questions about this period of his life, which answers were rechecked by Plekhanov before publication.

5. Venturi, *Roots of Revolution*, p. 574.

6. "Iz zhizni saratovskikh kruzhkov," pp. 8–9. Figner remembers that several of her companions also opted for Odessa; Figner, "Iz avtobiografii," *Byloe*, 1917, No. 2, p. 177. Others established a center at Tambov; see "K istorii 'Zemli

i voli,'" *Krasnyi arkhiv*, 19 (1926): 166–177. Venturi, *Roots of Revolution*, p. 579, refers to a "settlement" founded by Aleksandr Kviatkovskii at Nizhni Novgorod.

7. Figner, "Iz avtobiografii," *Byloe*, 1917, No. 2, pp. 178–79.

8. Figner, *Nacht*, p. 76.

9. Ibid., pp. 77–78.

10. Ivanchin-Pisarev, *Khozhdenie*, pp. 87–99.

11. Ibid., pp. 24–25.

12. Figner, *Nacht*, p. 81.

13. Ibid., p. 82.

14. Ibid., p. 89.

15. Ivanchin-Pisarev, *Khozhdenie*, pp. 29–30.

16. Ibid., p. 274.

17. Ibid., pp. 19–22.

18. Figner, "Iz avtobiografii," *Byloe*, 1917, No. 2, p. 177; Ivanchin-Pisarev, *Khozhdenie*, p. 23.

19. Ivanchin-Pisarev, *Khozhdenie*, pp. 30–31.

20. Ibid., p. 58.

21. Ibid., pp. 59–62.

22. Ibid., pp. 67–74.

23. Ibid., pp. 84–85.

24. Ibid., p. 64.

25. Ibid., pp. 85–87.

26. Ibid., pp. 24–26.

27. Ibid., pp. 95–148.

28. Ibid., p. 172.

29. Ibid., pp. 173–184.

30. Ibid., pp. 192–193, 215–233, 247–250.

31. Ibid., p. 195.

32. Ibid.

33. Ibid., pp. 195–196.

34. Ibid., p. 210.

35. Ibid., pp. 250–253.

36. Ibid., p. 265.

37. Ibid., pp. 263, 264.

38. Ibid., pp. 266–267.

39. Deich, *Za polveka*, I: 170–174.

40. Ibid., p. 174.

41. Ibid., p. 211.

42. Ibid., pp. 212–13.

43. Mikhail Rodionich Popov's charming account of this episode may be found in *Zapiski zemlevol'tsa* (Moscow: Politkatorzhan, 1933), pp. 115–140.

44. Ibid., pp. 135–39.

45. Ibid., p. 135.

46. Ibid., p. 209.

47. Evtikhii Pavlovich Karpov, "Stranichki iz vospominanii: Aleksandr Konstantinovich Solov'ev," *Katorga i ssylka* 13 (1924), 36–43; but this estimate of Solov'ev's incapacity is found in many sources.

48. S. E. Lion, "Ot propagandy k terroru (Iz odesskikh vospominanii semi-desiatnika)," *Katorga i ssylka*, 12 (1924): 17-20.

49. "Iz vospominanii L'va Gartmana," *Byloe* (London), 1903, No. 3, p. 183.

50. G. F. Cherniavskaia-Bokhanovskaia, "Avtobiografiia," *Katorga i ssylka*, 42 (1928): 54.

51. On the commune at Saratov, see the article "Iz zhizni saratovskikh kruzhkov," cited above. Ginev, "Revoliutsionnaia deiatel'nost'," p. 231, has a summary of police activities against the settlements, as does Venturi, *Roots of Revolution*, pp. 575-79.

52. Morozov, *Povesti*, II: 229, 246, 262 and elsewhere; I. P. Belokovskii, "Andrei Ivanovich Zheliabov: Otryvki iz vospominanii," *Byloe*, 1906, No. 2, p. 79.

53. Karpov, "Stranichki," pp. 42-43; Serebriakov, *Obshchestvo*, pp. 20-21; "Pokushenie A. K. Solov'eva na tsareubiistvo 2 aprelia 1879 goda," *Byloe*, 1918, No. 7, 144-45.

54. Stefanovich, *Zloba dnia*, p. 4. These numbers seem fairly accurate.

55. Popov, *Zapiski zemlevol'tsa*, pp. 88-89.

56. Figner, *Nacht*, p. 90.

57. Popov, *Zapiski zemlevol'tsa*, pp. 207-8.

58. Ibid., pp. 208-9.

59. Aptekman, *Obshchestvo*, pp. 344-45.

CHAPTER 3: THE ORIGINS OF VIOLENCE

1. L. Barrive, *Osvobozhditel'noe dvizhenie*, pp. 136-37.

2. Valk *et al.*, *Revoliutsionnoe narodnichestvo*, II: 29.

3. Ibid., p. 30.

4. Figner, "Natanson," *PSS*, V: 209-10.

5. Ibid., p. 209.

6. Figner, "Iz avtobiografii," *Byloe*, 1917, No. 2, p. 175.

7. This plan is confirmed in a letter from Aaron Zundelevich to Lev Deich, dated London, September 24, 1922, and published in the anthology *Gruppa "Osvobozhdenie truda"*, III: 210-11. Zundelevich wrote Deich that the wealthy nobleman Dmitrii Lizogub, a patron of the terrorist cause, gave 14,000 rubles specifically for the activation of Kablits's plan.

8. Figner, "Iz avtobiografii," *Byloe*, 1917, No. 2, p. 175.

9. Aptekman, *Obshchestvo*, pp. 196-98, reprinted in Serebriakov, *Obshchestvo*, p. 14.

10. Aptekman, *Obshchestvo*, p. 198.

11. E. A. Kolosov, "Revoliutsionnaia deiatel'nost' N. S. Tiutcheva v 1870-kh gg.," in N. S. Tiutchev, *Revoliutsionnoe dvizhenie 1870-1880 gg.* (Moscow: Politkatorzhan, 1925), p. 14.

12. Deposition, 23 June 1880, "Avtobiograficheskoe zaiavlenie," p. 164.

13. Aptekman, *Obshchestvo*, p. 198; although on p. 204, he contends that the society was highly centralized from the start.

14. Shiriaev, "Avtobiograficheskaia zapiska," pp. 85-86.

15. Iurii Bogdanovich, in a statement to the procuror dated May 5, 1882; "Iz narodovol'cheskikh avtobiograficheskikh dokumentov," pp. 216-17.

16. Koz'min, "K istorii 'Zemli i Voli' 70-kh godov."

17. "Iz zhizni saratovskikh kruzhkov," pp. 7-8.

18. Aptekman, *Obshchestvo*, p. 195; Serebriakov, *Obshchestvo*, pp. 13, 33.

19. Figner, *Nacht*, p. 73.

20. Kuklin, *Itogi*, Addendum, p. 25.

21. Venturi, *Roots of Revolution*, has an excellent account of these deeds in Chapter 20, "Zemlya i Volya."

22. Tsitsianov is described as a prince in Venturi, *Roots of Revolution*, p. 525. His militant reaction is cited by N. S. Rusanov, "Ideinye osnovy Narodnoi voli," *Byloe*, 1907, No. 9, p. 71, as one of the first acts of violence leading to the terrorism of 1879-81. On Myshkin, see A. A. Kunkl', "Iz perepiski I. N. Myshkina s tovarishchami po zakliucheniiu," *Katorga i ssylka*, 66 (1930): 71-90; V. S. Antonov, "Obshchestvenno-politicheskie vzgliady I. N. Myshkina," *Istoricheskie zapiski*, 72 (1962): 63-86; and others.

23. Serebriakov, *Obshchestvo*, p. 42; see the same opinion in M. F. Frolenko, "Nachalo 'narodovol'chestva,'" *Katorga i ssylka*, 24 (1926): 19.

24. Venturi, *Roots of Revolution*, p. 601.

25. V. Bogucharskii, *Aktivnoe narodnichestvo semidesiatykh godov* (Moscow: Izd. M. i S. Sabashnikovykh, 1912), pp. 323-33.

26. *Chronique du mouvement socialiste en Russie, 1878-1887* [St. Petersburg, 1890], pp. 429-30. This extraordinary document compiled by N. I. Shebeko for the use of the Ministry of the Interior was printed in 100 copies only and marked "confidentiel et exclusivement personnel," but a copy made its way into a European bookstore and was eventually published in French and in Russian. Hereinafter cited as *Chronique*.

27. This ugly episode is described by Philip Pomper in his *Sergei Nechaev*, Chapter IV.

28. B. P. Koz'min, "S. G. Nechaev i ego protivniki" in his *Revoliutsionnoe dvizhenie 1860-kh godov* (Moscow: Politkatorzhan, 1932). For a confirming opinion see Mikhail Frolenko, *Sobranie sochineniia v dvukh tomakh* (Moscow: Politkatorzhan, 1930-31), I: 178-80.

29. The gruesome details of the episode are reported in *Chronique*, pp. 159-61. For Deich's equally horrible account, see his *Za polveka*, II: 129-34.

30. Deich, *Za polveka*, II: 127-34; M. F. Frolenko's long footnote to A. Iakimova, "Pamiati Marii Aleksandrovny Kolenkinoi-Bogorodskoi," *Katorga i ssylka*, 31 (1927): 178-79. Several recent historians agree that Gorinovich was convicted without substantial evidence; see for example Ulam, *In the Name of the People*, pp. 260-61, and Jay Bergman, *Vera Zasulich: A Biography* (Stanford: Stanford University Press, 1983), pp. 27-28.

31. Deich, *Za polveka*, I: 59.

32. Serebriakov, *Obshchestvo*, p. 15.

33. Kolosov, "Revoliutsionnaia deiatel'nost' Tiutcheva," p. 17.

34. All evidence indicates that the Executive Committee was Osinskii's imaginative appellation for the Southern *buntari* group, rather than the administrative organ of a larger revolutionary party; see Deich, "Osinskii," *Katorga i ssylka*, 54

(1929): 30–32, and O. Liubatovich, "Dalekoe i nedavnee," *Byloe*, 1906, No. 5, pp. 215–16. Oddly enough Tvardovskaia takes this Executive Committee for real: "Krizis 'Zemli i voli,'" *Istoriia SSSR*, 1959, No. 4, p. 68.

35. Serebriakov, *Obshchestvo*, p. 43.

36. Figner, "Natanson," *PSS*, V: 210.

37. Figner, "Iz avtobiografii," *Byloe*, 1917, No. 2, p. 179, reports casually that the members of Land and Freedom "punished the worker Finogenov for his betrayal with death." This deed is listed in *Chronique*, p. 22.

38. Kolosov, "Revoliutsionnaia deiatel'nost' Tiutcheva," p. 30; see also *Chronique*, pp. 242–43. The report in *Chronique*, pp. 22–26, speculating that Nikonov had been killed by Ivan Ivichevich (along with a friend named Ludovic Brantner) is confirmed by Lev Tikhomirov, *Vospominaniia L'va Tikhomirova*, (Moscow-Leningrad: Gosizdat, 1927), p. 110. Popov, *Zapiski zemlevol'tsa*, pp. 162–63, credits a worker named Sentianin with the murder. Sentianin was later arrested.

39. Kolosov, "Revoliutsionnaia deiatel'nost' Tiutcheva," pp. 86–87; *Chronique*, pp. 23–25, 44–45, and 241–43.

40. Kolosov, "Revoliutsionnaia deiatel'nost' Tiutcheva," pp. 28–29; Zharkov's murder is also described in *Chronique*, pp. 241–43.

41. *Chronique*, pp. 37–42. Koval'skii, who was the son of a priest, was known for his militant temperament; he always carried a Smith and Wesson revolver. See the special section on Koval'skii in *Katorga i ssylka*, No. 45/46 (1928), especially Ts. Martynovskaia, "I. M. Koval'skii i pervoe vooruzhennoe soprotivlenie v Odesse," pp. 81–99; also Kraft, "Iz vospominanii ob I. M. Koval'skom," *Katorga i ssylka* 38 (1928).

42. Figner, "Iz avtobiografii," *Byloe*, 1917, No. 2, p. 179, and *passim*.

43. Deich, "Osinskii," pp. 18–20; M. F. Frolenko, "Kommentarii k stat'e N. A. Morozova 'Vozniknovenie Narodnoi voli,'" *Byloe*, 1906, No. 12, pp. 22–23.

44. For Zasulich's relationship to Nechaev, see Vera Zasulich, "Vospominaniia," *Byloe*, 1919, No. 14, pp. 96–97, and "Nechaevskoe delo" in *Gruppa "Osvobozhdenie truda"*, II: 69.

45. Wolfgang Geierhos, *Vera Zasulic und die russische revolutionäre Bewegung* (Munich-Vienna: Oldenbourg, 1977), pp. 30–31.

46. Ibid., p. 31; also Frolenko, "Komentarii," p. 23.

47. Geierhos, *Zasulic*, p. 37. On the withdrawn, shy, and unhappy personality of Zasulich and the even less attractive attributes of her roommate, see Bergman, *Zasulich*, p. 31; Kravchinsky, *Underground Russia*, p. 117; Deich, *Za polveka*, I: 254–263; Evtikhii Karpov, "V. I. Zasulich: Nakanune pokusheniia," *Vestnik literatury*, 1919, no. 6, pp. 2–4; and Iakimova, "Pamiati Kolenkinoi-Bogorodskoi," pp. 180–84. N. S. Tagantsev, "Iz perezhitogo," *Byloe*, 1918, No. 9, p. 149, describes Kolenkina as a "nervously ailing girl," and he had known her from childhood.

48. Geierhos, *Zasulic*, p. 37; Bergman, *Zasulich*, p. 38.

49. Geierhos, *Zasulic*, p. 40; Deich, "Osinskii," p. 24; Bergman, *Zasulich*, p. 38.

50. Deich, "Osinskii," p. 25; Zasulich seemed blissfully unaware that the Senate, the State Council, the tsar, and the police all could easily extend or change these sentences, as indeed was the case.

51. Geierhos, *Zasulic*, p. 41. Kolenkina intended to assassinate the Senate ober-procurer from the trial of 193 on the same morning, but she was unable to locate him so he escaped.

52. Bergman, *Zasulich*, especially pp. 41–42, and Geierhos, *Zasulic*, pp. 56–58; also Sh. M. Levin, "Dve demonstratsii," *Istoricheskie zapiski*, 54 (1955): 251–61.

53. Deich, "Osinskii," p. 22–24.

54. Aaron Zundelevich, as "foreign officer," arranged for Deich's escape abroad: Lev Deich, *Russkaia revoliutsionnaia emigratsiia 70-kh godov* (Petersburg: Gosizdat, 1920), pp. 3–4.

55. Geierhos, *Zasulich*, pp. 57–82, reports reactions of individuals and the press.

56. Figner, "Iz avtobiografii," *Byloe*, 1917, No. 2, p. 179.

57. Geierhos, *Zasulic*, pp. 62–63.

58. Zasulich, "Vospominaniia," p. 72. Dmitrii Klements described her as living in a dreamlike state, taking a long time to get back to reality again, and at one time even thinking of turning herself in to the police. L. G. Deich, "O D. A. Klementse," *Katorga i ssylka*, No. 60 (1929), pp. 151–52.

59. Sergei Kravchinskii, in the journal *Zemlia i volia*, his programmatic lead article in the first issue, October, 1878, reprinted in *Revoliutsionnaia zhurnalistika*, p. 77.

60. Popov, *Zapiski zemlevol'tsa*, p. 93.

61. Ibid., p. 94; statement of N. I. Kibal'chich in "Pokazaniia pervomartovtsev; Iz aktov predvarietel'nogo sledstviia," *Byloe*, 1918, No. 10/11, pp. 296–97.

62. Deich, "Osinskii," p. 27.

63. Liubatovich, "Dalekoe i nedavnee," *Byloe*, 1906, No. 5, 237. Kravchinskii told Liubatovich that "self-criticism" was "eating up" Zasulich during her first years in exile. See Deich's account in "O D. A. Klementse," pp. 151–52.

64. Serebriakov, *Obshchestvo*, pp. 42–43.

65. Ibid., p. 43, and Deich, "Osinskii," p. 29. Both credit Osinskii for this attempt, but other names are listed in *Chronique*, pp. 16–19; Frolenko, *Sobranie sochinenii*, I: 202; and R. A. Steblin-Kamenskii, "Grigorii Anfimovich Popko," *Byloe*, 1907, No. 5 (12), p. 189.

66. This proclamation, which contained threats against Police Chief Geiking because of his intensive search for Kotliarevskii's murderers, is described in *Chronique*, p. 19, and in *Obshchina* (Geneva), No. 3/4 (March/April, 1878), pp. 28–29.

67. *Chronique*, p. 19.

68. Ibid.

69. Ibid., p. 22. See also Steblin-Kamenskii, "Popko," pp. 179–204. Popko made no secret of his deed; he confided to his friend P. N. Fomin/A. F. Medvedev and probably to others: see P. Shchegolev, "Aleksei Medvedev," *Katorga i ssylka* 71 (1930), p. 102, and the casual references to Popko as assassin in M. Frolenko, "Nachalo 'narodovol'chestva'," p. 19–20, and S. E. Lion, "Ot propagandy k terroru," p. 12. Nevertheless, the revolutionaries managed to keep Popko's identity secret, and not even Grigorii Gol'denberg, a terrorist who turned informer, knew Popko's real identity. See his deposition in "Glava iz odnoi knigi sekretno izdannoi zhandarmami," *Byloe* (London), 1903, No. 4, p. 68.

70. Aptekman, *Obshchestvo*, pp. 286–96; Serebriakov, *Obshchestvo*, pp. 34–35.

71. Aptekman, *Obshchestvo*, p. 195, states the constitution was "temporary" in that it was subject to annual review. He is probably referring to the Mikhailov constitution of 1878, which was indeed reviewed by the membership the following year at Voronezh.

72. Ibid., pp. 295–96; Serebriakov, *Obshchestvo*, p. 35.

73. Aptekman, *Obshchestvo*, p. 296; Serebriakov, *Obshchestvo*, p. 35.

74. Serebriakov, *Obshchestvo*, p. 33; Aptekman, *Obshchestvo*, p. 301. The writer of these words was evidently Plekhanov, for Aptekman was not present at this session.

75. Valk *et al.*, *Revoliutsionnoe narodnichestvo*, II: 34–42.

76. Rosa Markovna Bograd, later Plekhanov's wife, reported that Mikhailov gave her the Catechism for her first revolutionary reading; R. M. Plekhanova, "Periferiinyi kruzhok 'Zemli i voli,'" *Gruppa "Osvobozhdenie truda,"* IV (1926): 91.

77. V. A. Tvardovskaia, "Organizatsionnye osnovy 'Narodnoi voli,'" *Istoricheskie zapiski*, 67 (1960): 106; Mikhailov made this statement to N. V. Kletochnikov, who later became the People's Will spy planted in the Third Section, or secret police.

78. Serebriakov, *Obshchestvo*, p. 34; Aptekman, *Obshchestvo*, 302.

79. Valk *et al.*, *Revoliutsionnoe narodnichestvo*, II: 35.

80. Ibid., p. 36.

81. Ibid., pp. 41–42.

82. Ibid., p. 37.

83. Ibid., p. 35.

84. Tvardovskaia, "Organizatsionnye osnovy," especially pp. 105–09.

85. The words are Figner's: Vera Figner, "Sof'ia Perovskaia, 1854–1881," *Byloe*, 1918, No. 10/11, p. 9. See the confirmation of her attitude in *Sof'ia L'vovna Perovskaia*, anonymous but written by Lev Tikhomirov (London: Zagranichnaia tip. Narodnoi voli, 1882), pp. 20–21, and Ilia Mirovich, *Sophja Perowskaja, die Maertyrer in der russischen Revolution: biographische Skizze nach russischen Quellen* (New York: Schaerr & Frantz, 1882), p. 13.

86. Tikhomirov, *Vospominaniia*, pp. 110–111. The relationship of Tikhomirov and Perovskaia is confirmed by S. S. Sinegub, *Zapiski chaikovtsa* (Moscow: Molodaia gvardiia, 1929), p. 192.

87. Extraordinary memoirs and tales exist regarding this episode. See, for instance, Morozov, *Povesti*, II: 292–302; Popov, *Zapiski zemlevol'tsa*, pp. 117–18 and 306–32; M. F. Frolenko, "Popytka osvobozhdeniia Voinaral'skogo 1–go iiulia 1878 g.," *Katorga i ssylka*, 41 (1928): 82–89 and 102–6; S. F. Kovalik, *Revoliutsionnoe dvizhenie*, pp. 24–26; Shchegolev, "Medvedev," pp. 66–71; and the ever-reliable *Chronique*, pp. 50–53.

88. Tikhomirov, *Vospominaniia*, p. 116.

89. See Kovalik, *Revoliutsionnoe dvizhenie*, pp. 25–26, and Frolenko, "Popytka osvobozhdeniia Voinaral'skogo," pp. 82–88. The coachman died.

90. See Popov, *Zapiski zemlevol'tsa*, pp. 117–18.

91. Frolenko, "Popytka osvobozhdeniia Voinaral'skogo," pp. 88–89; [Tikhomirov], *Perovskaia*, pp. 20–21; Liubatovich, "Dalekoe i nedavnee," *Byloe*, 1906, No. 5, pp. 219–220.

92. *Chronique*, pp. 52–53; Shchegolev, "Medvedev," pp. 72–73; Serebriakov, *Obshchestvo*, p. 43.

93. Morozov, *Povesti*, II: 329–33.

94. Deich, "Osinskii," p. 33; Serebriakov, *Obshchestvo*, p. 43. The best account of this rioting, in August 1878, emerges in *Chronique*, pp. 250–51, but see also Levin, "Dve demonstratsii," pp. 261–69.

95. Kravchinskii deserves a full-length biography in English; this author has seen only the dissertation by John E. Bachman, *Sergei Mikhailovich Stepniak-Kravchinskii: A Biography from the Russian Revolutionary Movement on Native and Foreign Soil*, The American University, 1971. In Russian, see Evgeniia A. Taratuta, *Russkii drug Engel'sa* (Moscow: Izd. Sovetskaia Rossiia, 1970), and Lev Deich, *Sergei Mikhailovich Kravchinskii-Stepniak: Baloven' sudby* (Petrograd, 1919).

96. *Obshchina* (Geneva), No. 3/4 (March/April 1878), p. 17.

97. Zasulich, "Vospominaniia," pp. 87–88, dates Kravchinskii's return as May 1878. On his decision to assassinate Mezentsev, see Frolenko, "Kommentarii," p. 24, including the note by Morozov appended here.

98. Deich, *Kravchinskii*, pp. 24–26; cf. the statement of T. I. Lebedeva to the court in "Protsess 20–ti narodovol'tsev v 1882 g.," *Byloe* (London), No. 1 (n.d.), p. 273, and Golovina-Iurgenson, "Moi vospominaniia," p. 104. A couple of Kravchinskii's indiscreet letters are published under the title "Iz zapisnoi knizhki arkhivista; Iz perepiski S. M. Kravchinskogo," *Krasnyi arkhiv*, 19 (1926): 195–202; also Zasulich, "Vospominaniia," pp. 81–82, and Sinegub, *Zapiski chaikovtsa*, pp. 220–24.

99. The dramatic account in *Chronique*, pp. 29–37, should be supplemented by Barannikov's equally sensational account to the court at his trial in 1882; see "Protsess 20–ti," pp. 98–99 and 112. See also Zundelevich to Deich, London, July 18, 1922, in *Gruppa "Osvobozhdenie truda"*, III: 198.

100. S. M. Kravchinskii, *Smert' za smert'; ubiistvo Mezentseva* (Petersburg: Gosizdat, 1920), a brochure that is, as Deich points out ("Osinskii," p. 34) both inconsistent and illogical.

101. *Zemlia i volia*, No. 1; reprinted in *Revoliutsionnaia zhurnalistika*, pp. 74–75.

102. See F. Volkhovskii's obituary of Kravchinskii, in *Letuchie listki* (London), No. 28 (January 18, 1896), p. 7.

103. Liubatovich, "Dalekoe i nedavnee," *Byloe*, 1906, No. 5, p. 223; Zasulich, "Vospominaniia," p. 90.

104. Deich, *Kravchinskii*, p. 38.

105. A year later when Deich, Zasulich, and Stefanovich slipped back into Russia, they had trouble persuading Kravchinskii not to go with them.

106. See the excellent article by N. S. Tiutchev, "Razgrom Zemli i voli v 1878 g. Delo Mezentsova," *Byloe*, 1918, No. 8 (30), pp. 157–79.

107. Tiutchev, "Razgrom," pp. 172–73; cf. Liubatovich, "Dalekoe i nedavnee," *Byloe*, 1906, No. 5, p. 221. Saburov was suspected of being the assassin, until it became clear that he was a much smaller man than the huge person who had accomplished the deed.

108. Popov, *Zapiski zemlevol'tsa*, p. 146; Tiutchev, "Razgrom," p. 160.

109. Liubatovich, "Dalekoe i nedavnee," *Byloe*, 1906, No. 5, p. 221. There is

an account of these arrests in *Chronique*, pp. 42–43, and in Tiutchev, "Razgrom," pp. 160–65; but the most detailed and interesting is that of the revolutionaries themselves, published in *Zemlia i volia*, No. 1, reprinted in *Revoliutsionnaia zhurnalistika*, pp. 100–102.

110. Tiutchev, "Razgrom," pp. 168–171, cf. Morozov, *Povesti*, II: 399–406.

111. Tiutchev, "Razgrom," pp. 169–70; Popov, *Zapiski zemlevol'tsa*, p. 107; *Chronique*, p. 43. See the fine account in *Listok zemli i voli*, No. 5 (June 8, 1879), reprinted in *Revoliutsionnaia zhurnalistika*, pp. 296–99.

112. *Chronique*, p. 46.

113. Serebriakov, *Obshchestvo*, p. 47.

114. *Chronique*, p. 44.

115. According to *Chronique*, p. 242; I have been unable to locate this reference.

116. N. V. Kletochnikov, who volunteered for this job, came to be of enormous usefulness to the revolutionaries; see A. Pribyleva-Korba, "Neskol'ko strok o N. V. Kletochnikove," *Katorga i ssylka*, 114/115 (1935): 146–154.

117. Testimony of T. I. Lebedeva at the trial of 20, 1882; see "Otchet o protsess 20–ti narodovol'tsev v 1882 godu," *Byloe*, 1906, No. 6, pp. 273–74; also V. L. Burtsev, "Severno-russkii rabochii soiuz: Stranitsa iz istorii rabochego dvizheniia v Rossii," *Byloe*, No. 1 (January, 1906), 173–74. The leader of the North Russian Workers Union, Stepan Khalturin, managed to go underground, later emerging as bomber of the Winter Palace.

118. Quoted from the revolutionaries' own report in *Listok zemli i voli*, No. 1, as reprinted in *Revoliutsionnaia zhurnalistika*, pp. 277–78.

119. Popov is identified as the murderer of Reinshtein by Aptekman, *Obshchestvo*, pp. 240–41, to whom he confessed details of the deed shortly after he committed the crime; see also the obituary written by M. Frolenko, "Mikhail Rodionovich Popov," *Golos minuvshego*, 7/8 (1917): 172; Morozov, *Povesti*, II: 406; S. Mitskevich, "Moskovskie revoliutsionnye kruzhki 2-i poloviny 1870-kh godov," *Katorga i ssylka*, 4 (1924): 61; and A. Pribyleva-Korba, "Vospominaniia o 'Narodnoi vole,'" *Golos minuvshego*, IV, No. 9 (1916), pp. 97–98.

120. *Chronique*, pp. 133–35; Deich, "Osinskii," p. 37.

121. *Chronique*, pp. 138–39.

122. An account of this episode appears in *Chronique*, p. 139.

123. Ibid. See the little pamphlet *Protsess sotsialistov Valer'iana Osinskogo, Sofii Leshern-fon-Gertsfel't, i Vartolomiaa Voloshenko; Kratkii otchet . . .* (Geneva: Tip. Rabotnik i Gromady, 1879); also "Sud i kazn' L. K. Brantnera, V. A. Svidirenko, i V. A. Osinskogo," *Katorga i ssylka*, 56 (1929): 68–76.

124. A description of this assassination is in *Chronique*, pp. 62–68.

125. Ibid., pp. 66–67.

126. Ibid., pp. 67–68; *Zemlia i volia*, No. 4, reprinted in *Revoliutsionnaia zhurnalistika*, pp. 226–28.

127. *Revoliutsionnaia zhurnalistika*, pp. 226–28.

128. For Gol'denberg's depositions, see "Svod ukazanii, dannykh nekotorym iz arestovannkh po delam o gosudarstvennykh prestuplenniakh," *Byloe*, 1907, No. 8, pp. 95, 113–15; and "Glava iz odnoi knigi sekretno izdannoi zhandarmami," *Byloe* (London), 1903, No. 4, pp. 66–75, and No. 5 (1903), pp. 61–74.

129. See Morozov, *Povesti*, II: 373–78.

130. Aptekman, *Obshchestvo*, p. 347.

131. Serebriakov, *Obshchestvo*, p. 48.

132. *Chronique*, pp. 73–79; Morozov, *Povesti*, II: 375–76.

133. Rosa Plekhanova, "Nasha zhizn' do emigratsii," *Gruppa "Osvobozhdenie truda"*, VI (1928): 73–75.

134. *Zemlia i volia*, No. 5, reprinted in *Revoliutsionnaia zhurnalistika*, pp. 270–71; Popov, *Zapiski zemlevol'tsa*, p. 89.

135. *Chronique*, p. 79.

136. Lev Deich in a footnote to one of Zundelevich's letters published in *Gruppa "Osvobozhdenie truda"*, III: 203.

137. Peter A. Zaionchkovsky, *The Russian Autocracy in Crisis, 1878-1882* edited, translated (from the original *Krizis samoderzhaviia na rubezhe 1870-1880-kh godov*), and with introduction by Gary Hamburg (Gulf Breeze, Florida: Academic International Press, 1979), pp. 39–40.

138. Ibid., p. 49.

139. Ibid., p. 75.

140. See the excellent analyses of the use of the judicial system against the *narodniki* by N. A. Troitskii, *Narodnaia volia pered tsarskim sudom* (Saratov: Izd. Saratovskogo univ., 1971) and *Bezumstvo khrabrykh; Russkie revoliutsionery i karatel'naia politika tsarizma, 1866-1882 gg.* (Moscow: Mysl', 1978).

141. Cf. *Chronique*, pp. 186–87, 266.

142. Zaionchkovsky, *Russian Autocracy*, p. 54; see also *Narodnaia volia: Sotsial'no revoliutsionnoe obozrenie* (Berlin [1924]), I: 24.

143. Serebriakov, *Obshchestvo*, p. 20; Figner, "Iz avtobiografii," *Byloe*, 1917, No. 3, p. 182; also "K biografii Very Nikolaevny Figner," *Byloe*, 1906, No. 5, pp. 8–9.

144. See Serebriakov, *Obshchestvo*, p. 52.

145. "Avtobiograficheskoe zaiavlenie Kviatkovskogo," p. 166.

146. Ginev, "Revoliutsionnaia deiatel'nost'," p. 239.

147. Figner, *Nacht*, pp. 89–90.

148. "K istorii partii Narodnoi voli," *Byloe*, 1906, No. 6, p. 5. This article contains written replies of Mariia Nikolaevna Olovennikova/Oshanina to questions submitted to her by a revolutionary historian (probably Serebriakov) in 1893.

149. [Tikhomirov], *Zheliabov*, p. 18.

150. M. F. Frolenko, "Lipetskii i voronezhskii s'ezdy," *Byloe*, 1907, No. 1, pp. 79–80.

151. Deich, *Kravchinskii*, p. 59; Stefanovich, *Zloba dnia*, pp. 7–8.

152. Sinegub, *Zapiski chaikovtsa*, p. 224.

CHAPTER 4: THE TERRORIST CONSPIRACY

1. Aptekman, *Obshchestvo*, pp. 301–02; Serebriakov, *Obshchestvo*, p. 33.

2. N. Bukh, "Pervaia tipografiia 'Narodnoi voli,'" *Katorga i ssylka*, 57/58 (1929): 57.

3. "Iz pokazanii V. N. Figner," *Byloe*, 1906, No. 7, p. 35. See also Morozov, *Povesti*, II, Chapter XV; Tikhomirov, *Vospominaniia*, pp. 125–27; Popov,

Zapiski zemlevol'tsa, p. 221; Plekhanov as quoted in Aptekman, *Obshchestvo*, pp. 331–32.

4. The phrase is from Tikhomirov, *Vospominaniia*, p. 10.

5. Plekhanova, "Periferiinyi kruzhok," p. 91.

6. A. D. Mikhailov, *Vospominaniia* (Geneva: Izd. G. A. Kuklina, 1903), pp. 27–38, in the accompanying report (anonymous, but written by Plekhanov) "Vospominaniia ob A. D. Mikhailove." See also Mikhailov's own memoir in the same volume, pp. 9–10. This material was republished in the volume *Aleksandr Dmitrievich Mikhailov* (Leningrad, 1925), edited by A. P. Pribyleva-Korba and V. N. Figner.

7. Mikhailov, *Vospominaniia*, pp. 29–33.

8. Popov, *Zapiski zemlevol'tsa*, pp. 195–96, describes him thus; Tikhomirov says he took on the air of a *raskolnik* himself and was beginning to talk theology even with his revolutionary friends; see Mikhailov, *Vospominaniia*, Tikhomirov's note on p. 16.

9. "Vospominaniia o Mikhailove," pp. 33–34.

10. Mikhailov, *Vospominaniia*, p. 14. On the attitude of his comrades, see also Tikhomirov, *Vospominaniia*, pp. 93–94.

11. Mikhailov, *Vospominaniia*, p. 35; Serebriakov, *Obshchestvo*, p. 33.

12. The new principles of organization, incorporated thereafter into the statute of *Zemlia i volia*, are discussed in Chapter 3 above.

13. The following description is drawn from Tikhomirov's notes to Mikhailov, *Vospominaniia*, pp. 11–14.

14. Ibid., p. 12.

15. Plekhanova, "Periferiinyi Kruzhok," pp. 91–92.

16. In October 1878, having hit the officer who had just arrested him, he managed to escape by ducking down alleys and into courtyards. *Chronique*, p. 46. Cf. Tikhomirov, *Vospominaniia*, p. 95, and Mikhailov, *Vospominaniia*, p. 14.

17. Tikhomirov, *Vospominaniia*, p. 126.

18. Ibid., p. 111, Sof'ia Ivanova, "Vospominaniia o S. L. Perovskoi," *Byloe*, 1906, No. 3, p. 87; Koz'min, "K istorii partii Narodnoi voli," pp. 7–8.

19. Plekhanova, "Periferiinyi Kruzhok," p. 92.

20. Tikhomirov in Mikhailov, *Vospominaniia*, note on p. 5, quoting Andrei Zheliabov; see also "Vospominaniia o Mikhailove," pp. 40–41.

21. Mikhailov, *Vospominaniia*, pp. 3–6, esp. Tikhomirov's note, pp. 5–6.

22. Plekhanov, as quoted in Deich, "O bylom i nebylitsakh," p. 24.

23. Aptekman, *Obshchestvo*, p. 330; Mikhailov, *Vospominaniia*, p. 18.

24. A. Tyrkov, "K sobytiiu 1-go marta 1881 goda," *Byloe*, 1906, No. 5, p.143.

25. Mikhailov, quoted in Popov, *Zapiski zemlevol'tsa*, p. 140.

26. Zharkov was murdered by Andrei Presniakov; see chapter 3.

27. An account of this gruesome operation appears in chapter 3.

28. See chapter 3.

29. Popov, *Zapiski zemlevol'tsa*, p. 142.

30. Deich, "O bylom i Nebylitsakh," p. 35.

31. On these individuals see for example Ek. Breshkovskaia, "Vstrecha s N. I. Kibal'chichem," *Revoliutsionnaia Rossia*, No. 27, pp. 8–10; [Lev Tikhomirov], *Nikolai Ivanovich Kibal'chich* (London: Zagranichnaia tip. Narodnoi voli, 1882); "Avtobiograficheskaia zapiska i pis'ma S. Shiriaeva," pp. 70–107; Plekhanova,

"Periferiinyi kruzhok," pp. 98–99; L. Deich, "Aaron Zundelevich: Odin iz pervykh sotsial-demokratov v Rossii," *Gruppa "Osvobozhdenie truda,"* II (1924): 185–216.

32. Popov, *Zapiski zemlevol'tsa*, p. 201.

33. Mikhailov, quoted in V. A. Tvardovskaia, "Krizis 'Zemlia i volia'," p. 65.

34. Kviatkovskii to the court, from Kuklin, *Itogi*, Addendum, p. 25.

35. Morozov, *Povesti*, II: 334, 349–51, 394–97.

36. Ibid., II: 349–51.

37. Tikhomirov, *Vospominaniia*, chapter entitled "Epokha 'Zemli i voli,' 'Ispolniitel'nogo komiteta,' i 'Narodnoi voli.'"

38. Tikhomirov wrote under the name I. Kol'tsov (or simply the initials I. K.) in *Delo*; Mikhailovskii later contributed to the journal *Narodnaia volia* under the name Gron'iar.

39. Liubatovich, "Dalekoe i nedavnee," *Byloe* 1906, No. 5, p. 217; cf. Tikhomirov's agreement in his *Vospominaniia*, pp. 127–28.

40. *Revoliutsionnaia zhurnalistika*, pp. 103–113.

41. Plekhanov's lead articles, clearly the most erudite and intelligent of them all, appeared in *Zemlia i volia*, Nos. 3 and 4; they concentrate even in this early stage of his development on the urban workers. The lead article in number 5, written by Tikhomirov, again returns to the terrorist argument; at the time it was published, Plekhanov had left town to avoid the police roundup after Solov'ev's assassination attempt, and Tikhomirov blatantly substituted his own article for one of Plekhanov's that had already been written and accepted. See Aptekman, *Obshchestvo*, pp. 363–64.

42. Six issues of the *Listok* went to press between March and June, 1879; they are reprinted in *Revoliutsionnaia zhurnalistika*.

43. *Listok zemlia i volia*, No. 1, reprinted in *Revoliutsionnaia zhurnalistika*, p. 280.

44. Tikhomirov, *Vospominaniia*, pp. 132–35; Deich, "Iz otnoshenii G. V. Plekhanova k narodovol'tsam," pp. 9–10.

45. See *Listok zemli i voli*, No. 2/3, March 22, 1879, as republished in *Revoliutsionnaia zhurnalistiki*, pp. 282–83. Tikhomirov's account of disagreements among the terrorist leaders is in *Vospominaniia*, pp. 132–25.

46. Plekhanov, quoted in Deich, "O bylom i nebylitsakh," p. 33.

47. As is apparent from his actions at the time that Land and Freedom split; see Chapter 5.

48. The best source on Solov'ev is the three-part, unsigned article that appeared in *Byloe*, 1918, under the title "Pokushenie A. K. Solov'eva na tsareubiistvo, 2 aprelia 1879 goda," No. 7, pp. 133–51; No. 8, pp. 88–107; and No. 9, pp. 184–203; this material is summarized in *Chronique*, pp. 82–91. See also Karpov, "Stranichki iz vospominanii," pp. 31–47.

49. "Pokushenie Solov'eva," *Byloe*, No. 9, pp. 186, 187, 188.

50. Figner, "Aleksandr Solov'ev," *PSS*, V: 193–94.

51. "Pokushenie Solov'eva," *Byloe*, No. 9, p. 193; also Part II of this article in *Byloe*, No. 8, p. 101.

52. "Pokushenie Solov'eva," *Byloe*, No. 9, pp. 184, 186, and elsewhere.

53. This weird, rambling, and often contradictory female indictment is contained in "Pokushenie Solov'eva," Part III, *Byloe*, No. 9, pp. 187–203; its gen-

eral effect (whether or not intentional) is to emphasize Solov'ev's instability and weakness of character.

54. Figner, "Solov'ev," p. 198.

55. Ibid.

56. In his depositions after his arrest, Solov'ev described his own peregrinations ("Pokushenie Solov'eva," Part I, *Byloe*, No. 7, pp. 138–47); his description of the passport problem is on p. 145. Similar descriptions appear in Karpov, "Solov'ev," pp. 45–47, and in *Chronique*, pp. 82–84.

57. See the account in Serebriakov, *Obshchestvo*, pp. 19–21.

58. Vera Figner, "Evgeniia Nikolaevna Figner," *Katorga i ssylka*, No. 9, 1924, p. 21.

59. Ibid. Solov'ev made a similar representation of his ideas to his friend Karpov when he returned shortly to St. Petersburg; Karpov, "Solov'ev," pp. 43–45.

60. "Pokushenie Solov'eva," Part I, *Byloe*, No. 7, p. 147; also p. 145.

61. Karpov, "Solov'ev," p. 45.

62. Ibid.

63. Mikhailov in a deposition before his trial; "Protsess 20–ti narodovol'tsev v 1882 g.," p. 292.

64. Mikhailov to the court at his trial in 1882; Vladimir Burtsev, "Protsess 20–ti," *Byloe* (London), No. 2 (n.d.), 99–101.

65. *Chronique*, pp. 87–89; this account is based on Gol'denberg's later depositions. See also Aptekman, *Obshchestvo*, pp. 358–60; Serebriakov, *Obshchestvo*, pp. 49–52; Morozov, *Povesti*, II: 415.

66. Accounts of this meeting appear in Aptekman, *Obshchestvo*, pp. 358–60; Morozov, *Povesti*, II: 415–17; Deich, "Iz otnoshenii G. V. Plekhanova k narodovol'tsam," pp. 11–12; and Popov, *Zapiski zemlevol'tsa*, pp. 201–2.

67. Popov, *Zapiski zemlevol'tsa*, p. 202.

68. Morozov, *Povesti*, II: 415.

69. Aptekman, *Obshchestvo*, pp. 358–59.

70. Ibid., pp. 359–60.

71. Plekhanov, quoted in Deich, "O bylom i nebylitsakh," p. 36.

72. This possibility, suggested in *Chronique*, pp. 96–98, was drawn from the testimony of Gol'denberg, who in any case was not present.

73. Popov, *Zapiski zemlevol'tsa*, p. 202; see Aptekman's contradiction of this quotation in *Obshchestvo*, p. 360, footnote.

74. Plekhanov, quoted in Deich, "O bylom i nebylitsakh," p. 37.

75. Zundelevich to Lev Deich, London, August 24, 1922, published in *Gruppa "Osvobozhdenie truda"*, III: 207.

76. Plekhanov, quoted in Deich, "O bylom i nebylitsakh," p. 36.

77. Ibid., p. 37.

78. Ibid.

79. Popov, *Zapiski zemlevol'tsa*, p. 202; Morozov, *Povesti*, II: 415.

80. Popov, *Zapiski zemlevol'tsa*, pp. 202–3.

81. Aptekman, *Obshchestvo*, pp. 356–60.

82. Popov, *Zapiski zemlevol'tsa*, pp. 146–47.

83. Ibid., p. 147.

84. There is an account of Solov'ev's assassination attempt in *Chronique*, pp. 85–87, but the most detailed treatment appears in the revolutionaries' own

chronicle *Listok zemli i voli*, No. 4, April 6, 1879, reprinted in *Revoliutsion-naia zhurnalistika*, pp. 290–91. In the following issue of *Listok*, Morozov published a long, detailed, and gruesome account of Solov'ev's execution; *Revoliutsionnaia zhurnalistika*, pp. 295–96.

85. Veimar was tried in May 1880 with a group of eleven *Zemlia i volia* members, including Adrian Mikhailov and Ol'ga Natanson. He was sentenced to ten years at hard labor and died in Kara in 1885. See German Lopatin, "K istorii osuzhdeniia d-ra O. E. Veimara," *Byloe*, 1907, No. 15, p. 122; and "K protsessu Adriana Mikhailova, Veimara, i drug," *Krasnyi arkhiv*, 39 (1930): 149–76.

86. Morozov, *Povesti*, II: 416.

87. A. V. Iakimova, "Gruppa 'Svoboda ili smert'," *Katorga i ssylka*, 24 (1926), pp. 14–16.

88. Ibid., pp. 15–16. The revolutionaries often found it desirable to mask their activities by posing as ordinary spouses and living together as man and wife. Considering the isolation, tension, and emotional commitment in the situation, the results were often predictable: thus Sof'ia Ivanova gave birth to Kviatkovskii's child while she was in prison; Iakimova bore a child in Petropavlovsk (1882); Ges'ia Gel'fman's pregnancy by Kolodkevich caused her to be excused from the scaffold after the assassination of the tsar; Liubatovich bore Morozov's child in Switzerland; and Shiriaev fathered a child, by his own admission, in the spring of 1879.

89. Ibid., p. 15; see also Shiriaev, "Avtobiograficheskaia zapiska," pp. 93–94.

90. Figner, *Nacht*, p. 98.

91. *Listok zemli i voli*, No. 4, dated April 6, 1879, reprinted in *Revoliutsion-naia zhurnalistika*, pp. 293–94. On Kletochnikov, see Pribyleva-Korba, "Neskol'ko strok o N. V. Kletochnikove," pp. 146–54. A number of Kletochnikov's notes on such matters as government agents, "spies," and prospective arrests have been published in *Byloe* in 1908: No. 7, pp. 146–52; No. 8, pp. 156–58; No. 9/10, pp. 248–51.

92. Many memoirs credit the "terrorist faction" with desiring such a meeting: Olovennikova/Oshanina in "K istorii partii Narodnoi voli," p. 4; Frolenko, "Nachalo 'narodovol'chestva'," p. 20; Grigorii Gol'denberg, in his deposition after his arrest, republished in "Glava iz odnoi knigi," p. 70; and Tikhomirov in R. M. Kantor, "K istorii revoliutsionnogo dvizheniia 1870-1880-kh godov (Neizdannaia zapiska L'va Tikhomirova)," *Katorga i ssylka*, 24 (1926): 120. On the other hand, Morozov, *Povesti*, II: 418–19, credits the *narodniki*, and Popov, a *narodnik*, was surely put in charge of local arrangements (*Zapiski zemlevol'tsa*, pp. 215–16).

93. The location was later changed to Voronezh; see chapter 5.

94. Popov, *Zapiski zemlevol'tsa*, p. 203; Morozov, *Povesti*, II: 418.

95. Deich, *Russkaia revoliutsionnaia emigratsiia*, p. 48, and by the same author, *Sergei Mikhailovich Kravchinskii-Stepniak*, pp. 50–51. See also Morozov, *Povesti*, II: 429.

96. Frolenko's account of this odyssey appears in most detail in his article "Lipetskii i voronezhskii s'ezdy," pp. 68–73, but he also writes an account in "Nachalo 'narodovol'chestva'," pp. 20–22.

97. Frolenko, "Lipetskii i voronezhskii s'ezdy," p. 72.

98. This author has found extremely useful the tables appended by N. A. Troitskii to his excellent works on the political trials: *Narodnaia volia pered tsarskim sudom, 1880-1891 gg.*, pp. 164-199; *Tsarskie sudy protiv revoliutsionnoi Rosii: Politicheskie protsessy 1871-1880 gg.* (Saratov: Izd. Saratovskogo univ., 1976), pp. 338-390; and *Bezumstvo khrabrykh*, pp. 314-22.

99. After their dramatic rescue from Kiev central prison in spring 1878.

100. Figner, *Nacht*, p. 95.

101. Frolenko, "Lipetskii i voronezhskii s'ezdy," p. 70.

102. Ibid.

103. Frolenko, "Nachalo 'Narodovol'chestva,'" p. 22.

104. Frolenko, "Lipetskii i voronezhskii s'ezdy," p. 68.

105. Ibid., p. 69. Zheliabov was well known for his zestful, dramatic, and sometimes tall tales, but apparently the bull was for real; he had tackled him head on, with a pitchfork.

106. Zundelevich had met Mikhailov by accident on a train shortly before the congresses. Zundelevich to Deich, London, August 24, 1922, *Gruppa "Osvobozhdenie truda,"* III: 208.

107. Frolenko, "Lipetskii i voronezhskii s'ezdy," p. 72.

108. Ibid.

109. Ibid., p. 71.

110. Ibid.

111. From Gol'denberg's testimony; "Glava is odnoi knigi," pp. 70-72.

112. M. Frolenko, "O Gol'denberge," *Katorga i ssylka*, 57/58 (1929): 279-82; Mikhailov to the court, Burtsev, "Protsess 20-ti," p. 109.

113. Zundelevich to Deich, London, January 15, 1923, *Gruppa "Osvobozhdenie truda"*, III: 214-215.

114. "Avtobiograficheskaia zapiska," p. 92. Shiriaev thereafter met Popov, who was recruiting for the Tambov congress on behalf of the *narodnik* element. Taking Shiriaev for a supporter of his faction, Popov invited him thence, but it is interesting that Shiriaev gave an equivocal answer and never mentioned the plan for Lipetsk, which was kept a dark secret. Popov, *Zapiski zemlevol'tsa*, p. 197.

115. Morozov, *Povesti*, II: 420.

116. The following summary is based on Morozov, *Povesti*, II: 407-32; Frolenko, "Lipetskii i voronezhskii s'ezdy;" Tikhomirov, *Vospominaniia*, and by the same author the little volume *Zheliabov*, pp. 19-25; and to a certain extent, the depositions of Gol'denberg as published under the titles "Svod ukazanii . . ." and "Glava is odnoi knigi," both cited previously. The account in *Chronique*, pp. 100-111, based on Gol'denberg's testimony and other police investigations, is surprisingly accurate.

117. Frolenko, "Lipetskii i voronezhskii s'ezdy," p. 74.

118. Morozov, *Povesti*, II: 420.

119. Frolenko, "Lipetskii i voronezhskii s'ezdy," p. 76.

120. Ibid., p. 75.

121. As reported in Ludwig Kulczycki, *Geschichte der russischen Revolution* (Gotha: F. A. Perthes, 1910-1914), II: 284.

122. Frolenko, "Lipetskii i voronezhskii s'ezdy," p. 73.

123. Morozov, *Povesti*, II: 425.

124. Ibid.

125. This is the contention of Gol'denberg: "Svod ukazanii," p. 118, and "Glava iz odnoi knigi," p. 71. Frolenko, "Lipetskii i voronezhskii s'ezdy," p. 75, and also in his "Kommentarii k stat'e N. A. Morozova," pp. 31-32, plays down the amount of time given to discussion of the assassination and claims that the decision about taking the tsar's life had long since been made. In a deposition in 1881, N. N. Kolodkevich insisted that no decisions were made about practical matters at all: "Iz narodovol'cheskikh avtobiograficheskikh dokumentov," pp. 210-11. At his trial, Mikhailov contended the subject was never brought up: Burtsev, "Protsess 20-ti," p. 109. However it is clear from Morozov, *Povesti*, II: 425, that from this time on, assassination was the matter of first priority.

126. Morozov, *Povesti*, II: 421.

127. Frolenko, "Lipetskii i voronezhskii s'ezdy," p. 77.

128. Zheliabov to the court: "Iz rechei na sude A. I. Zheliabova, N. I. Kibal'-chicha, i S. L. Perovskoi," *Byloe*, 1906, No. 3, p. 66.

129. Frolenko, "Lipetskii i voronezhskii s'ezdy," pp. 75-77; Morozov, *Povesti*, II: 422-23.

130. Morozov, *Povesti*, II: 421.

131. Ibid., p. 424.

132. Ibid.

133. Shiriaev, "Avtobiograficheskaia zapiska," p. 93.

134. Frolenko, "Lipetskii i voronezhskii s'ezdy," pp. 74-75.

135. Shiriaev, "Avtobiograficheskaia zapiska," p. 93.

136. Described in Tikhomirov, *Vospominaniia*, pp. 98-99.

137. Cf. Morozov, *Povesti*, II: 246.

138. Kantor, "K istorii revoliutsionnogo dvizheniia," p. 120.

139. Morozov, *Povesti*, II: 426.

140. Gol'denberg reports that after Lipetsk he traveled back to St. Petersburg; he did not participate in the Voronezh conference at all. There are some indications—although he does not state it with absolute clarity—that Shiriaev did the same. See Shiriaev, "Avtobiograficheskaia zapiska," p. 93, and Gol'denberg's testimony in "Svod ukazanii," pp. 117-19, and "Glava iz odnoi knigi," pp. 71-72.

CHAPTER 5: THE SCHISM

1. See the list in Popov, *Zapiski zemlevolt'sa*, p. 215. The presence of the Figner sisters at Tambov and Vera's decision before the meetings to enter the organization Land and Freedom (ibid., p. 143; Figner "Iz avtobiografii," *Byloe*, 1917, No. 3, p. 179) clearly indicate that the two sisters anticipated continuing their provincial propaganda efforts, working through Land and Freedom instead of independently.

2. Popov, *Zapiski zemlevol'tsa*, pp. 215-16.

3. Ibid., p. 216.

4. Ibid., p. 143.

5. Ibid., p. 216.

6. Frolenko, "Kommentarii k stat'e Morozova," p. 31.

7. Popov, *Zapiski zemlevol'tsa*, p. 216. Participants' memories failed them with the result that we have no completely accurate list of those who attended

the conference at Voronezh. Popov presents the longest list of participants, but his list is demonstrably inaccurate in several regards. This author has made such careful comparative studies of data (from Popov, *Zapiski zemlevol'tsa*, p. 216; Plekhanov, in Deich, "O bylom i nebylitsakh," pp. 39-42; and Aptekman, *Obshchestvo*, pp. 199-200, as well as other more casual references) as to conclude that no reliable list can be made of participants. In this regard, no two memories agree.

8. Plekhanov, quoted in Deich, "O bylom i nebylitsakh," p. 40; see also p. 41.
9. Ibid., p. 40.
10. Ibid.
11. Ibid., p. 39-40.
12. Ibid., p. 42.
13. Popov, *Zapiski zemlevol'tsa*, p. 216; Aptekman, *Obshchestvo*, p. 248.
14. Again there is disagreement among the several sources about the identity of these individuals, although all agree that Zheliabov was one of them. Cf. Morozov, *Povesti*, II: 426; Figner, *Nacht*, pp. 98-99; Tikhomirov, *Zheliabov*, p. 25; Frolenko in two separate writings—"O Gol'denberge," p. 282, and "Nachalo 'narodovol'chestva,'" p. 23; and Aptekman, *Obshchestvo*, pp. 199-200. Morozov states that he "barely suppressed a smile" at the fact that the added terrorists brought the two factions to a remarkably similar numerical total (*Povesti*, II: 426); if he is right, we must presume the admission of at least four new terrorist members.
15. Figner, *Nacht*, p. 99; Frolenko, "Kommentarii k stat'e Morozova," p. 33.
16. Frolenko, "O Gol'denberge," p. 282, and "Nachalo 'narodovol'chestva,'" p. 23.
17. Kantor, "K istorii revoliutsionnogo dvizheniia," p. 121.
18. Morozov, *Povesti*, II: 429, confirmed by Aptekman, *Obshchestvo*, p. 200. Anna Pribyleva-Korba, "Vospominaniia o 'Narodnoi voli,'" p. 99, believes that Deich and Stefanovich actually attended the Voronezh meetings. All other testimony belies this.
19. Morozov, *Povesti*, II: 427.
20. Plekhanov, quoted in Deich, "O bylom i nebylitsakh," p. 39.
21. Ibid.
22. Morozov, *Povesti*, II: 427. Aptekman, *Obshchestvo*, pp. 369-70, gives a similar but less dramatic account of this episode.
23. Morozov, *Povesti*, II: 427.
24. Ibid., 428; cf. Figner, *Nacht*, p. 100.
25. Morozov, *Povesti*, II: 428.
26. See Nikolai Morozov, "Vozniknovenie 'Narodnoi voli'," *Byloe*, 1906, No. 12, pp. 17-18. In *Povesti*, the reprint of this article does not include the phrase about being close to tears; *Povesti*, II: 428.
27. Morozov, "Vozniknovenie," p. 19; this passage is not in *Povesti*.
28. Morozov, *Povesti*, II: 428.
29. Figner, *Nacht*, p. 101.
30. Tikhomirov, *Zheliabov*, p. 27.
31. Vera Figner, "Sof'ia Perovskaia, 1854-1881," *Byloe*, 1918, No. 10/11, p. 9; Figner uses the word "enraptured" to describe how she thought Perovskaia was reacting.

32. Popov, *Zapiski zemlevol'tsa*, pp. 218-19. Aptekman, *Obshchestvo*, p. 369, disagrees on the nature of the debates, stating that the proposal on political terrorism was debated "so passionately and stormily that the president only with great difficulty succeeded in establishing order."

33. Popov, *Zapiski zemlevol'tsa*, p. 219.

34. Vera Figner, in the introduction to *Andrei Ivanovich Zheliabov . . . Materialy dlia biografii* (Moscow, 1930), p. 34.

35. Tikhomirov, *Zheliabov*, pp. 42-43.

36. Popov, *Zapiski zemlevol'tsa*, p. 219.

37. Ibid., p. 216; Frolenko, "Lipetskii i voronezhskii s'ezdy," p. 84.

38. Popov, *Zapiski zemlevol'tsa*, p. 217.

39. Ibid.

40. Ibid., p. 216; Figner, *Nacht*, p. 100; Aptekman, *Obshchestvo*, p. 268.

41. Popov, *Zapiski zemlevol'tsa*, p. 217.

42. Ibid.; Frolenko, "Lipetskii i voronezhskii s'ezdy," p. 84; Morozov, *Povesti*, II: 429; Aptekman, *Obshchestvo*, pp. 373-74.

43. Morozov, *Povesti*, II: 429.

44. Ibid.; Aptekman, *Obshchestvo*, p. 200.

45. Valk *et al.*, *Revoliutsionnoe narodnichestvo*, II: 42, published this statement from a note written in Morozov's hand and entitled "Obligatory decrees of the congress of Land and Freedom, 19 June in Voronezh."

46. Frolenko, "Lipetskii i voronezhskii s'ezdy," p. 84.

47. Tvardovskaia, "Organizatsionnye osnovy," especially pp. 105-07.

48. Plekhanova, "Periferiinyi Kruzhok," p. 92.

49. Ibid., p. 115.

50. Ibid., pp. 115-16.

51. Ibid., p. 116.

52. [Tikhomirov], *Zheliabov*, p. 28; cf. Kulczyski, *Geschichte der russischen Revolution*, II: 290.

53. Gol'denberg so reported later to the police: *Chronique*, pp. 111-12.

54. Frolenko, "Lipetskii i voronezhskii s'ezdy," pp. 85-86.

55. Liubatovich, "Dalekoe i nedavnee," *Byloe*, 1906, No. 6, pp. 110-11.

56. Pribyleva-Korba, "Vospominaniia o 'Narodnoi vole,'" especially pp. 98-104.

57. Figner, *Nacht*, pp. 103-04; N. Bukh, "Pervaia tipografiia," p. 67.

58. On her romance with Morozov, see Liubatovich, "Dalekoe i nedavnee," *Byloe*, 1906, Nos. 5 and 6.

59. For interesting details, see Zundelevich to Deich, London, 12 November, 1922, in *Gruppa "Osvobozhdenie truda"*, III: 197.

60. Pribyleva-Korba, "Vospominaniia o 'Narodnoi vole,'" p. 98-99; Korba was wrong in believing that Zasulich was there during the Voronezh meetings.

61. Morozov, *Povesti*, II: 429.

62. Korba lists these two along with Plekhanov as the most difficult comrades to lose; see her "Vospominaniia o 'Narodnoi Vole,'" p. 101.

63. See details later in this chapter.

64. Lev Deich, "G. V. Plekhanov v 'Zemle i voli,'" *Gruppa "Osvobozhdenie truda"*, III: 61.

65. Plekhanova, "Nasha zhizn' do emigratsii," p. 67.

66. Ibid., pp. 65–66.

67. Deich, "Plekhanov v 'Zemle i voli,'" p. 61.

68. Morozov, "Vozniknovenie 'Narodnoi voli,'" p. 19. Not in *Povesti.*

69. Lizogub had inherited a considerable estate and intended to leave it to the revolutionary cause, but after his execution, much of the money was diverted elsewhere by the friend he left in charge.

70. The history of this press is nicely described by S. Livshits in an article "Podpol'nye tipografii 60–kh, 70–kh, i 80–kh godov," *Katorga i ssylka* 43 (1928): 60–78, and in less detail by E. Koval'skaia, "Pervaia tipografiia 'Chernogo peredelia,'" *Katorga i ssylka*, 50 (1929): 61–63. On Mariia Konstantinovna Krylova, see also K. Breshkovskaia, "Iz vospominaniia (S. A. Leshern, N. A. Armfel'd, T. I. Lebedeva, M. K. Krylova, G. M. Gel'fman)," *Golos minuvshego*, 1918, No. 10/12, pp. 219–30.

71. Tikhomirov, *Vospominaniia*, pp. 134–35.

72. Morozov, *Povesti*, II: 430.

73. Ibid.

74. Frolenko, "Nachalo narodovol'chestva," p. 25.

75. Livshits, "Podpol'nye tipografii," p. 78; Koval'skaia, "Pervaia tipografiia," pp. 61–62.

76. Liubatovich, "Dalekoe i nedavnee," *Byloe*, 1906, No. 6, p. 109.

77. Morozov, *Povesti*, II: 430.

78. Liubatovich, "Dalekoe i nedavnee," *Byloe*, 1906, No. 6, pp. 109–10.

79. E. N. Koval'skaia, "Moi vstrechi s S. L. Perovskoi: Otryvki iz vospominanii," *Byloe*, 1921, No. 16, pp. 47–48.

80. Ibid., p. 48.

81. Deich, "Iz otnoshenii Plekhanova k narodovol'tsam," pp. 12–14.

82. Popov, *Zapiski zemlevol'tsa*, pp. 217–18.

83. Ibid., p. 224.

84. Ibid., p. 173.

85. Morozov remarks on this in his article: "Otgolosok davnikh dnei: Po povodu stat'i M. R. Popova: 'Iz moego revoliutsionnogo proshlogo,'" *Byloe*, No. 22, p. 241.

86. Frolenko, "Lipetskii i voronezhskii s'ezdy," pp. 85–86.

87. Aptekman, *Obshchestvo*, p. 376.

88. Koval'skaia, "Pervaia tipografiia," p. 62; N. Sergievskii, "'Chernyi peredel'' i narodniki 80–kh godov," *Katorga i ssylka*, 74 (1931): 8–10; Zundelevich to Deich, London, August 30, 1923, *Gruppa "Osvobozhdenie truda"*, II: 199.

89. Zundelevich to Deich, London, 24 September 1922, *Gruppa "Osvobozhdenie truda"*, III: 210–11.

90. Sergievskii, "'Chernyi peredel','" pp. 9–10.

91. Koval'skaia, "Vstrechi s Perovskoi," p. 48.

CHAPTER 6: THE MYSTIQUE OF TERRORISM

1. Deich, "Osinskii," p. 27.

2. These instances of contact and communication have been mentioned previously, Chapter 3.

3. Figner, *Nacht*, p. 93.

4. Shiriaev, "Avtobiograficheskaia zapiska," p. 86.

5. Tikhomirov, *Vospominaniia*, p. 129.

6. Ibid., pp. 125–26.

7. See chapter 3. For similar reactions, see also Deich, *Kravchinskii*, p. 50; Stefanovich, *Zloba dnia*, pp. 7–8; Frolenko, both in "Nachalo 'narodovol'-chestva,'" pp. 25–26, and "Lipetskii i voronezhskii s'ezdy," p. 79; Oshanina, "K istorii partii 'Narodnoi voli,'" pp. 5–6; and Tikhomirov in "K istorii revoliutsion-nogo dvizheniia," pp. 119–20.

8. See chapter 4.

9. Figner, *Nacht*, p. 93.

10. Tikhomirov, *Vospominaniia*, pp. 125–26.

11. Sergievskii, "'Chernyi peredel', i narodniki," pp. 7–8, includes with his list of members of *Chernyi peredel'* and *Narodnaia volia* the names of several former members of *Zemlia i volia* who refused to join either new organization and opted to go back to their work in the countryside.

12. This is the subject of Aptekman's sad last chapter in *Obshchestvo.*

13. Vera Figner, "Grigorii Prokof'evich Isaev," *Golos minuvshego*, 1917, No. 9/10, p. 148.

14. Figner, *Nacht*, p. 78; Ivanchin-Pisarev, *Khozhdenie*, pp. 103–30; Deich, *Za polveka*, I: 211–213.

15. Figner, "Solov'ev," *PSS*, V: 198.

16. N. I. Sergeev, quoted in Ginev, "Revoliutsionnaia deiatel'nost'," p. 240.

17. On Lenin, see G. I. Ionova and A. F. Smirnov, "Revoliutsionnye demo-kraty i narodniki," *Istoriia SSSR*, 1961, No. 5 (September-October), p. 133; see also Tvardovskaia, "Krizis 'Zemli i voli,'" pp. 60–61.

18. These and other episodes have been described previously.

19. Ginev, "Revoliutsionnaia deiatel'nost'," p. 243.

20. A. V. Iakimova, "Iz dalekogo proshlogo," *Katorga i ssylka*, 8 (1924): 8–9.

21. Morozov, *Terroristicheskaia bor'ba* (London: Russkaia tip., 1880), p. 10.

22. Pribyleva-Korba, "Vospominaniia o 'Narodnoi vole,'" p. 95.

23. Shiriaev to the court, Kuklin, *Itogi*, Addendum, p. 26.

24. Sof'ia Ivanova, "Vospominaniia o S. L. Perovskoi," *Byloe*, 1906, No. 3, p. 86.

25. One of the rare such instances is recorded by Popov, *Zapiski zemlevol'tsa*, pp. 207–8.

26. "Pokushenie Solov'eva na tsareubiistvo 2 aprelia 1879 goda," *Byloe*, January-March, 1918. The thoroughness of the police is apparent in all these documents; after Solov'ev's arrest, they interviewed witnesses and pursued leads throughout Russia. But nowhere is there evidence that Solov'ev had been under any kind of police suspicion before his attempt on the tsar.

27. Figner's statement to the court on 27 January 1884; "K biografii," pp. 5–7.

28. Figner, *Nacht*, p. 87. Note Figner's contradictory evaluations of her ex-perience.

29. These episodes have been described previously in chapters 1 and 2.

30. Figner's claim (cf. *Nacht*, p. 87) to have been converted to terrorism in January 1879 at the time of Solov'ev's visit to the village where she and her

sister were working is actually belied by her other statements, as for instance her description of her mood at Voronezh in "Sof'ia Perovskaia," p. 5.

31. See chapter 4.

32. Popov, *Zapiski zemlevol'tsa*, p. 224.

33. Ibid., p. 88.

34. Liubatovich, "Dalekoe i nedavnee," *Byloe*, 1906, No. 5, p. 218.

35. Aptekman, *Obshchestvo*, p. 344.

36. Serebriakov, *Obshchestvo*, p. 47.

37. Aptekman, *Obshchestvo*, p. 343.

38. Figner, "Sof'ia Perovskaia," p. 5.

39. Pribyleva-Korba, "Vospominaniia o 'Narodnoi voli,'" p. 108.

40. Ivanova, "Vospominaniia o S. L. Perovskoi," p. 86. Tyrkov found her reaction angry, because the tsar had "torn her from her peaceful, quiet work as a propagandist;" Tyrkov, "K sobytiiu 1 marta 1881 goda," p. 143.

41. Mirovich, *Sophja Perowskaja*, p. 21; see also Sergei Ivanov, "Iz vospominanii o 1881 gode," *Byloe*, 1906, No. 4, pp. 236–37, and [Tikhomirov], *Perovskaia*, pp. 19–21.

42. Frolenko, "Lipetskii i voronezhskii s'ezdy," p. 81.

43. According to Popov, who writes that he had a letter from her in 1880 affirming this; *Zapiski zemlevol'tsa*, pp. 196–97. Tikhomirov confirms Perovskaia's attitude, when he reports that she proposed her services only in regard to Alexander's assassination and no more; see Kantor, "K istorii revoliutsionnogo dvizheniia," p. 122.

44. Zheliabov, quoted in Rusanov, "Ideinye osnovy Narodnoi voli," p. 76.

45. Popov, *Zapiski zemlevol'tsa*, p. 196.

46. Baron, *Plekhanov*, p. 32.

47. Debagorii-Mokrievich, *Vospominaniia*, III: 492.

48. Kantor, "K istorii revoliutsionnogo dvizheniia," p. 120.

49. Morozov, *Terroristicheskaia bor'ba*, p. 4.

50. Ibid., p. 12.

51. Morozov was particularly irritated when editors of *Zemlia i volia* criticized or refused to publish his articles; *Povesti*, II: 396–98.

52. Zheliabov to the court; *Delo pervogo marta*, p. 336.

53. Kantor, "K istorii revoliutsionnogo dvizheniia," p. 120. In his *Vospominaniia*, p. 128, Tikhomirov writes of Morozov: "Nikolai Morozov remained almost a boy, but he was caught up by terror and not interested in anything else. . . . In essence he did nothing for the circle, although by his undoubted courage and young fervor he was always ready to put his life on the line."

54. Iakimova, "Iz dalekogo proshlogo," p. 9.

55. Bukh, "Pervaia tipografiia 'Narodnoi voli,'" p. 64.

56. V. G. Korolenko, *Sobranie sochineniia* (Moscow: Pravda, 1953–56), VII: 265.

57. Ibid., pp. 265–66.

58. There is a fine study of Zaichnevskii by B. P. Koz'min in *Iz istorii revoliutsionnoi mysli v Rossii* (Moscow: Akad. Nauk, 1961).

59. On this point see S. S. Volk, *Narodnaia volia, 1879–1882* (Leningrad: Nauka, 1966), pp. 240–44, and G. V. Plekhanov, "Politicheskie zadachi russkikh sotsialistov" (1883) in *Na dva fronta: Sbornik politicheskikh statei* (Geneva: Tip.

partii [RSDRP], 1905), p. 9, and "Sotsializm i politicheskaia bor'ba" (1889) in the same source, pp. 128–29.

60. "K istorii partii Narodnoi voli," pp. 1–10.

61. N. S. Rusanov, *Iz moikh vospominanii* (Berlin: Izd. Z. I. Grezhebina, 1923), pp. 126–27.

62. Tvardovskaia, "Organizatsionnye osnovy 'Narodnoi voli,'" p. 136; see also Vera Figner's introduction to *Vospominaniia L'va Tikhomirova*, p. xxiii. Tikhomirov's calls for the seizure of power did not appear in the underground press until after he had fled abroad and had begun to publish the journal *Vestnik Narodnoi voli* in Switzerland: see V. A. Tvardovskaia, "Problema gosudarstva v ideologii narodovol'chestva (1879–1883 gg.)," *Istoricheskie zapiski*, 74 (1963): 172.

63. Tvardovskaia, "Problema gosudarstva," pp. 172–75; Volk, *Narodnaia volia*, pp. 238–50.

64. See Popov, *Zapiski zemlevol'tsa*, pp. 95–97.

65. Bogucharskii, *Aktivnoe narodnichestvo*, p. 327. On this point, see the very interesting discussion about Zaichnevskii's ties with the constitutional group in Orel, presented by Rusanov in *Vospominaniia*, pp. 122–23.

66. Bogucharskii, *Aktivnoe narodnichestvo*, pp. 323–27.

67. Tikhomirov credits Osinskii (*Zheliabov*, p. 16), and so does Deich ("Osinskii," p. 27), but Bogucharskii's conclusions seem better documented.

68. Frolenko, "Lipetskii i voronezhskii s'ezdy," p. 80.

69. [Tikhomirov], *Zheliabov*, p. 23.

70. Zheliabov to the court, *Delo pervogo marta*, p. 333. Cf. the conclusions of Tvardovskaia, "Problemy gosudarstva," p. 148.

71. Zheliabov, in a statement on 26 March 1881; *Delo pervogo marta*, p. 5.

72. Mikhailov, in "Otchet o protsesse 20-ti narodovol'tsev," p. 254.

73. Morozov, "Vozniknovenie 'Narodnoi voli,'" p. 4; this phrase does not appear in Morozov's *Povesti*. Cf. the interesting account in Tyrkov, "K sobytiiu 1-go marta 1881 goda," pp. 139–40.

74. The controversy over Morozov and the philosophy of the *politiki* was one of the causes of the sad demise of I. A. Teodorovich, long-time editor of the journal *Katorga i ssylka*, which was forced to cease publication in 1935. See in particular Teodorovich's long article, "Rol' N. A. Morozova v revoliutsionnom proshlom," *Katorga i ssylka*, No. 92 (1932), pp. 7–60.

75. Bukh, "Pervaia tipografiia," p. 64.

76. Bogucharskii, *Aktivnoe narodnichestvo*, p. 324.

77. Mikhailov to the court, "Otchet o protsesse 20-ti narodovol'tsev," pp. 254–55.

78. Krylova reported to Morozov in regard to Stefanovich's arguments; Morozov, *Povesti*, II: 430.

79. "Iz zhizni saratovskikh kruzhkov," p. 13.

80. Walicki uses as the title of his book *The Controversy over Capitalism* (Oxford: Clarendon Press, 1969), and therein on pp. 132–53 is included an excellent discussion of Plekhanov's views on *narodnichestvo* and his difficult transition to Marxism. See also Baron, *Plekhanov*, pp. 48–55.

81. Walicki, *Controversy*, chapter III.

82. Ibid., pp. 80–81; see also Rem Blium, *Poiski putei k svobode* (Tallin: Eesti Raamat, 1985), chapter VII.

83. Cf. Korolenko, *Sobranie sochinenii*, VII: 263–66; Debagorii-Mokrievich, *Vospominaniia*, II: 491; V. Figner, "I. A. Ivanchin-Pisarev," *PSS*, V: 199–204. For a discussion of the *narodnik* program, see Chapter 2.

84. Plekhanova, "Nasha zhizn' do emigratsii," p. 69.

85. Deich, "Plekhanov v 'Zemli i voli,'" p. 60.

86. Kolosov, "Revoliutsionnaia deiatel'nost'," in Tiutchev, *Revoliutsionnoe dvizhenie*, pp. 29–30.

87. Deich, "Osinskii," p. 9.

88. Aptekman understood Plekhanov's potential impatience with village work, but he was also sad about its results; see *Obshchestvo*, p. 219.

89. Kolosov in Tiutchev, *Revoliutsionnoe dvizhenie*, p. 19.

90. Debagorii-Mokrievich, *Vospominaniia*, III: 499–500.

91. Morozov in *Povesti*, II: 264.

92. Stefanovich, *Zloba dnia*, pp. 3–4.

93. Morozov, *Povesti*, II: 246.

94. Ibid., 262; this is a rather charming episode, in that they were all trying not to hurt each other's feelings.

95. Ibid., 265.

96. Ibid., II: 264–65.

97. Popov, *Zapiski zemlevol'tsa*, p. 149.

98. Liubatovich, "Dalekoe i nedavnee," *Byloe*, 1906, No. 5, p. 221.

99. *Chronique*, p. 431; this view is confirmed by Tyrkov, "K sobytiiu 1 marta 1881 goda," p. 144.

100. Dmitrii Kuz'min, *Narodovol'cheskaia zhurnalistika* (Moscow: Polit-katorzhan, 1930), pp. 91–92; Ivanchin-Pisarev, *Khozhdenie*, p. 291.

101. Liubatovich, "Dalekoe i nedavnee," *Byloe*, 1906, No. 6, pp. 123–24.

102. Tikhomirov, *Vospominaniia*, p. 86; Figner, "Ocherki avtobiograficheskie," *PSS*, V: 162.

103. Figner, *Nacht*, pp. 75, 88.

104. Shiriaev, "Avtobiograficheskaia zapiska," pp. 91, 90.

105. See chapter 5.

106. Popov, *Zapiski zemlevol'tsa*, p. 149.

107. Popov strongly advocated adoption of agrarian terrorism as a major party plank at the meetings of Voronezh; Aptekman, *Obshchestvo*, p. 241.

108. Frolenko, "Lipetskii i voronezhskii s'ezdy," p. 69; these and the following episodes have been described previously in Chapter 4.

109. In the words of Ivanova, "Vospominaniia o S. L. Perovskoi," p. 86.

110. Sergievskii, "Chernyi peredel'," p. 46.

111. Tikhomirov in "K istorii revoliutsionnogo dvizheniia," p. 113.

112. Stefanovich, *Zloba dnia*, p. 14; Tikhomirov, *Vospominaniia*, p. 125.

113. "Avtobiograficheskoe zaiavlenie Kviatkovskogo," p. 165.

114. Sergievskii, "Chernyi peredel'," p. 46.

115. M. Klevenskii in a review of Ivanchin-Pisarev's biographical *Khozhdenie v narod*, published in *Katorga i ssylka*, 59 (1929): 214–15.

116. Aptekman, *Obshchestvo*, p. 345.

117. Frolenko, "Lipetskii i voronezhskii s'ezdy," p. 82.

118. Thomas G. Masaryk, *The Spirit of Russia* (New York: Macmillan, 1955), II: 108.

119. Cf. Tikhomirov's phrase in "K istorii revoliutsionnogo dvizheniia," p. 113. This is one of the most perceptive analyses of the revolutionary movement.

120. Liubatovich, "Dalekoe i nedavnee," *Byloe*, 1906, No. 6, p. 109.

121. Deich, "Osinskii," p. 26.

122. Tikhomirov, *Vospominaniia*, p. 107.

123. *Chronique*, p. 27.

124. Popov, *Zapiski zemlevol'tsa*, p. 222.

125. Aptekman, *Obshchestvo*, p. 380.

126. Masaryk, *Spirit of Russia*, II: 106.

127. Frolenko, "Lipetskii i voronezhskii s'ezdy," p. 83.

128. *Chronique*, p. 27.

129. Masaryk, *Spirit of Russia*, II: 106.

130. P. F. Alisov, *Aleksandr II osvoboditel'* (Geneva [1879]), p. 12.

131. In "K istorii revoliutsionnogo dvizheniia," p. 120.

132. Morozov, *Povesti*, II: 412.

133. Frolenko, "Nachalo 'narodoval'chestva,'" p. 17. See also Vl. Vilenskii-Sibiriakov, "Narodovol'tsy," *Katorga i ssylka*, 24 (1926): 10.

134. Serebriakov, *Obshchestvo*, p. 52.

135. Frolenko, "Lipetskii i voronezhskii s'ezdy," pp. 82-83.

136. Aptekman, *Obshchestvo*, p. 349.

137. Tikhomirov, *Vospominaniia*, p. 105.

138. Perovskii, "Vospominaniia," p. 72.

139. P. S. Ivanovskaia, "L. D. Terent'eva," *Katorga i ssylka*, 76 (1931): 146; see also Liubatovich, "Dalekoe i nedavnee," *Byloe*, 1906, No. 6, 126.

140. "K istorii partii Narodnoi voli," pp. 6-7.

141. See Aptekman, *Obshchestvo*, pp. 348-49. Popov's account of his work in Kiev and his early arrest may be found in *Zapiski zemlevol'tsa*, pp. 225-260.

142. Stefanovich, *Zloba dnia*, p. 8.

SELECTED
BIBLIOGRAPHY

MEMOIRS AND DOCUMENTS

This work is based primarily on memoirs of revolutionaries, depositions to authorities, official revolutionary programs, and police reports. Such sources were frequently published in revolutionary journals, early Soviet periodicals, and collections edited by Soviet scholars. The following items proved most useful.

Aleksandr Dmitrievich Mikhailov. Edited by V. N. Figner and A P. Korba. Leningrad, 1925.

Aptekman, O. V. "Dve dorogie teni. Iz vospominanii o G. V. Plekhanove i M. A. Natansone kak semidesiatnikakh." *Byloe,* 1921, No. 16, 3-14.

———. *Obshchestvo "Zemlia i volia" 70-kh godov; po lichnym vospominaniiam.* Petrograd: Kolos, 1924.

Arkhiv "Zemli i voli" i "Narodnoi voli." Edited by S. N. Valk *et al.* Moscow: Politkatorzhan, 1932.

"Avtobiograficheskoe zaiavlenie A. A. Kviatkovskogo." *Krasnyi arkhiv,* 14 (1926): 159-75.

"Avtobiograficheskaia zapiska i pis'ma S. Shiriaeva." *Krasnyi arkhiv,* 7 (1924): 70-107.

Bukh, N. "Pervaia tipografiia 'Narodnoi voli.'" *Katorga i ssylka,* 57/58 (1929): 54-93.

Burtsev, Vladimir. "Protsess 20-ti." *Byloe* (London), No. 2, n.d., pp. 91-135.

Chronique du mouvement socialiste en Russie, 1878-1887. [St. Petersburg: Impr. officielle du Ministre de l'intérieur, 1890.]

Debagorii-Mokrievich, V. *Vospominaniia.* Paris: J. Allemane, 1894-98.

Deich, Lev. "Aaron Zundelevich: Odin iz pervykh sotsial-demokratov v Rossii." *Gruppa "Osvobozhdenie truda"* (Moscow: Gosizdat, 1923-28) II: 185-216.

──── . "G. V. Plekhanov v 'Zemle i voli.'" *Gruppa "Osvobozhdenie truda"*, III (1925): 44-67.

──── . "Iz otnoshenii G. V. Plekhanova k narodovol'tsam." *Katorga i ssylka*, 7 (1923): 9-20.

──── . "O bylom i nebylitsakh: Iz literaturnogo nasledstva G. V. Plekhanova s dopolneniiami L. Deicha." *Proletarskaia revoliutsiia*, 1923, No. 3(15), pp. 29-44.

──── . *Russkaia revoliutsionnaia emigratsiia 70-kh godov.* Peterburg: Gosizdat, 1920.

──── . *Sergei Mikhailovich Kravchinskii-Stepniak: Baloven' sud'by.* Petrograd, 1919.

──── . "Valer'ian Osinskii (k 50-letiiu so dnia kazni)." *Katorga i ssylka*, 54 (1929): 7-43.

──── . *Za polveka.* Berlin: Izd. "Grani," 1923. Reprint: Cambridge: Oriental Research Partners, 1975.

Delo pervogo marta 1881 g. Protsess Zheliabova, Perovskoi i dr. Pravitel'stvennyi otchet, so stat'ei i primechaniiami L'va Deicha. St. Petersburg: Tip. V. Ia. Mil'steina, 1906.

"Doklady A. P. Drentel'n Aleksandru II." *Krasnyi arkhiv*, 40 (1930): 125-75.

Figner, Vera. "Iz avtobiografii Very Figner." *Byloe*, 1917, No. 2, pp. 153-82; No. 3, pp. 166-91; No. 4, pp. 57-89.

──── . "Iz pokazanii V. N. Figner." *Byloe*, 1906, No. 7, pp. 27-43.

──── . "K biografii Very Nikolaevny Figner." *Byloe*, 1906, No. 5, 3-13.

──── . "Mark Andreevich Natanson." *Katorga i ssylka*, 56 (1929): 141-50.

──── . *Memoirs of a Revolutionist.* Westport, Conn.: Greenwood Press, 1968. Reprint of 1927 edition; translation of *Zapechatlennyi trud.*

──── . *Nacht über Russland.* Berlin: Malik Verlag, 1926.

──── . *Polnoe sobranie sochinenii v semi tomakh.* Moscow: Izd. V.O.P., 1932.

──── . "Sof'ia Perovskaia, 1854-1881." *Byloe*, 1918, No. 10/11, 3-11.

Frolenko, M. F. "Iz vospominanii o Vere Ivanovne Zasulich (k piatiletiiu so dnia smerti)." *Katorga i ssylka*, 10 (1924): 241-47.

──── . "Khozhdenie v narod v 1874 goda." *Katorga i ssylka* 11 (1924): 9-14.

──── . "Kommentarii k stat'e N. A. Morozova, 'Vozniknovenie Narodnoi voli.'" *Byloe*, 1906, No. 12, pp. 22-33.

──── . "Lipetskii i voronezhskii s'ezdy." *Byloe*, 1907, No. 13, 67-86.

──── . "Mikhail Rodionovich Popov." *Golos minuvshego*, 1917, No. 7/8, 171-79.

──── . "Nachalo 'narodovol'chestva.'" *Katorga i ssylka*, 24 (1926): 17-26.

──── . "Popytka osvobozhdeniia Voinaral'skogo, 1-go iiulia 1878 g." *Katorga i ssylka*, 41 (1928): 82-89.

──── . *Sobranie sochinenii v dvukh tomakh.* Moscow: Politkatorzhan, 1930-31.

Gartman, L. "Iz vospominanii L'va Gartmana." *Byloe* (London), No. 3 (February 1903), 180-87.

"Glava iz odnoi knigi sekretno izdannoi zhandarmami." *Byloe* (London), No. 3 (February 1903): 187-91; No. 4 (May 1903): 66-75; No. 5 (December 1903): 61-74.

Gruppa "Osvobozhdenie truda". 6 vols. Iz arkhivov G. V. Plekhanova, V. I. Zasulich, i L. G. Deicha. Moscow: Gosizdat, 1924-28.

Iakimova, A. V. "'Bol'shoi protsess' ili 'protsess 193-kh:' O revoliutsionnoi propaganda v imperii." *Katorga i ssylka*, 37 (1927): 7-31.

——— . "Gruppa Svoboda ili smert'." *Katorga i ssylka* 24 (1926): 14-16.

——— . "Pamiati A. A. Fomina." *Katorga i ssylka*, 106 (1922): 126-40.

——— . "Pamiati Marii Aleksandrovny Kolenkinoi-Bogorodskoi." *Katorga i ssylka*, 31 (1927): 177-86.

Ivanchin-Pisarev, A. I. *Khozhdenie v narod.* Moscow: Molodaia gvardiia, 1929.

——— . "Pobeg. kn. P. A. Kropotkina." *Byloe*, 1907, No. 13, pp. 37-42.

Ivanov, Sergei. "Iz vospominanii o 1881 gode." *Byloe*, 1906, No. 4, pp. 228-42.

Ivanova, Sof'ia. "Vospominaniia o S. L. Perovskoi." *Byloe*, 1906, No. 3, pp. 83-89.

"Iz narodovol'cheskikh avtobiograficheskikh dokumentov." *Krasnyi arkhiv*, 20 (1927): 205-31.

"Iz perepiski S. M. Kravchinskogo." *Krasnyi arkhiv*, 19 (1926): 195-202.

"Iz zhizni saratovskikh kruzhkov (Iz mater'ialov O. i I. Markovykh)." *Byloe* (London), No. 4 (May 1903), 3-21.

"K istorii partii Narodnoi voli." *Byloe*, 1907, No. 6, pp. 1-10.

"K istorii 'Zemli i voli' 70-kh godov (Programma tambovskogo poseleniia zemlevol'tsev)." *Krasnyi arkhiv*, 19 (1926): 166-77.

Karpov, Evtikhii Pavlovich. "Stranichki iz vospominanii: Aleksandr Konstantinovich Solov'ev." *Katorga i ssylka*, 13 (1924): 31-47.

——— . "V. I. Zasulich: Nakanune pokusheniia." *Vestnik literatury*, 1919, No. 6, pp. 2-4.

Klements, D. A. *Iz proshlogo.* Leningrad, 1925.

Koni, Anatolii Fedorovich. *Vospominaniia o dele Very Zasulich.* Moscow: Academiia, 1933.

Kovalenskii, Mikhail Nikolaevich. *Russkaia revoliutsiia v sudebnykh protsessakh i memuarakh.* 4 vols. Moscow: Mir, 1923-25.

Kovalik, S. F. *Revoliutsionnoe dvizhenie semidesiatykh godov i protsess 193-kh.* Moscow: Politkatorzhan, 1928.

Koval'skaia, E. N. "Moi vstrechi s S. L. Perovskoi: Otryvki iz vospominanii." *Byloe*, 1921, No. 16, pp. 42-48.

——— . "Stranichka iz zhizni G. V. Plekhanova." *Katorga i ssylka*, 13 (1924): 25-30.

Kravchinskii, Sergei Mikhailovich. *Smert' za smert'; ubiistvo Mezentseva.* Petersburg: Gosizdat, 1920.

——— . *Underground Russia: Revolutionary Profiles and Sketches from Life.* London: Smith, Elder, 1883.

Kropotkin, Prince Peter. *Memoirs of a Revolutionist.* Boston and New York: Houghton, Mifflin, 1899.

Kuklin, G. A. *Itogi revoliutsionnogo dvizhenii v Rossii za sorok let (1862-1902 gg.): Sbornik programm* . . . Geneva: Izd. G. A. Kuklina, 1903.

Kunkl', A. A. "Vokrug dela Very Zasulich." *Katorga i ssylka*, 38 (1928): 57-66.

Lavrov: Gody emigratsii. Arkhivnye materialy v dvukh tomakh. Ed. by Boris Sapir. Dordrecht and Boston: Reidel, c. 1974.

Lion, S. E. "Ot propagandy k terroru (Iz odesskikh vospominanii semidesiatnika)." *Katorga i ssylka*, 12 (1924): 9-24.

Liubatovich, Ol'ga. "Dalekoe i nedavnee." *Byloe*, 1906, No. 5, pp. 206-41; No. 6, pp. 108-54.

Mikhailov, Aleksandr Dmitrievich. *Vospominaniia.* Geneva: Izd. G. A. Kuklina, 1903.

Morozov, N. A. *Povesti moei zhizni.* Moscow: [Akademiia nauk], 1961.

———. *Terroristicheskaia bor'ba.* London: Russkaia tip., 1880.

———. "Vozniknovenie 'Narodnoi voli:' Iz vospominanii o lipetskom i voronezhskom s'ezdakh letom 1879 goda." *Byloe*, 1906, No. 12, pp. 1-21.

"Otchet o protsesse 20-ti narodovol'tsev v 1882 godu." *Byloe*, 1906, No. 6, pp. 237-93.

Perovskoi, V. L. *Vospominaniia o sestre.* Moscow: Gosizdat, 1927.

Plekhanov, G. V. *Na dva fronta: Sbornik politicheskikh statei.* Geneva: Tip. partii [RSDRP], 1905.

Plekhanova, R. M. "Nasha zhizn' do emigratsii." *Gruppa "Osvobozhdenie truda",* VI (1928): 65-119.

———. "Periferiinyi kruzhok 'Zemli i voli.'" *Gruppa "Osvobozhdenie truda",* IV (1926): 81-116.

"Pokazaniia pervomartovtsev: Iz aktov predvaritel'nogo sledstviia." *Byloe*, 1918, No. 10/11, pp. 230-325.

"Pokushenie A. K. Solov'eva na tsareubiistvo, 2 aprelia 1879 goda." *Byloe*, 1918, No. 7, pp. 133-50; No. 8, pp. 88-107; No. 9, pp. 184-203.

Popov, M. R. *Zapiski zemlevol'tsa.* Moscow: Politkatorzhan, 1933.

Pribyleva-Korba, Anna. "Vospominaniia o Narodnoi voli." *Golos minuvshego*, 1916, No. 9, pp. 90-113.

"Protsess 20-ti narodvol'tsev v 1882 g." *Byloe*, 1906, No. 1, 227-300.

Protsess 193-kh. S predisloviem V. Kallasha. Moscow, 1906.

Protsess Very Zasulich: Sud i posle suda. St. Petersburg, n.d.

Revoliutsionnoe narodnichestvo 70-kh godov XIX veka. 2 vols. Edited by B. S. Itenberg, S. N. Valk, *et al.* Moscow: Nauka, 1964-65.

Revoliutsionnaia zhurnalistika semidesiatykh godov. Edited by B. Bazilevskii. Paris: Societé nouvelle de librairie et d'édition, 1905.

Rusanov, N. S. "Ideinye osnovy Narodnoi voli." *Byloe*, 1907, No. 9, pp. 37-70.

———. *Iz moikh vospominanii.* Berlin: Izd. Z. I. Grezhebina, 1923.

Shishko, Leonid. *Sergei Mikhailovich Kravchinskii i kruzhok chaikovtsev; Iz vospominanii i zametok starogo narodnika.* St. Petersburg: Izd. Vl. Raspopa, 1906.

Sinegub, S. S. *Zapiski chaikovtsa.* Moscow: Molodaia gvardiia, 1929.

Stefanovich, I. V. *Zloba dnia: Deistvuiushchim i gotovym deistvovat' sotovarish-cham moim, moe druzhee [sic] poslanie.* n.p., 1880.

"Svod ukazanii, dannykh nekotorym iz arestovannykh po delam o gosudarstven-nykh prestuplenniakh." *Byloe*, 1907. No. 18, pp. 118-52; No. 19, pp. 141-68; No. 20, pp. 89-123.

[Tikhomirov, L. A.] *Andrei Ivanovich Zheliabov.* London: Vol'naia russkaia tip., 1882.

———. *Nikolai Ivanovich Kibal'chich.* London [Zagranichnaia tip. Narodnoi voli], 1882.

———. *Sof'ia L'vovna Perovskaia.* London: Zagranichnaia tip. Narodnoi voli, 1882.

Tikhomirov, L. A. *Vospominaniia L'va Tikhomirova.* Moscow-Leningrad: Gosiz-dat, 1927.

———. "K istorii revoliutsionnogo dvizheniia 1870-1880-kh godov. Neizdannaia zapiska L'va Tikhomirova." Ed. by R. M. Kantor. *Katorga i ssylka*, 24 (1926): 110-22.

Tyrkov, A. "K sobytiiu 1 marta 1881 goda." *Byloe*, 1906, No. 5, pp. 139-60.

Vpered! 1873-1877 gg. 2 vols. Materialy iz arkhiva Valer'iana Nikolaevicha Smirnova. Edited by Boris Sapir. Dordrecht: D. Reidel, 1970.

Zasulich, Vera. *Vospominaniia.* Moscow: Politkatorzhan, 1931.

SECONDARY WORKS

Of the many scholarly analyses, the following are probably most useful:

Asheshov, N. P. *Sof'ia Perovskaia: Materialy dlia biografii i kharakteristiki.* Petersburg, Gosizdat, 1920.

Balabanov, M. S. *Istoriia revoliutsionnogo dvizheniia v Rossii.* [Kiev] Gosizdat Ukrainy [1925].

Baron, Samuel H. *Plekhanov: The Father of Russian Marxism.* Stanford: Stan-ford University Press, 1963.

Barrive, L. *Osvobozhditel'noe dvizhenie v tsarstvovanie Aleksandra vtorogo; istoricheskie ocherki.* Moscow: Tip. russkogo tovarishchestva, 1909.

Bergman, Jay. *Vera Zasulich: A Biography.* Stanford: Stanford University Press, 1983.

———. "Vera Zasulich, the Shooting of Trepov, and the Growth of Political Terrorism in Russia, 1878-1881." *Terrorism*, IV (1980): 25-51.

Berman, L. "Otkliki na ubiistvo shefa zhandarmov Mezentsova." *Katorga i ssylka*, 114/115 (1935): 155-59.

Billington, James H. *Mikhailovsky and Russian Populism.* Oxford: Clarendon Press, 1958.

Blium, Rem. *Poiski putei k svobode.* Tallin: Eesti Raamat, 1985.

Bogucharskii, V. *Aktivnoe narodnichestvo semidesiatykh godov.* Moscow, Izd. M. i S. Sabashnikovykh, 1912.

———. "V 1878 godu: Vsepodanneishee donesenie shefa zhandarmov." *Golos minuvshego*, 1917, No. 7/8, pp. 124-68.

———. *Iz istorii politicheskoi bor'by v 70-kh i 80-kh gg. XIX veka.* Moscow: Russkaia mysl', 1912.

Deiateli revoliutsionnogo dvizheniia v Rossii: Bio-biograficheskii slovar'. 5 vols. Moscow: Politkatorzhan, 1927-34. Reprint, Leipzig: Zentralantiquariat der deutschen demokratischen Republik, 1974.

Filippov, R. V. *Ideologiia bol'shego obshchestva propagandy 1869-1873 gg.* Petrozavodsk: Karel'skoe knizhnoe izd., 1963.

Footman, David. *Red Prelude: The Life of the Russian Terrorist Zhelyabov.* New Haven: Yale University Press, 1945.

Geierhos, Wolfgang. *Vera Zasulic und die russische revolutionäre Bewegung.* Munich-Vienna: Oldenbourg, 1977.

Ginev, V. N. "Revoliutsionnaia deiatel'nost' narodnikov 70-kh godov sredi krest'ian i rabochikh srednogo povolzh'ia." *Istoricheskie zapiski*, 74 (1963): 220-44.

Gorev, B. I. *Revoliutsionnoe narodnichestvo semidesiatykh godov.* Moscow: Politkatorzhan, 1932.

Hardy, Deborah. *Petr Tkachev: The Critic as Jacobin.* Seattle and London: University of Washington Press, 1977.

Ionova, G. I., and A. F. Smirnov. "Revoliutsionnye demokraty i narodniki." *Istoriia SSSR*, 1961, No. 5, pp. 112-40.

Itenberg, B. S. "Nachalo massovogo 'khozhdeniia v narod.'" *Istoricheskie zapiski*, 69 (1961): 142-76.

Kappeler, Andreas. "Zur Charakteristiken russischer Terroristen (1878-1887)." *Jahrbücher fur Geschichte Osteuropas*, 1979, No. 27.

Koz'min, B. P. *Iz istorii revoliutsionnoi mysli v Rossii.* Moscow: Akad. nauk, 1961.

———. *Revoliutsionnoe dvizhenie 1860-kh godov.* Moscow: Politkatorzhan, 1932.

Kucherov, Samuel. "The Case of Vera Zasulich." *Russian Review*, XI (1952): 86-96.

Kulczycki, Ludwig. *Geschichte der russischen Revolution.* 3 vols. Gotha: F. A. Perthes, 1910-1914.

Kuz'min, Dmitrii. *Narodovol'cheskaia zhurnalistika.* Moscow: Politkatorzhan, 1930.

Levin, Sh. M. *Dmitrii Aleksandrovich Klements: Ocherk revoliutsionnoi deiatel'-nosti.* Moscow, 1929.

———. "Dve demonstratsii (Iz istorii revoliutsionnoi situatsii kontsa 70-kh godov XIX v.)." *Istoricheskie zapiski*, 54 (1955): 251-70.

———. *Obshchestvennoe dvizhenie v Rossii v 60-70e gody XIX veka.* Moscow: Izd. sotsial'no-ekon. literatury, 1958.

Lifshits, G. M., and Liashenko, K. G. "Kak sozdavalas' programma vtoroi 'Zemli i voli.'" *Voprosy istorii*, 1965, No. 9, pp. 36-50.

Livshits, S. "Podpol'nye tipografii 60-kh, 70-kh, i 80-kh godov." *Katorga i ssylka*, 41 (1928): 23–33; 43 (1928): 60–78; 50 (1928): 64–80; 51 (1929): 57–74; 55 (1919): 44–60.

Masaryk, Thomas G. *The Spirit of Russia.* New York: Macmillan, 1955.

Miller, Martin A. *Kropotkin.* Chicago and London: University of Chicago Press, 1976.

Mindlin, I. V. "Perekhod G. V. Plekhanova ot narodnichestva k marksizmu." *Voprosy istorii*, 1956, No. 12, pp. 3–16.

Mirovich, Ilia. *Sophja Perowskaja, die Maertyrerin der russischen Revolution: biographische Skizze nach russischen Quellen.* New York: Schaerr & Frantz, 1882.

Pomper, Philip. *Peter Lavrov and the Russian Revolutionary Movement.* Chicago and London: University of Chicago Press, 1972.

——. *The Russian Revolutionary Intelligentsia.* New York: Thomas Y. Crowell, 1970.

——. *Sergei Nechaev.* New Brunswick: Rutgers University Press, 1979.

Serebriakov, E. A. *Obshchestvo Zemlia i volia.* London: Tip. Zhizni, 1901. Reprinted from first edition, London, 1894.

Sergievskii, N. "'Chernyi peredel'' i narodniki 80-kh godov." *Katorga i ssylka*, 74 (1931): 7–58.

Seth, Ronald. *The Russian Terrorists.* London: Barrie & Rockliff, 1966.

Shchegolev, P. "Aleksei Medvedev." *Katorga i ssylka*, 71 (1930): 65–110.

Steblin-Kamenskii, R. A. "Grigorii Anfimovich Popko (12-go aprelia 1852 g.–20-go marta 1885 g.). Opyt biografii." *Byloe*, 1907, No. 17, pp. 179–204.

Teodorovich, I. A. "Rol' N. A. Morozova v revoliutsionnom proshlom." *Katorga i ssylka*, 92 (1932): 7–60.

Tiutchev, N. S. "Razgrom Zemli i voli v 1878 g. Delo Mezentsova." *Byloe*, 1918, No. 8, pp. 157–79.

——. *Revoliutsionnoe dvizhenie 1870–1880 gg. Stat'i po arkhivnym materialam.* Moscow: Politkatorzhan, 1925.

Tkachenko, P. S. *Revoliutsionnaia narodnicheskaia organizatsiia 'Zemlia i volia' (1876–1879 gg.).* Moscow: Izd. Vysshaia shkola, 1961.

Troitskii, N. A. *Bezumstvo khrabrykh; Russkie revoliutsionery i karatel'naia politika tsarizma, 1866–1882 gg.* Moscow: Mysl', 1978.

——. *Bol'shoe obshchestvo propagandy 1871–1872-kh godov (Tak-nazyvaemye chaikovtsy).* Saratov: Izd. Saratovskogo univ., 1963.

——. *Narodnaia volia pered tsarskim sudom, 1880–1891 gg.* Saratov: Izd. Saratovskogo univ., 1971.

——. "Protsess 193-kh." In *Obshchestvennoe dvizhenie v poslereformennoi Rossii.* Moscow: Nauka, 1965.

——. *Tsarskie sudy protiv revoliutsionnoi Rossii: Politicheskie protsessy, 1871–1880 gg.* Saratov: Izd. Saratovskogo univ., 1976.

Tun, A. *Istoriia revoliutsionnykh dvizhenii v Rossii.* Perevod V. Zasulich, D. Kol'tsova, & dr. Moscow: Izd. "Proletarii," 1924.

Tvardovskaia, V. A. "Krizis 'Zemlia i volia' v kontse 70-kh godov." *Istoriia SSSR*, 1959, No. 4, pp. 60-74.

———. "Organizatsionnye osnovy 'Narodnoi voli.'" *Istoricheskie zapiski*, 67 (1960): 103-44.

———. "Problemy gosudarstva v ideologii narodnichestva (1879-1883 gg.)" *Istoricheskie zapiski*, 74 (1963): 148-86.

Ulam, Adam. *In the Name of the People: Prophets and Conspirators in Prerevolutionary Russia.* New York: Viking Press, 1977.

Venturi, Franco. *Roots of Revolution: A History of the Populist and Socialist Movements in Nineteenth-Century Russia.* New York: Alfred A. Knopf, 1960.

Volk, S. S. *Narodnaia volia, 1879-1882 gg.* Leningrad: Nauka, 1966.

Yarmolinsky, Avrahm. *Road to Revolution: A Century of Russian Radicalism.* New York: Macmillan, 1959.

Zakharina, V. F. "Revoliutsionnye narodniki 70-kh godov: Ideologi krest'-ianskoi demokratii." *Istoriia SSSR*, 1963, No. 5, pp. 101-16.

INDEX

Activism, revolutionary need for, 155–57

Agrarian terrorism, 153

Aksakov, landowner, 34–35, 41

Aksakova, Mme., 35

Aksel'rod, Pavel, 114

Alexander II, tsar of Russia, 1855–81: assassination of, x, 79, 99, 129, 145, 157–58, 163; Solov'ev attempt on, 62, 77, 91–94, 95, 153; mentioned, 137. *See also* assassination

Alexander III, tsar of Russia, 1881–94, 142, 158

Alisov, P. F., 157

Anarchists, in "crazy summer," 10

Annenskii, A. F., 72

Aptekman, O. V., 108, 158; on "crazy summer," 11; on disorganization group, 50–51, 55–56; hopes for unity, 121; on Land and Freedom organization, 17, 19, 23–24, 26, 49, 52, 53, 64; as propagandist, 44–45, 118, 129, 136; on terrorism, 92, 156, 157; on villager revolutionism, 154–55; at Voronezh congress, 109, 114

Assassination, 157–58, 163–64; anticipated results of, 138–47; in revolu-

tionaries' program, 101–102, 114; Solov'ev attempt at, 91–95

Bakunin, Mikhail, x, 30, 33, 141

Bakuninism, 18–20, 27, 39, 139

Bakuninists, Southern, 26, 48. *See also buntari*, Southern

Balkan wars, effects on violence, 54, 152

Barannikov, Aleksandr: as disorganizer, 68, 70, 142, 154; at Lipetsk, 98–99, 100; and propaganda, 64, 137, 144

Baron, Samuel H., xii

Bell, The, 21

Berman, L., xi

Black Repartition, 73, 122, 129, 158

"Blow to the center," concept of, 48–49

Bobokhov, Sergei, 72–73

Bogdanovich, Iurri, 140, 141, 150; in Figner circle, 8, 9, 16; and Kropotkin escape, 8; on Land and Freedom program, 19, 27, 52; as propagandist, 15, 32, 34–35, 36, 38, 42, 43, 89, 151; and Solov'ev, 90

Bogdanovich, Mariia Pavlovna, 15, 89

Bogdanovich, N. N., 15, 89, 91

118, 120, 122–23; and "liberation" of prisoners, 67–68, 152–53; and Mikhailov, 82; in People's Will, 122, 158; and Plekhanov, 83; as propagandist, 14, 42, 43, 136–37, 144, 151; seeks vitality, 153; and Tikhomirov, 87, 104; on violence, 78, 99, 109–10; at Voronezh, 109, 112

Peter the Great, tsar of Russia, 1682–1725, 100

Petrovskii agricultural school, riots at, 63

Petrunkevich, I. I., 54, 143

Plekhanov, G. V., 83–84, 85, 114, 117; arguments against capitalism, 120, 145–46, 147; arguments for propagandists, 118–19, 120–21, 129, 147, 163; emigration of, 122, 158; failure to attract support, 129; on Kravchinskii, 83; on *Land and Freedom*, 88, 94, 127; and Mikhailov, 84–85, 115–16, 118, 121; and Natanson circle, 17; and Perovskaia, 126; propandizing, 8, 21, 29–30, 31, 86–88, 148–49; on terrorism, 75, 92–93, 128; at Voronezh, 97, 107–108, 109–12

Police measures, against revolutionaries, 71–73, 74, 76–78, 96–97, 128, 131–35, 158, 162–63

Political revolution, endorsed by terrorists, 146–47

Politiki, 140, 142, 145, 155

Polonskaia. *See* Oshanina, M. N.

Pomper, Philip, xii

Popko, G. A., 59, 63, 68, 143

Popov, father of M. R. Popov, 76

Popov, M. R., 72, 137, 147; on Kviatkovskii, 85; on Land and Freedom split, 121, 122; on Mikhailov, 84; murders

Reinshtein, 73, 84; as propagandist, 40–41, 43, 118, 129, 131, 135, 151, 158; on revolutionary mood, 153; on violence, 64, 92–94, 156; and Voronezh, 97, 107–108, 109, 113, 114; on Zasulich, 62

Popov, N. S., 31

Preobrazhenskii, A. I., 109, 113, 118, 122, 137

Presniakov, A. S., 56, 57–58, 63, 73, 85, 149

Prisoners, liberation of, in revolutionary program, 50. *See also* names of individuals

Propagandists: argue with terrorists, 117–22; on capitalism, 145–47; comradeship, need for, 24–25, 151–52; in "crazy summer," 9–16; demoralization of, 1–3; and disorganization group, 51–52, 76–78; experiences of, 31–43; heroism as attractive to, 61, 152–53; jobs held by, 43; in Land and Freedom, 51–53, 107, 122; numbers of, estimated, 29–30; organization of, 23–25; principles of, 16–23; program of, analyzed, 26–28; program of, approved, 25–26; recruited to terrorism, 112–13, 116–17, 125, 129, 137–44; revolutionism of, 26–27, 154–55; on social revolution, 146–47; Solov'ev as, 88–91; on violence, 63–65, 75–76, 77–78, 91–94; at Voronezh, 109–115. *See also* "flying" propaganda; Land and Freedom; names of individuals; villagers

Ptitsa, typesetter, 119

Reinshtein, N. V., 73, 85

Revenge, as revolutionary motive, 162

ABOUT THE AUTHOR

DEBORAH HARDY is Professor of History at the University of Wyoming. She is the author of *Petr Tkachev: The Critic as Jacobin* and *Wyoming University: The First Hundred Years.* Her articles have appeared in such journals as *Slavic Review, Canadian Slavic Studies* and *Russian Review.*